Profiles from the Susquehanna Valley

Profiles from the Susquehanna Valley

Past and present vignettes of its people, times and towns

PAUL B. BEERS

Paul B. B[signature]

Stackpole Books

PROFILES FROM THE SUSQUEHANNA VALLEY

Copyright © 1973 by
THE STACKPOLE COMPANY

Published by
STACKPOLE BOOKS
Cameron and Kelker Streets
Harrisburg, Pa. 17105

Printed in U.S.A.

Library of Congress Cataloging in Publication Data

Beers, Paul B
   Profiles from the Susquehanna Valley.

   1. Susquehanna Valley--History. I. Title.
F157.S8B43   917.48   73-1603
ISBN 0-8117-1380-6

Contents

Part I.   Around the Neighborhood

Old Front Street
. . . Gracious Living, Elms, and Superbourgeois

Generations of Harrisburg's finest enjoyed its prestige, proximity, and pleasures until the unhappy domestic facts of the post-World War II years brought its demise.

Sin City
. . . Godliness and Gaiety

Within sight of church steeples, the Harrisburg Area had its brothels, speakeasies, bathtub gin, and slot machines. A new generation pursues the sins of the flesh no less vigorously but with more hypocrisy.

Black Harrisburg
. . . From Hercules to Manhood

Tolerated but never fully accepted in 200 years, the black rightfully no longer acquiesces in a submissive role. With historic irony, white suburbia is now challenged to break its pattern of separatism and assert the American dream of brotherhood.

Weather Worries
. . . Most Like It Hot

Nobody lives in Central Pennsylvania because the weather is ideal, but there are autumn days that make this, quite simply, one of the most beautiful and enjoyable spots on earth.

The Lamb's Gap double slaying, the Case of the Missing Body, and the Babes in the Woods mystery were Midstate murder tales in the 1920s and 1930s that retain public interest.

After generations of indifference, the Harrisburg Area developed a community college, a medical center, an upper-level college, thriving business schools, a burgeoning suburban educational system, and a City school district modernizing to face as great a challenge as any.

The DeCoux Penn, the Milles doors, Rothermel's and Savage's murals, and Barnard's nudes are distinctive works of art, but the locals also enjoy Penrose in the park, Miss Penn, General Hartranft on his horse and even the $20,000 marbled Matt Quay.

Though it has yet to produce a nationally known artist, the Susquehanna Valley today has its liveliest art scene. Painters, craftsmen, curators, and buyers all make it active.

Show business started with the Harrisburg Company of Comedians and has continued, with triumphs and pratfalls, in Shakespeare Hall and the Grand Opera House, at the Community Theater, Allenberry, Gretna, and Totem Pole, with names like John Durang, Joe Jefferson, Billy Welsh, Jasper Deeter, Charles Coghlan, Richard North Gage, Charlton Heston, and Donald Oenslager brightening the scene.

Though music is the most precise of the arts, it is the most fully appreciated in Central Pennsylvania. The biggest stars, from Jenny Lind and Pablo Casals to Fred Waring and the Dorsey Brothers, have toured the area, while the Harrisburg Symphony, the Choral Society, and the local talent play on.

Part III. The Politicians

Excitement in politics is rare and two-party competition even
rarer for the Susquehanna Valley, which has never ranked
politicians very high. The history is the GOP, or "Generally
Only Republicans," but now that is changing some.

John the First had the good sense to settle and prosper, and
John the Second had even better sense to set aside "four acres
and 13 perches" for the State Capitol and make the community
what it is.

Tall, dour, brilliant William Maclay helped found the world's
oldest political party and even sought the nation's capital for
the banks of the Susquehanna, but he is little appreciated today.

Meeting in Zion Lutheran Church in 1839, "The Whippables" ignored the obvious choice of Henry Clay to nominate a winner.
Harrisburg is America's smallest town to have a presidential
convention.

It was shameful enough that the old Capitol burned down at
noontime on a working day, but when the politicians stole the
new Capitol blind, it was a national story and a great trial.

No Simple Simon, this Harrisburger created the greatest statewide political machine in American history by remaining true
to his friends and ruthless to his enemies.

Don never had the charm of his amazing father, but he was an
astute political leader and an equally smart businessman. He
married the Jacqueline Kennedy of his era, half his age, and
was the talk of the social and literary world.

Acknowledgments

On a rainy Friday afternoon, May 26, 1961, I had a conference with James R. Doran, editor of the *Harrisburg Patriot-News* since 1951. I had been a staff reporter for four years, and my immodest suggestion was that I do a column for the *Evening News*. As my journal notes for that day: "Boy oh boy, did he want a column. He used to do one himself, for seven years. Later, about 3 P.M., he came bubbling out across the office to me and said, 'Hey, what about the construction of the post office across the street? People like destruction and construction.' He was smiling and swinging his shoulders. I replied, 'Sure, sure, sure.' " And so on June 9, the Reporter At Large column began. The first was about razing old buildings; people like destruction best. The column has continued ever since, some 1,800 of them, the longest-running column Harrisburg has ever had. For that opportunity, and the encouragement and friendship he has given unstintingly ever since, this book on the community for which he has worked so diligently is dedicated to Jim Doran.

A note of appreciation also goes to the late James Rietmulder and Robert H. Fowler. Jim Rietmulder, president of Stackpole Books, was the editor of *The Pennsylvania Sampler* and worked on the preliminaries of this book. A capable and generous man with his talent and time, Jim Rietmulder was a friend. Bob Fowler, publisher of *American History Illustrated* and *Civil War Times Illustrated*, was a former newspaper colleague and for 15 years has been an adviser on the vagaries of writing and publishing. The articles on Simon Girty and Simon Cameron first appeared, in slightly different form, in his publications. To William Eppleman, sincerest thanks for permission to use, from his outstanding collection, the Walt Huber painting which appears on the cover.

I am also indebted to the publishers acknowledged below for permission to reprint excerpts from their books. The excerpts are from *A Rage to Live* and *Appointment in Samarra*, both by John O'Hara, and *No Country for Old Men*, by Warren Eyster, with permission of the publisher, Random House, Inc., copyright by the authors; *Mencken Chrestomathy*, by H. L. Mencken, with permission of the publisher, Alfred A. Knopf, Inc., copyright by the author; *Roll River*, by James Boyd, with permission of the publisher, Charles Scribner's Sons, copyright by the author; and *Abraham Lincoln: The War Years*, by Carl Sandburg, with permission of the publisher, Harcourt Brace Jovanovich, Inc., copyright by the author.

And, lastly, a smile back to Philip Benjamin Beers, a native Harrisburger who was born as this book was being conceived. His zest and delight in greeting each new morning of another Central Pennsylvania day gave added incentive to the recording of facts and stories about his part of the world that someday maybe he will want to read, or even better, rewrite.

Introduction

. . . A Particular Place

President George Washington slept over in Harrisburg on October 3, 1794, on his way to Western Pennsylvania to put down the Whiskey Rebellion. He spoke a mere 152 words to a crowd gathered in Market Square, calling Harrisburgers "zealous and efficient patriots" even though he knew a majority of these Central Pennsylvanians sympathized with the whiskey-making and tax-evading insurgents.

Today Harrisburg is the center of the fastest-growing metropolitan area in Pennsylvania, some 420,000 people from Gettysburg to Palmyra. It is still the land of "zealous and efficient patriots," perplexing at times but capable of making remarkable efforts, such as their cooperative rebuilding feats after the disastrous Flood of 1972.

The equal in population to a state like Alaska or a nation like Swaziland, the Harrisburg Area is a particular place with a particular tradition. It does things its way for its own reasons, and its cautious life style ties the present to the past and contemporaries to posterity.

"To be deeply rooted in a place that has meaning is perhaps the best gift a child can have," wrote the late Christopher Morley, a native Pennsylvanian. "If that place has beauty and a feeling of permanence, it may suggest to him unawares that sense of identity with this physical earth which is the humblest and happiest of life's intuitions."

The Peace Movement came to Harrisburg in 1972 with the Harrisburg 8 trial. "The heartland of Middle America," charged the supporters of the Rev. Philip Berrigan. A hub of overzealous and too-efficient superpatriots, they said. "A folksy kind of place," reported pundit Joseph Kraft. Syndicated columnist Mary McGrory observed hundreds of natives leading what appeared to be "humdrum lives," and the dreadful thought came to her, "Harrisburg might indeed be America." Tony Scoblick, one of the defendants, said the white rural society of the Harrisburg Area is "almost an alien culture." He complained, "It's impossible to get a jury of our peers from this group." Sister Elizabeth

McAlister, another defendant, announced that a fairer trial could be had in New York, Washington, or Baltimore. But after the jury on April 5 dealt the government's heavy-handedness a crushing blow by declaring the defendants innocent of all major charges, Sister Elizabeth acknowledged that the people had treated her fairly and Scoblick admitted, "We underestimated the jury."

Though almost indifferent to the tragedies of the Vietnam War, unreceptive to the philosophy of dissent, and only bemused by the social activists, the Harrisburg Area in the spotlight of the Harrisburg 8 trial rose to the occasion. Justice was rendered without a fuss, the nation's self-respect was not tarnished. And Central Pennsylvanians returned to their own unobtrusive concerns.

For generations, visitors and newcomers have misconceived this benign Susquehanna sector of Pennsylvania as dull, provincial, and somnolent, with rubes and the petit bourgeois setting the pace. "What a pimple on the ass of progress this burg is," John O'Hara has a character complain.

Charles Dickens in 1842 was shocked to see the town's leading lights chuck tobacco juice on the hotel rug rather than "yield to the prejudice" of a spittoon or "abandon themselves, for the moment, even to the conventional absurdity of pocket handkerchiefs." Anthony Trollope jotted in his journal in 1861: "There is nothing special at Harrisburg to arrest any traveler. The appearance of the members of the Legislature of Pennsylvania did not impress me very favorably." When Babe Ruth at the height of his baseball career in 1928 came to town, he inspected the nightlife, yawned, returned to his hotel room and was in his purple pajamas before midnight. King George VI and Queen Mary in 1939 never got out of the train. "Bet he's having breakfast in bed. That's what I'd do if I were king," said an idle Harrisburger at the depot.

A Penn State student from Pittsburgh wrote a thesis about the 1970 Legislature and noted: "In some respects Harrisburg is the ideal setting to do research. There is very little excitement, few dramatic events and a near total absence of nightlife to distract the researcher from his study."

This place—Latitude 40–15–44 and Longitude 76–52–66—sometimes is called "Chicken Corn Soup Country," after its favorite dish. Perhaps it is the bland soup that has been the common ingredient, fortifying the predominant White Anglo-Saxon Protestant culture and assimilating most minorities. An impression can be that all are "happy in their dullness," as James Boswell observed of the Dutch when he toured 18th Century Holland. The degree of contentment often is astounding. In 1971 Susquehanna Township had a two-week sanitation strike apparently without anyone's smelling it. "Why wasn't it in the newspapers?" a resident questioned. "Because there weren't any complaints," replied a township commissioner.

There are four basic reasons for the life style of Central Pennsylvania. It has a conservative Pennsylvania German background. Its economic foundation is government, which gives it a soft-spoken, acquiescent, bureaucratic stability. Of the 192,400 jobholders in Dauphin, Cumberland, and Perry counties, 45,200 are government employees. There are many transients because of the state capital, the transportation industry, and the military. And, lastly, in the past 15 years, the Harrisburg Area has had an influx of professionals, coming in to work in the fields of government, medicine, law, and engineering.

So Central Pennsylvania is a blend of the sophisticated with the unsophisticated, most of whom are relaxed with middle-class aspirations in a relatively recession-proof economy.

"No matter how big Harrisburg grows, it will always be a country town. It has country-town ideals," the late J. Horace McFarland, the nationally known conservationist and local civic leader, used to say.

Bil Gilbert described it as a "benign environment" when he wrote about Millersburg in the *Saturday Evening Post*. Gilbert, of Adams County and a free-lance writer, went to this Upper Dauphin County community in 1968 to discover why its citizenry was so indifferent to the tragedy of Vietnam. He found that its abundance of good water, food, air, privacy and leisure, its proximity to employment and its absence of vermin, disease, violence, and congestion created "The Millersburg Way, the enshrinement of security, the disparagement of all but the mildest stimulation as a kind of animality." What happens elsewhere to other people just does not excite Millersburgers, Gilbert concluded.

Outward friendliness is not a common trait in Central Pennsylvania. "We Fort Penn people," writes John O'Hara in *A Rage to Live*, "we're harder to get to know than most, I guess. . . . more stand-offish than Lancaster or Altoona maybe, or Reading." It is a characteristic that contributes to the prefabricated privacy, where Harrisburgers share their warmth and hospitality only among themselves. It takes floods, like those in 1936 and 1972, or the end of World War II to buckle the taciturnity.

Privacy is highly regarded, perhaps too much. Most of the social life is private, from Elks clubs and American Legion posts to swimming pool associations and country clubs. Communities divide into a multiplicity of enclaves, with a minimum of intercooperation. It is not a coincidence that the West Shore has a population of 105,000 and is larger than Harrisburg, Scranton, and all but four cities in Pennsylvania, yet many inhabitants think of themselves as residents of little boroughs and townships, a delusion of village intimacy not dispelled by the city-sized traffic jams.

There is little enthusiasm for politics, though the state capitol is one of the nation's most partisan arenas. Political ideas, philosophies, and personages seldom are regarded as important; or, rather, politics is seen as a distraction from the comforts of private life. The great issues in American history—slavery, economic justice, suffrage, civil rights, consumerism, war protest, environmental protection, and women's liberation—never excited Harrisburgers, except when the opinionated shouted, displayed poor manners, and became an annoyance. "The people here are difficult to arouse and even when they're aroused, they're not very aroused," explained former Associated Press reporter and politician John M. Lynch to visiting newsmen during the Berrigan trial.

It is easy to build a case that Central Pennsylvanians today are much as they have always been—cautious, emotionally restrained, obstinate, suspicious of the new, publicity stingy, and quietly self-indulgent. But they are also hard-working, religious, privately generous, humorous in their way, basically tolerant if not always at first understanding, slow to become cynical, and unusually law-abiding (the Harrisburg Area was 200th of 227 metropolitan areas in the nation with the least crime per capita, according to the 1971 FBI Uniform Crime Report).

Samuel Coleridge never saw Central Pennsylvania, but in 1794 he had a dream: "I . . . formed a plan as harmless as it was extravagant, of trying the experiment of human perfectibility on the banks of the Susquehanna; where our little society . . . was to have combined the innocence of the Patriarchal Age with the knowledge and general refinements of European culture; and where I dreamed that in the sober evening of my life I should behold the cottages of independence in the undivided dale of industry."

Though human perfectibility and European refinement are yet to be realized, if even desired, the Susquehanna society does retain much innocence and sobriety with its independence, industry, and knowledge.

John Updike grew up in nearby Reading and Berks County, and his 1970 comment about the land of his youth could apply to the Harrisburg Area: "Reading is neither the sticks nor the megalopolis. There's a nice blend, a freedom. I think you have a lot of options here if you want to use them . . . It's really a very lovely place to begin." He added that there's a beauty to such an American place. "It's a kind of honest beauty, the beauty of doing real work."

Old Front Street

. . . *Gracious Living, Elms, and Superbourgeois*

"After supper they sat upstairs in the library," writes James Boyd in *Roll River*. "In his dark blue smoking jacket with braided cuffs, he leaned back and smoked a long, thin cigar. Each of their roles was understood. She supplied for his consideration the gossip and small talk of the town, while he, enthroned on the red-leather chair and wreathed in the smoke of the havana, offered comments, footnotes, ribaldry, and judgment. From time to time, he leaned forward with his legs still crossed, and trapped his cigar against the toe of his slipper; the ash flew neatly into the fireplace; he leaned back, pleased with himself but not deceived; it was a compensation to her to see crumbs of news from her petty world consumed by clouds of fine havana smoke and flashes of derision. For after all, it was desirable that a husband should be a demigod, and if one could not be a demigod among men, one might, at least, be a demigod among gossip."

That passage is from Boyd's 1935 novel, published by Scribner's, about Harrisburg and old Front St. between 1880 and 1930.

The Rand family lived near the Camelback Bridge and makes its money as a coal distributor, as did Boyd's own family. Harrisburg is Midian and Front St. is River St. It takes 117 pages of the 603-page

FRONT STREET

novel for John Rand's daughter Clara to march to the Market Square Presbyterian Church and marry a Philadelphia dude named Fitz-Greene Rankin, whose family is in the wholesale hardward business. For a wedding present from a neighbor, Clara receives an enameled Chinese incense burner.

The marriage lasts less than a year. Rankin is a bounder and commits suicide, a popular denouement used by Great Depression novelists like Boyd or the younger John O'Hara. During the skating party on the Susquehanna, Fitz-Greene Rankin takes his own life by skating near Island Park where the ice is thin. Firemen from the Good Hope Company are unable to reach him in time.

The Widow Clara lives the rest of her life on Front St., holding her chin high and keeping an immunity from "the narrow iron shell of life in this and other little places." Nothing disturbs her stateliness, not the automobiles replacing the horses on the street, not the new Harrisburg Country Club near the farm she bought for $2,600, not even the "knowing glances, naive and slightly vulgar with which society in Midian greeted all particular relationships."

There is Clara's sister-in-law up the street, "indeed a splendid figure of a woman, but hard to love, like a show-ring horse." There is nephew Tommy Rand, who after Yale goes into the family coal business. Tommy marries Julia Wilton, an ash blonde in the neighborhood who turns out to be "a woman not difficult to get along with, once a man had given up all idea of being fond of her."

Tommy heads off to world War I and is wounded. In a Paris hospital he meets nurse Jeanne Thompson, from way up at 718 River St. It is Jeanne he should have married, but she was not a true Front Streeter. Tommy returns from the war, thinks of Jeanne, and almost goes to pieces drinking too much Old Highspire rye. He is saved from utter self-destruction only because his wife Julia dies of pneumonia and because he has an opportunity to be a hero in a coal disaster. Bucking up, Tommy endures his frustrations until his son Tad wins an engineering degree from Cornell and finds a girl to marry who is not from Front St., not even from the Harrisburg Area. In the end, Tommy dies at peace with the world and himself in the Harrisburg Hospital, while the Widow Clara smiles bravely out at the rolling river.

Before he dies, Tommy reflects on what was Harrisburg's last generation of the Front St. establishment. "Their way of life together, its freedom, humorous mutual contempt, and easy license was destructive in other more immediate ways. Yet those who survived it were tempered and sure, as he had never been, as he was not now. He wondered what new mistakes they would invent and bequeath to succeeding generations as the characteristic of their age."

James Boyd was born July 2, 1888, at 124 Pine St., but he had relatives around the corner on Front St. He was graduated from the Hill School, Princeton, and Trinity College at Cambridge, and worked briefly for the *Patriot* as a reporter and for the Harrisburg Academy as a teacher. After serving in World War I, he lived most of his adult life in Southern Pines, N.C., and wrote four novels, the best of which is *Drums*. In literary circles, he was respected as a poet. He died Feb. 25, 1944, and in his obituary picture he resembles Eugene O'Neill. Boyd Hall is a legacy of his family.

Boyd's Harrisburg story retains its fascination, but how well he caught the atmosphere of old Front St. is questionable. The families really were more patrician than aristocratic, a sort of superbourgeois. Boyd was able to picture their need for comfort, status, and money, but, like an even surer artist, John O'Hara with his Fort Penn in *A Rage to Live*, Boyd showed less understanding of their commitment to *noblesse oblige*, education, and professionalism. Disappointing as the Front Streeters could be, they were not decadent.

The decline of Front St. might be attributed to deterministic social evolution and a weakening of the superbourgeois. Higher property taxation, the passing of the $20-a-month, sleep-in servant, the increased auto and truck traffic, and many other unhappy domestic facts of post-World War II American life doomed the prime inner-city neighborhoods. In the still moderately populated Harrisburg Area, it was simpler, more expedient, and even more ego-satisfying to recolonize gentry ghettoes in the restricted reaches of suburbia than to cope with old mansions and in-town annoyances. Furthermore, because of their commercial value, the Front St. homesteads brought ample cash for the sons and daughters to rebuild indulgently, if less substantially, out in the greenbelt.

It would be interesting if Boyd and O'Hara could describe the modern-day suburban squires and technocrats, because they saw the old Front Streeters as insular. "I often told her that most of the Fort Penn people gave me a pain in the ass," says O'Hara's outsider, Sidney Tate, "and she understood that but thought I could make an effort, and I'd simply say I'd married her and not Nesquehela County." "Well," replies Tate's friend, "maybe she resented your attitude. Maybe inside her she was thinking that you were a stranger. And Grace, unless she's changed, she never gave a damn what went on outside the county line."

The zenith of the Front St. set, gracious Harrisburg living, and unmitigated male chauvinism occurred on March 3, 1897. On that night some 400 of the town's plutocrats were at the grand opening of the

Harrisburg Club at Front and Market Streets. Attendants dressed in livery of dark blue and gold braid stood by to provide service.

The club had solid oak walls in every room, and electric lights were shaped like bell globes. The billiard room was on the first floor. There was a grand stairway and a balcony, and the dining room was on the second floor. Membership dues were high.

Boies Penrose went from the State Senate to the U.S. Senate that winter, but he kept his bachelor suite in the nearby Senate Hotel. When he was in town, Big Boies was always slipping over to the Harrisburg Club to do his drinking, which he considered second only to politics as serious business.

Before the Harrisburg Club closed at the beginning of World War II, O'Hara visited it at least once. He probably used it as a model for his Fort Penn Club in his 1949 novel. O'Hara said the club effected "a revolutionary change in the social life of Fort Penn," meaning that the Front Streeters starting going there for lunch instead of strolling from their offices to their homes. He said it was the code of the club that in the dining room you chose your company, while in the grill anyone could sit at your table. A written rule was that no breakfast was served after 9:30 A.M., no matter how late some members wished to get to work.

Two doors up from the Harrisburg Club was the University Club, founded in 1916 but not located on Front St. in the old Alricks home until 1922. This club had beautiful woodwork too, a dining room, a billiard parlor and all, but its bar was in the basement and dormitory rooms were on the upper floors. It had an attractive initiation fee of $10 and annual dues of $20, and for its banquets had such notable guest speakers as Lowell Thomas, Henry Drinker, Carveth Wells, Count Von Luckner, and H. V. Kaltenborn.

The University Club was for "intimate contact with 200 fellow college and university men; men who have followed a path similar to yours; who speak the same language; who will help you move up the ladder of success."

A high percentage of the University Club members had gone to Yale or Princeton. Harrisburg was a big Yale and Princeton town. The Hickok, Bailey, Reily, Stackpole, McCormick, and Gross namesakes of Front St. went to Yale, for example. "And then for some reason a lot of boys started to go to Princeton," as a Kunkel once explained.

Front St. had the clubs. The Engineers Club was next to the Harrisburg Hospital in what later became the law office of Huette F. Dowling and his nephew, now Judge John C. Dowling. The Civic Club was given by the widow of William R. Fleming in 1916. It was built in 1890 as a mansion, the only one on the west bank of the street.

Within walking distance of a man's home on Front St. was his business, his church, his bank, his schools, his restaurants, his hospital, the Court House, and the Capitol, all the necessities. When you lived on Front St., you had time to be somebody.

In 1925 there was no need to look elsewhere but Front St. to find who ran Harrisburg. In the 32 blocks between the John Harris Mansion and Division St. lived: 12 politicians, including the governor, the congressman, the Republican state chairman, and a former Prohibition candidate for President; 10 lawyers, including four who were or would be judges; three newspaper executives; three bankers; two clergymen; two manufacturers; the state's leading educator; an architect; one of five former mayors from Front St., and a bevy of physicians. Among the family names were: Kunkel, Swallow, Brady, Haldeman, Metzger, Kelker, McCreath, Herr, Hoffer, Gross, McCormick, Wharton, Hickok, Gilbert, Fox, Dull, Darlington, Weiss, Bailey, Cameron, Boas, Mitchell, Baker, Wickersham, Cunningham, Green, Sohn, Reily, Doutrich, Stackpole, Tracy, Payne, Bergner, Schuddemage, Herman, Knisely, Wallower, Hamilton, Reese, and Royal.

The late Rachel Fox, widow of Judge E. Fox, was one of the most charming of the Front Streeters and could recite the names of all 91 families without hesitation. Her brother, the late Prof. Beverly Waugh Kunkel, in 1967 spoke to the Historical Society on "The Genetics and Genealogy of Front St." Dr. Kunkel had been born there in 1880, and after earning his Ph.D. in biology (at Yale, of course), became an authority on vertebrate embryology for four decades at Lafayette College—founded by another Front Streeter, Judge James Madison Porter, the brother of still another Front Streeter, Gov. David Rittenhouse Porter.

The Kunkels were a Front St. breed whom Boyd and O'Hara did not see. From Christian Kunkel I, the burgess of Harrisburg in 1796, descended two congressmen, two judges, two state senators, nine lawyers, five physicians, three scientists, and one minstrel comic. Beverly Kunkel said he had "genetic relatives"—not "blood relatives," because he was a geneticist—up and down Front St. Once when Mrs. Fox underwent an operation, she told her brother that she was "surrounded by an army of Kunkel doctors," and she was.

Many Front Streeters parlayed their talent and money by marrying within the neighborhood. Porters married Reilys, Kunkels married Grosses, Baileys married Reilys, and a McCormick even married a Cameron. It was a neat mixture of heredity and environment that fascinated geneticist Beverly Kunkel. His own father, Charles, who ran the

Mechanics Bank on Market St., married Eliza B. Waugh, whose father conducted the Harrisburg Female College at the John Harris Mansion until he floundered in hard times and sold the home to Simon Cameron.

There were Lutherans and Methodists, and even a few Catholics, but the prevailing faiths on Front St. were Presbyterianism and Episcopalianism. To the Market Square Church went the Harrises, Hamiltons, Flemings, Alricks, Hickoks, Gilberts, Reilys, and Baileys, while to Pine Street went the McCormicks, Camerons, Grosses, and Boyds. The Olmsteds, Naumans, Paynes, Foxes, Boases, Reeses, Haldemans, and Whartons were among the illustrious at St. Stephen's Cathedral. Old Salem Reformed had Calders, Kelkers, Kunkels, Royals, and Grosses.

Though the Front Streeters had pride and self-esteem, few were outright snobs. It is a mistake to misjudge this older generation's deliberate sense of propriety for arrogance. What pretensions were enjoyed cannot compare to the blatant aloofness of some of the contemporary isolated *nouveau riche*. Many of the Front Streeters indeed were narrow in their social attitudes and politics, but they were realistic people. After all, they were only a block away from the real world.

The most noted feature of Front St. were the mansions, which actually were modestly conspicuous for the elite but were wonderfully extravagant in the eyes of the proletarian Harrisburg Germans. With the dignity of a row of dowagers, the mansions faced the Susquehanna. For handsomeness, nothing in Central Pennsylvania has ever equalled the picturesque scene of these stately homes and the wide, serene river, with 550 American elms lining its Harrisburg shore.

Donald McCormick had a mansion of 32 rooms, including two libraries, four marble fireplaces, an elevator, and towers and gables, plus three hitching posts and carriage steps outside. His place at 101 N. Front St. is now part of the Harrisburg Library.

David E. Tracy, president of the old Harrisburg Pipe and Pipe Bending Co., had a 30-room mansion, erected in 1908 with mural paintings, all concrete floors covered with the best hardwood, masonry walls, an iron-cage elevator, an immense cedar closet, and a coal bin so big it was later used as a dining hall. The entrance was actually on Muench St., but Tracy got himself a Front St. address. He had five live-in domestics, including his chauffeur. Tracy Hall at Bishop McDevitt High School is named for him, and in 1951 his home became the Osteopathic Hospital for 20 years.

Henry Schuddemage (pronounced "Shoed-a-mayge") in the 1890s built a 17-room mansion, with 19 windows on the first floor. A former councilman, Schuddemage wanted a Victorian palace. He had two-inch stonework, and hardwood floors were on all three stories. The Schuddemage mansion was razed in 1962, and the demolishers said it was as difficult to rip down as an armory.

The Maclay Mansion at Front and South Sts. was built in 1791 by the U.S. Senator with 2½-foot-thick limestone walls and solid mahogany woodwork. It launched the Front St. tradition for modest splendor. In 1908 the second part of the home was added, duplicating even the glasswork. From 1827 to 1908 the Harrisburg Academy used the mansion. Jacob F. Seiler, out of Yale, became headmaster at age 28 and remained until his death in 1907. Professor Seiler was one of the delights of Front St. He was a mathematician, a linguist, a historian, a trout fisherman, one of Harrisburg's few prominent Democrats, and a founder of the Pine Street Church, where he was a ruling elder for 44 years and a Sunday School teacher for 49 years. Before the Pennsylvania Bar Association took over full use of the mansion in 1972, George Reily Bailey, president of the old Harrisburg National Bank, lived there for 25 years.

The governors resided at 311–313 N. Front St. from the Civil War until 1960, when Gov. David L. Lawrence sold the property. Gov. Raymond P. Shafer moved out of the Indiantown Gap residence and into the new Georgian house at Front and Maclay Sts. for Christmas of 1968. Meanwhile, a half-century before, DeWitt Fry wanted his home at 311 S. Front St. to look like the old Governor's Mansion, so he put a brownstone entrance on it to match.

The least disturbed important piece of architecture on the street is St. Stephen's Cathedral House with its small Grecian portico, built in the 1840s.

The decline of Front St. quickened with the end of World War II. "We never dreamed for one minute in those days of the changes that would come," said Mrs. Fox in 1963. The family lines expired, others moved away, the young went off to college and did not return to Harrisburg, and business interests were lost. The street became one-way south on Sept. 17, 1956. Even earlier, in 1952, the Dutch elm blight began. By 1961, 45 percent of the street was commercial and 11 office buildings had macadam parking lots in front.

No one had the slightest idea of how to save Front St., or even why it should be saved. The simplest solution—move back and start a renaissance of Harrisburg gracious living—was not even considered by a generation which, as James Boyd foresaw, would invent "new mistakes" to "bequeath to succeeding generations as the characteristic of their age."

Sin City

EMPTYING BOOZE

... *Godliness and Gaiety*

The mores of the Harrisburg Area always have been strange and baffling.

"Fort Penn, the City Beautiful, but as dead as a doornail on Sunday afternoon," wrote John O'Hara in *A Rage to Live*. Yet at the time, Harrisburg had one of the most thriving red-light districts in the East and was a center for the trafficking of bootleg booze, while Dauphin County had 77,816 illegal slot machines, according to a federal government report.

Harrisburg long has been a community divided down the middle between the blue-blooded and devout church-goers and the indulgent sensualists. The two are worlds apart in living style, but are wonderfully scrupulous not to annoy the other's pursuit of happiness; and always there is a curiosity about the one side's godliness and rectitude and the other's depravity and gaiety.

Prurient curiosity is the Harrisburg weakness. As O'Hara's fictional editor said: "If the telegraph wire said a thousand people had been killed in an earthquake in Chile, the important news in Fort Penn would still be that a rich and beautiful young girl was going to bed with a handsome, more or less unknown city slicker. It's regrettable, out of proportion, but it's true. Or, God damn it, is it regrettable? Come to think of it, if the people of Fort Penn were more interested, morbidly interested in the earthquake and a thousand people killed, I'd quit the newspaper business, or at any rate I'd get out of Fort Penn."

The American Social Health Association on Sept. 24, 1968, gave Harrisburg an "A" rating for its efforts to keep the City and its environs

24

free of streetwalkers and pickups in bars, lobbies, and taverns. "We are delighted, but we are mindful that it must be a continuing campaign," said Mayor Albert H. Straub. The very next day, the State Police arrested eight persons in a vice raid and the following day arrested six more, all within a mile of City Hall. But cleanliness is next to godlessness too. Each prostitute proved to be medically clean, even the veteran who was 47 years old.

When the Rev. Malcolm Boyd, the poet and lecturer, visited Harrisburg in 1972 during the Harrisburg 8 trial, he jokingly observed, "They have a lot of church buildings in Harrisburg, so I consider it a very dangerous place."

The religious influence indeed has always been strong. As early as 1851, the *Harrisburg Telegraph* noted that the town of 7,000 persons had 11 churches and a denomination meeting hall, a ratio higher than that of Utica, N.Y., which supposedly had the most churches per capita.

Harrisburg since 1919 has had community Holy Week services. In the 1930s and 1940s there were 98 churches in or near the City, but as John Gunther wrote in *Inside U.S.A.*, "Both Army and Navy threatened during World War II to put its [Pennsylvania's] capital out of bounds, because the venereal rate was so high." There were more than 100 prostitutes working Mulberry St., Cherry Alley, Dewberry Alley, and up in "The Ward" on Verbeke, Sixth, and Seventh Sts. District Attorney Carl B. Shelley made a famous raid on May 26, 1939, hitting 38 bawdy houses and bars and arresting 152 persons. Selling sex was big business, and not even the church-going politicians—as all of them have always been in the Harrisburg Area—dared to disturb the flesh trade. Crackdowns came only after officials insisted that the public's health, not its morals, was endangered by the visible depravity. One of the town's leading attorneys with clients in the red-light district eventually advanced himself to the position of honorable judge.

The brothel business declined with the end of World War II, only to be replaced by pickups and call girls. The most notable exception was in staid Carlisle, of all places, where the free enterprise system struggled on. The legendary Bessie Jones at age 82 was slain on Oct. 1, 1972, after operating a house of ill repute in her clapboard home on Locust Ave. for more than a half-century. Mrs. Jones, a black proprietress, inherited the house from her mother, Mrs. Cora Andrews, who in turn had inherited it from her mother, supposedly a camp follower with the Confederate Army who stayed in Carlisle after the Battle of Gettysburg. Bessie usually had two girls, one black and one white, for a week's stay on the circuit, and in later years charged $15. She was arrested only nine times for operating a bawdy house, four times for selling liquor without a license, and once for failing to file her income tax. Internal Revenue discovered she had $192,000 in the bank under her own name and $80,000 in a pink pillow slip. The citizenry cheered in 1959 when her attorney, Hyman Goldstein, once a famous Dickinson quarterback who played against Jim Thorpe, compared her in court to Molly Pitcher, Thorpe, Dickinson College, and the Dickinson Law School as "a fine old institution" in Carlisle. "She supplies something needed in the community," he asserted. Bessie's untimely death ended an era.

A lenient attitude always existed about hard drinking in the Harrisburg Area, understandably so because of the Scotch-Irish and German heritage. The late historian A. Boyd Hamilton said that the first person arrested in Harrisburg was a bootlegger named Nicole Godin, but he was let go after the Indians complained.

Harrisburg, which thinks of itself as a law-and-order town, was wet during the 13 years of Prohibition, from Jan. 17, 1920, to Dec. 4, 1933. The establishment, especially the newspapers, favored Prohibition, but the people did not. On the first day of what H. G. Wells called "the crowning silliness," the *Patriot* reported, "Few Mourners at Barleycorn's Bier." A reporter wrote: "John Barleycorn is dead. Thirsty booze-hounds ran swiftly from bar to bar last evening." The *Telegraph* was even drier than the *Patriot*, and more wrong in its social predictions. It editorialized on the first day: "Those who believe that 'booze will come back' are barking up an empty tree. Booze has gone to stay." The churches rejoiced and the Dauphin County Women's Christian Temperance Union held a celebration at Stevens Memorial Methodist Church, where the song "Goodbye Saloon" was sung. The Warhorse of Prohibition," the Rev. Dr. Silas Comfort Swallow, made an appearance. "His countenance fairly beamed as he told of his years of work in the dry cause, and he added that he is not through yet," the newspaper reported.

But Prohibition never had a chance in Harrisburg. "It was kind of an open town," wrote Robert Louis Lyon in 1971. He had been with the United Press in Harrisburg in the twenties and thirties. "Prohibition was in force, but there were all kinds of interesting apartment speakeasies, usually run by large, genial, suicide blondes. Some of the original saloons were still doing business behind their unlocked swinging doors, supposed to be selling nothing stronger than 0.5 percent beer. Naturally the feds and the local cops bought that story, or rather the saloon-keepers bought them. And, of course, there were the two wide-open red light districts to liven things up."

Prohibition wiped out Highspire Pure Rye Whiskey, a favorite since 1823; Old Put, another rye; Liquorine, a Highspire-made "unequalled

cure for coughs and colds," and such wonderful local beer as Graup-
ner's and Fink's.

Replacing the old standards, Harrisburg got "Moony," "Four Aces,"
"White Mule," bathtub gin, and other assorted beverages. Illicit booze
was expensive, with beer selling for 25 cents a glass and hard liquor for
75 cents. Prince Farrington, "the king of the bootleggers," shipped
down some of his better stuff from Jersey Shore. Farrington was pro-
ducing 2,000 gallons of 190 to 195 proof alcohol every 24 hours even
after Prohibition in 1934, when the federal agents arrested him for
depriving the government of $12,000 a day in tax revenue. Nobody
ever called Farrington's whiskey "rotgut." The bourgeoisie had it delivered to the door. In fact, the last Prohibition bootlegger caught in Harrisburg was a gentleman running a five-gallon jug in a burlap bag from his
car to a customer's home.

An estimated 50 speakeasies were between North and Reily Sts. A
candy store sold booze, as did a bakery. In Steelton, they drank what
they called "hot tea." A man in the ward had 85 barrels of mash on his
second floor, and police could not understand why the floor did not
collapse. Harrisburgers soaked old trousers in kegs to give the alcohol
more flavor.

Bootleggers pumped steam into old whiskey barrels and then added
brown sugar or caramel to a soaking concoction of grain alcohol and
distilled water. It was "steam whiskey," often murderous. Bathtab gin
actually was made in Harrisburg bathtubs, with grain alcohol, distilled
water, and extracts. In one winter, 13 Harrisburgers died because kero-
sene got into the booze. Needled beer was a mixture of grain alcohol
forced through needles into barrels of near beer.

The end of the Prohibition joyride was followed a decade later by the
end of bawdy houses. For the last 35 years, with no standards, the sins
of the flesh have been dispersed and, though thriving, the sensuality is a
good deal less glamorous.

Drinking and even prostitution were not always harmful, but nar-
cotics are. A 1972 study by Juniata College of eight Central Pennsylvania counties revealed that one out of five high school students have
tried drugs. Other social indicators in the Harrisburg Area are not
reassuring either. Illegitimacy in Dauphin County in the 1960s increased by 15 percent. There were 925 divorces in Dauphin, Cumberland, and Perry counties in 1970. The suicide rate in this part of Pennsylvania is usually above average. The old weaknesses of the flesh were
out in the open and tolerated, remarkably so. The new maladjustments
are just as visible and appear to be far more perverse, but are ignored as
beyond remedy though they can produce far worse consequences.

Black Harrisburg

LINGO TEMPLE

. . . From Hercules to Manhood

Blacks have lived in the Harrisburg Area from the earliest pioneering days. One, named Hercules, played the heroic role in Harrisburg's finest tale of folklore. Yet the blacks as a people for 250 years have never been fully accepted.

While much anti-Negro sentiment always has existed in the community, spreading to suburbia in the postwar era, the more accurate description of Harrisburg racial history is that bigotry has not so much prevailed as the white man's unmindfulness. Overt white-black hostility has been rare. If more affirmative confrontation had come in less tense days before the 1960s and 1970s, the community might have broken out of its separatism that still could lead to attitudinal apartheid and increased physical isolation in the future.

The blacks from the beginning were trapped by their pigmentation and inherited poverty, and they became the subservient class in the Harrisburg Area. Educational opportunity, jobs, and housing were not easily accessible. The growing white middle class quickly judged the black man as its unequal and ostracized him.

The black was not barred outright from politics, churches, business, professional life, and culture, but he was not accepted either, and there was surprisingly little tokenism. Central Pennsylvania buried the black under a blanket of history and circumstance, narrowed its almost consensus view about proper ideas and behavior, and ignored the vitality, warmth, sensitivity, and personal elegance of the black man and his way of life.

Until this generation, the black Harrisburger all too often acquiesced in his supportive role, and his docility was not even appreciated. When the notorious zero-vote district, the Sixth Precinct of the Seventh Ward, gave Barry Goldwater a 75-vote majority in 1964, and was the one exception in the entire nation for black neighborhoods, Harrisburgers took the oddity for granted. Two years later at a public meeting, a local black announced that his people were "tired of $2 and a glass of wine in exchange for a vote." One hundred years of "plantation politics"—a term a white Harrisburg politician used—began to crumble.

28

The shocks often have had to come from outside the Midstate. In 1969 segregationist Sen. John C. Stennis, speaking in the U.S. Senate, used government statistics to show that Harrisburg's school racial imbalance was as bad, or worse, than segregation in his own Mississippi.

The Irvis suit in the U.S. Supreme Court against Harrisburg Moose Lodge 107, located within yards of the State Capitol, was unnerving. K. Leroy Irvis, a Pittsburgh black lawyer and Democratic majority leader in the State House, as well as perhaps the most skilled orator in Pennsylvania politics, accompanied a white Moose member to the club on Dec. 29, 1969, and was denied service.

"I'm from California," a black resident wrote to the *Patriot* in 1971, "and I won't pretend that there is no discrimination in that state, but comparatively speaking, black people in Central Pennsylvania are openly and terribly discriminated against." He was criticizing the refusal of some golf courses to admit blacks.

The July 15, 1968, report for the Greater Harrisburg Movement stated: "Suburban communities, particularly on the West Shore, generally have no Negro population whatsoever. Although no one in an official position will identify this as a problem, it is perhaps the single greatest barrier to effective communication and cooperation among local officials. Suburban officials are happy not to have to become involved with the City and thereby run the risk of becoming involved with or having to take a public position on open housing and the other racial issues."

A newspaper series in 1968 by Wilbur Pennewill concluded with the article: " 'What More Do They Want?' Attitude Points Up White Racism, Negroes Say."

Yet black history in the Harrisburg Area is too complex to be wrapped up in polemics.

Though thwarted at almost every turn by white hypocrisy, black Harrisburgers have had no worse a chance for leading fulfilling lives than they do in almost any other community in this nation that is fretfully emerging from its cultural patterns of discrimination. Though still the exception, there are enough white-black friendships to refute assertions that locally the races are split inseparably. Racial violence and bitterness, especially in 1968 and 1969, surfaced and two youths—a white boy and a black boy—were killed; yet the more prolonged trouble that should have been expected was avoided. Black leadership, dormant or head-nodding for decades, increasingly has become more articulate and persuasive. And the Harrisburg School District, to the point of being perhaps overambitious for a Central Pennsylvania institution, is one of the nation's leaders in its attempt to desegregate its classrooms, economically as well as racially.

Black history in Harrisburg started with the legend—never proven true—of Hercules, the slave of the pioneer John Harris. About 1720, shortly after Harris started his trading post, a band of Indians returning from the south demanded rum. Harris refused. The Indians carried him to the nearby mulberry tree on River Park and prepared to burn him. Meanwhile, Hercules escaped to the West Shore, rounded up friendly Shawnee Indians, and saved his master, according to the tale told years later by the pioneer's grandson, Robert Harris, a congressman. Hercules is buried near Harris and an infant Harris daughter in River Park. Ironically, for centuries afterward, Harrisburg had no integrated cemeteries.

There were not many slaves in frontier Harrisburg. Pennsylvania in 1780, thanks to the Quakers, became the first slave state to abolish slavery, but it did so on a gradual basis. The last known slave was registered in Harrisburg on Aug. 29, 1825. That same year, on April 21, there was a runaway slave riot at the local jail. Blacks, infuriated by the capture of a fugitive, stormed the jail. Nineteen persons were arrested and 12 found guilty. One of the convicted escaped, but the others were punished on the treadmill.

While white Harrisburgers did not consider the Negro as their equal, they did abhor slavery. Gov. Joseph Ritner (1836–1838), an Anti-Mason and later a founder of the Pennsylvania Republican Party, made his home at Newville and risked political popularity to be an abolitionist. Ritner to this day is the only professional politician of the Area, with the exception of his colleague Thaddeus Stevens from Gettysburg and Lancaster, to take a stand for the blacks at the inconvenience of the white community.

Famed black spokesman Frederick Douglass and his white advocate, William Lloyd Garrison, held an antislavery meeting at the Dauphin County Courthouse in mid-August of 1847. Harrisburgers apparently were vexed by a black man's assuming he was equal. A "volley of unmerchantable eggs," in Douglass's words, were thrown through the courthouse window, and when Douglass stood to speak more eggs were tossed and "again scented the house with Slavery's choice incense." The crowd chanted, "Throw out the nigger, throw out the nigger." Garrison was hit by an egg. Bricks were thrown and a flying stone caught Douglass above one eye. He grabbed a chair to protect himself, while there was a debate over whether the police should be called to quell the mob.

Douglass had to leave the courthouse with another black. "A white lady kindly offered to walk with me and protect me from the mob," he wrote, but he declined because "such an arrangement would exasperate the mob."

"Harrisburg one day will be ashamed of it," Douglass jotted in his journal. The next morning, a Sunday, he spoke in the local black churches and at the courthouse again in the afternoon, but no trouble ensued. One church in which he must have appeared is Bethel AME, founded in 1843. Another was the old Wesleyan Union, founded in 1829, located where the South Office Building is today.

A major disturbance occurred on Aug. 24, 1850, when some Virginians and a Mr. Littlejohn of Baltimore came to Harrisburg to arrest three runaway slaves, George Brocks, Sam Wilson, and a man called Billy. While the slave-catchers were at the office of the U.S. Commissioner on Walnut St., a crowd attacked them. Bricks were torn from the Third St. pavement and hurled, one striking Littlejohn. The slaves were jailed, but Brocks and Wilson escaped. Before taking Billy back to Virginia, Littlejohn went to eat at the Herr House at the southwest corner of Third and Market Sts., but the black waiters refused to serve him. Sixty-one persons were indicted. The incident, however, was so upsetting that the town's most prominent whites, including J. M. Haldeman, John C. Kunkel, F. K. Boas, R. J. Fleming, Lyman Gilbert, H. A. Kelker, John H. Berryhill, and P. K. Boyd, paid the costs and had all criminal charges dropped.

Blacks did much of the manual labor in Central Pennsylvania, including helping to build the canals and railroads. They earned minimal wages to erect the fortifications of Harrisburg and the West Shore prior to the Battle of Gettysburg.

The leading black man of Harrisburg's 19th century was William Howard Day (1825–1900). Day was elected to the School Board in 1878 and was its president from 1891 to 1893, perhaps the first black city school board president in any white American community. It has never been satisfactorily explained why in Harrisburg a black was so honored; it has not happened in any suburban school system in the area, and Harrisburg did not get its second black president until 1969. But Dr. Day was an exceptional man.

He was born Oct. 19, 1825 in New York City and earned his bachelor's and master's degree at Oberlin College. In later life he was awarded an honorary doctorate from Livingstone College in North Carolina. He was distinguished long before coming to Harrisburg. He edited two black weekly newspapers, one in Cleveland, and was a prominent teacher and lecturer in Latin, Greek, mathematics, rhetoric, vocal music, and shorthand. He was a guest of honor in the British Isles and spoke before the Lord Mayor of Dublin and 3,000 others at the music hall. Prior to the Civil War, he directed the education of 50,000 underground-railroad blacks in Canada.

Day came to Harrisburg's uptown Eighth Ward in 1872 and was a clerk in the corporation bureau of the Auditor General. In 1876 he was elected secretary of the General Conference of the AME Zion Church, a post he held the rest of his life. At his death on Dec. 3, 1900, he was given the first front-page obituary for a black man in the *Harrisburg Telegraph*, which said: "By all he was recognized as one of the leading men of his race." He was buried at Lincoln Cemetery in Penbrook. A newer cemetery in Steelton later was named for him, as well as a Harrisburg public housing project.

In the 1880s Peter S. Blackwell, a college graduate, came to Steelton, which had 1,200 blacks. He founded the *Steelton Press*, which together with the *Harrisburg Sentinel Gazette* constituted the black weekly press. The outspoken Blackwell campaigned in Washington in 1904 to demand that Republicans enforce the 15th Amendment, and that same year he was elected Steelton councilman by 27 votes. Though Steelton had a hard-working black community, with a Home Club and a Black Union Republican Club, its schools were segregated until after World War I, and fewer than 40 blacks won diplomas. At least twice, the white steel bosses imported blacks as strike-breakers.

W. Justin Carter (1866–1947) was Harrisburg's first black attorney, and, following the death of Dr. Day, was the leader of the black community. A native of Richmond, Va., Carter studied at Harvard, taught two years in Maryland, and came to Harrisburg in 1894. He practiced law here for 53 years, and was one of the town's foremost orators. He was private secretary to political boss Lieutenant Governor Ed Beidleman, and later in the Earle Administration he helped rewrite the Workmen's Compensation Law. He was an assistant district attorney, and within local Republican circles was a persistent advocate of the black man's rights.

Day and Carter made breakthroughs that were not sustained. It was not until Aug. 24, 1967, that City Hall got its first black official. Glenn E. Williams, Jr., 40, the son of a Penn-Harris Hotel doorman, was sworn in as city controller. In November of 1969, Stanley R. Lawson, a Republican, won election as the first black city councilman, at the same time Mrs. Miriam Menaker, also a Republican, became the first woman and Jewish council member. In 1971, LeRoy Robinson, Jr. ran on the Democratic ticket for City Council and lost by only 86 votes.

Harrisburg is just 36 direct miles from the Mason-Dixon Line, so it has always had a sizable black population. During the Civil War the Tri-

County Area had a population of 109,647, of whom 3,168 were blacks; and 1,321 of them lived in the City. In the next 80 years, the total population doubled, but the black community more than tripled. In the 50 years between 1920 and 1970, the area population doubled again, and once again the black population more than tripled, though in 1925 only 13 percent of the blacks in Harrisburg and Steelton owned their own homes.

In 1970 there were 26,271 blacks in Dauphin County, 1,797 blacks in Cumberland County, and 35 blacks in Perry County. One hundred years before, Perry County had 140 blacks. In the 1960s, Cumberland County's blacks actually declined by 50.

What has happened is an obvious increased separatism. In the 1960s, suburbia got even more predominantly white as Harrisburg's black community increased by almost 40 percent to 20,911. Carlisle's 961 blacks represented more than half of Cumberland County's.

Harrisburg's white population in the Sixties fell by 17,739 as its blacks increased by 5,815, and by 1970 the City was 30.7 percent black, second in Pennsylvania only to Philadelphia's 33.6 percent.

The growing local heterogeneity of the races took place at a time of rising national tensions, and conflict was not unexpected in the Harrisburg Area; in fact, it might have been a self-fulfilling prophecy.

The new era dawned in 1963. The first integrated public housing opened in a poorer section of Swatara Township, the Mayor's Human Relations Committee was established, and on June 11 the first black fireman was hired. Interestingly enough, the City had black policemen from the turn of the century. In 1967 Steelton set a Pennsylvania precedent by appointing the state's first black police chief, a capable young man whose name appropriately enough was Frederick Douglas.

The first Freedom March was held in Harrisburg on Aug. 3, 1963. "It certainly would be a real novelty in Harrisburg to see a Negro reading an electric meter or a gas meter," the Rev. Franklin Henley, a local black, told the 600 marchers.

Trouble broke out in 1968. At the February 9 basketball game between William Penn and John Harris high schools, Ben David Darden, Jr., 16, a black of deficient intelligence, stabbed to death Frank Ament, 15, a white from Susquehanna Township, outside the Camp Curtin gymnasium. It was an isolated incident, but spread fear throughout the white community.

Harrisburg's sister city, York, had serious weekend civil disturbances in the summer of 1968. In August a York white man shot and wounded 11 black citizens before he was disarmed by William Orr, a black. On Christmas morning, Orr was murdered in his kitchen by a shotgun blast from a passing automobile. York, with only 6,300 blacks, that summer had the first curfew ever enforced for racial troubles in Central Pennsylvania. A York lawyer explained the problem as arising from "indecisiveness, lack of preparation, and the simple fact that York's best talent has moved to the suburbs."

In the fall of 1968, for the first time a majority of pupils in Harrisburg schools were black. In 1930 there had been 1,643 black pupils, or 12 percent, and by 1970 there were 7,245 blacks, or 58 percent. The enrollment of all pupils hit a peak in 1967 with 13,751, and started to drop after that. Meanwhile, the Pennsylvania Human Relations Commission, while conceding that Camp Hill, the West Shore, Lower Dauphin, and Derry Township had virtually all-white, de facto segregated districts, ordered the Harrisburg system to integrate.

Only one suburban area willingly made an effort at integration. In the fall of 1968, Susquehanna Township, the most innovative of the suburban districts, converted the previously all-black Glenwood Elementary School of Edgemont into a kindergarten for the entire district. The township accepted the change with unusual equanimity.

All but two of Harrisburg's 18 schools in 1969 were racially imbalanced, with 99 percent blacks in Downey and Hamilton, 97 percent in Ben Franklin, 95 percent in Woodward, and 88 percent in Lincoln, all elementary schools.

"The Pennsylvania Human Relations Commission got our attention by hitting us over the head with a mandate for racial balance," Superintendent David H. Porter wrote in 1971. "The Commission's order, though castigated by many, may well have been precisely the right thing at the right time. Not only did it wake us up to our responsibilities in race relations but it made us aware of the educational and administrative flaws that ran through our entire system."

In the two years prior to the School Board's 1970 plan for racial balance, Harrisburg had the worst social crisis in its history.

There were school incidents of extortion and assault and battery in the fall of 1968. On Feb. 18, 1969, Harris, Penn, and Camp Curtin were closed for the first time after there were three minor fires and several physically abused pupils. "Open rebellion" occurred at Harris, in the words of Superintendent Glenn Parker, and Harris shut again on February 20 while police patrolled the halls.

Dr. Parker resigned in June of 1969 after five years' service in an increasingly difficult situation. A veteran of 30 years in the Harrisburg system, the low-keyed but committed Dr. Porter was appointed, proving to be a remarkable choice. That fall James H. Rowland, Sr., a local lawyer and a member of the State Board of Education, became the first black School Board president since Dr. Day. Like Porter, Rowland's strength was his calmness, his reasonableness, and his courage to be progressive in a period when much of the national mood was reactionary.

A sign of the white exodus to the suburbs was that in September of 1969, the Central Dauphin District, with 13,294 pupils to Harrisburg's 12,932, became the largest in Dauphin County.

The year of the moon landing, 1969, was the worst Central Pennsylvania ever had.

The Harrisburg Riot broke out on June 23, when a former black school teacher started a boycott of a pharmacy at 13th and Market Sts. Two days earlier she had been arrested on a disorderly conduct charge after she sought to purchase a pack of cigarettes as the store was closing. Incensed because she was taken off to police headquarters in a paddy wagon, she organized a march at the pharmacy the following Monday night. Violence broke loose at 7:40 P.M., with flying bricks and tear gas, and the Allison Hill neighborhood did not quiet down until 3 A.M. It was like a noisy, all-night block party, except that 13 persons were arrested, seven of whom, including the school teacher, were convicted in September.

The following Tuesday night, June 24, the violence continued, and 18-year-old Charles A. Scott, a black, was killed by a blast from a shotgun fired by an 11-year veteran on the police force. The same night there were eight cases of arson, many false alarms, and 50 State Troopers arrived to make three more arrests.

Mayor Albert H. Straub, on constant duty, clamped down a week-long curfew on the City, and the first night 34 persons were arrested for violating that. Meanwhile the Black Coalition issued a statement, asking, among other things, "Immediate removal of all occupational forces from our community so that our community can have law and order."

At the State Human Relations Commission hearings, a police official testified that the riot was planned. That assertion lacked full substantiation, but tensions were high enough to make a riot possible without preplanning. City Hall estimated that the violence cost taxpayers a minimum of $100,000.

Within a month of the Harrisburg Riot, there were four days of civil disturbance in York, in which there was sniping and the arrest of 57 persons. A nonresident black woman was killed and a white policeman fatally injured, as Neil Armstrong and Edwin Aldrin walked on the moon. The National Guard answered the call at York.

The racial troubles contributed to political upsets in both communities. That November the Harrisburg voters turned out Mayor Straub and the Republican organization for the first time in 57 years. Harold A. Swenson, a Democrat, was elected by 50 votes. In York, Dr. Eli Eichelberger, also a Democrat, won election by 400 votes.

Tension peaked in Harrisburg, and there was no major incident again until September of 1971, when the new Harrisburg High School Cougars played its first football game at Cedar Cliff. The Colts won in the last minutes of play, 17–14, and trouble ensued, for which Harrisburg received virtually all the blame. Within four months, the two schools met again in basketball, and Harrisburg won, 55–54, its first basketball victory in the new school's history. There was no trouble. The aftermath of the football game, however, raised new questions about how far suburbia would understand and cooperate with an inner-city school. Cedar Cliff announced withdrawal from the Central Penn League and the Pennsylvania Interscholastic Athletic Association arbitrarily placed a probation order against Harrisburg, for an incident in which there was misbehavior by both whites and blacks and City and suburban youths.

During this period, Harrisburg's problems were compounded because of the State Capitol, where much picketing occurred. Marches by welfare recipients, many of them black, became more of an irritant to onlooking whites than similar demonstrations by other protestors. Though the state school teachers were as ill-mannered as any, Harrisburg Area residents were more upset when Roxanne Jones, chairman of the Philadelphia Welfare Rights Organization, riantly threw her shoe through the transom of Governor Shafer's reception room on June 2, 1970. Miss Jones, a black, later served five days of a two-month term in Dauphin County Prison.

It was in this social tempest that the Harrisburg School Board, by a vote of 6–2 on May 8, 1970, adopted racial and economic desegregation for the purpose of individual scholastic achievement and citizenship awareness. The Dauphin County Court upheld the decision, and in September of 1970 the new school mix and the cross-town busing began. "We think the requirements are morally, constitutionally and educationally right and good," Dr. Porter asserted. The community, however, was glum, but remarkably law-abiding in face of its doubts whether classroom achievement and racial understanding could be realized. "Lucky Kids Go to Harrisburg Schools This Fall" was an early public relations slogan, but quickly was changed to a more appropriate "Give the Kids and the Schools a Chance."

The new program started in 1970 with a school district 58 percent black, which became even blacker because perhaps 800 white youngsters were withdrawn after the plan was announced. Harrisburg had to bus more than a third of its pupils, at a cost of almost $500,000. "The alternative is to return to what we were and this is unacceptable," said Dr. Porter. "Our schools were dying."

As Harrisburg was integrating in 1970, so was Rochester, N.Y., Chapel Hill, N.C., and Berkeley and Riverside, Calif. White Plains, N.Y. had started as early as 1964 and Hartford, Conn. in 1966.

The school experiment is so linked to national racial attitudes that an early assessment of its progress is impossible. It would seem, however, that it did start to stop much of the deterioration, especially the violence, in the classrooms. There appears to be a gradual rebuilding of civic morale, if not yet of racial acceptance, in the community. At the same time there is a noticeable hardening of suburbia's neighborliness toward Harrisburg. While the City struggled with its historic rejuvenation in 1970 and 1971, ironically the headlines on the West Shore told of litigation against middle-class white male youngsters wanting to wear hair longer than promulgated school codes permitted.

The busing issue never became explosive in the Harrisburg Area, perhaps because it was buffered by a prevailing, and this time favorable, hypocrisy. Virtually all the suburban districts bus heavily, including Central Dauphin, which takes youngsters from Paxtang, which is within walking distance of John Harris, and Susquehanna, which picks up pupils within three blocks of William Penn. Students living across the street from the Steelton-Highspire Junior-Senior High School are bused, incredibly enough, to Central Dauphin, because Steel-High is located in Swatara Township but does not serve that community. Furthermore, 42 percent of American school children in 1971, according to the *New York Times*, were carried by 256,000 yellow buses.

Harrisburg in September of 1971 advanced its program by making one high school, its first unified school since 1893. Had surrounding metropolitan areas within walking distance of Harris and Penn been in the school system, the two high schools could have been retained and had a fairly good integrated and scholastic mix.

York adopted its desegregated program in 1971. W. Russell Chapman, a black leader with a master's degree in chemistry from Cornell, cast the deciding 5–4 vote from his chair at the top of the stairway in his home. "I'm voting for it," he said dramatically, and four days later, at age 73, Mr. Chapman was dead from cancer.

The future of black history in Harrisburg now lies, not so much within the City, but within the metropolitan area. The blacks and whites of the City endured the 1960s with more valor and optimism than could have been expected after 250 years of separatism. The crisis of citizenship now spills out to the affluent white suburbs, where the fundamental unresolved issue of American history, that of true brotherhood, is to be tested.

Weather Worries

... *Most Like It Hot*

Central Pennsylvania weather is so distressingly disappointing that the natives get eccentric about it.

The winters are mild, so the burghers perversely hate what chill there is and are pathologically opposed to snow. They put winter treads on their automobiles at the end of September, though Harrisburg seldom gets an inch of snow before Thanksgiving Day. Deaf to Thoreau's "frozen music" of winter, Harrisburgers endure tight-lipped until mid-April.

There is a "Valley Forge syndrome" that contradicts the fact that the mean snowfall is only 36.3 inches, half of what covers Syracuse, N.Y. in a season. Harrisburgers look back in horror on the record snowfall of 81.3 inches in the winter of 1960–61.

The winter average temperature is 31.7 degrees. The Lower Susquehanna's record low is a minus 25, but Harrisburg's low was a minus 14 degrees on Jan. 14, 1912. For 12 days that January, the minimum never got higher than 13 degrees above, the unhappiest cold siege ever in the City. Harrisburg averages 5,205 degree days a year, which are the year's accumulated degrees above 65 that thermostats are set. The town is a bit colder than Pittsburgh, Philadelphia, and Reading, but much less harsh than Erie, Scranton, or State College. What is annoying is not the cold, but Harrisburg's freezing-thawing type of winter.

It is rare when Harrisburg has as much as six inches of snow on the ground for 30 days of winter. Yet a snowstorm can panic the natives. Dwight Eisenhower left the presidency in 1961 during a week when the Midstate was "weather-beaten and snow-weary," in the words of the *Patriot-News*, because 18.7 inches had fallen. Ike agreed with his neighbors that it was unpleasant, and he quickly departed Gettysburg for quail shooting in sunny Georgia.

Central Pennsylvania seldom enjoys many springlike days. From a mild, damp winter, it usually heads into a prolonged and sticky summer. There is not even an abundance of rain. Twenty days a month are rain-free, on the average, and there are three hail storms and 30 to 35 thunderstorms a year. The normal annual precipitation is 40 to 44 inches.

Yet a cloudless day is a rarity. Harrisburg's annual sunshine is only 60 percent of the maximum possible. There are only 85 clear days a year, on the average. Between June and September, the normal humidity at 7 P.M. is from 61 to 68 percent. As John Updike wrote in *Rabbit Redux*, "The sky is cloudless yet colorless, hovering blanched humidity, in the way of these Pennsylvania summers, good for nothing but to make green things grow. Men don't even tan; filmed by sweat, they turn yellow."

Gen. Robert E. Lee got a sample of the July doldrums. Showers preceded the Battle of Gettysburg, and then on the first day it was clear and hot. A Gettysburg College professor measured the temperature at 87 degrees in the shade. The second and third days the weather began hazy and ended with high humidities and temperatures above 90. On the fourth day, Lee retreated and there was a terrific downpour.

As a climatological report put it: "Although temperatures as high as 107 degrees have been reported in southern countries, extremes of 100 are rare, occurring only once every few years. Temperatures in excess of 90 degrees, however, are experienced normally on 20 to 30 days from May to September each year and at times may be accompanied by high relative humidity and little wind movement. When lasting for more than one or two days, conditions become oppressive. Fortunately, such periods seldom extend beyond five to seven days at a time." What happens is that the southern and Atlantic summer winds flow into the Cumberland Valley. Semipermanent high pressures hover over the Carolinas and seal the humidity in, while the prevailing westerlies do not move fast enough over the Alleghenies to clear the atmosphere and bring cool relief. North beyond the Blue Mountains and Clarks Ferry, there is higher elevation and the weather improves.

Autumn is the reward for living through a Harrisburg summer. It comes late, but by mid-October is rich and lustrous in its apple-yellow fullness, as Thomas Wolfe wrote about Adams County, the birthplace of his father. Often through November a light-topcoat autumn prevails, making Central Pennsylvania one of the most beautiful and enjoyable spots in the world.

The Great Flood of '72

. . . A Drenching That
Became a Disaster

There was stillness. The birds and insects disappeared. Vehicular and rail traffic vanished. The bridges, streets and sidewalks were deserted. Houses and buildings were abandoned, many with their doors ajar. The strange ghostliness of another planet was broken only by the commotion overhead of helicopters, clattering like lawn mowers as they crossed the sky. And in every crevice was a pungent, clammy smell. The aftermath of destruction was coated with a light chocolate-colored ooze from which the acrid odor permeated through the stricken community. What the brownish water touched was contaminated, made unappealingly old with its lustre removed.

'72 FLOOD

This was the Flood of 1972, the greatest natural calamity the Harrisburg Area ever had. For a full week after June 22, there was displaced water. Then gradually it seeped away, leaving behind mud and corrosive slime and on buildings a film of blackish oil.

A disaster unduplicated—and in many cases incalculable—the Flood of 1972 became a historical turning point. People talked of "before the flood" and "after the flood," recognizing a discernible moment when the chronology of their lives and their community was interrupted. The effect was cumulative, and as the months passed the Flood of 1972 remained fixed in the people's consciousness.

Central Pennsylvanians always have been amazingly complacent and unrealistic about the possibilities of flooding, though they live in one of the worst flood plains in the eastern United States. It is a particular community-wide aberration that had persisted for generations, to the point that the populace and its politicians left themselves defenseless against the catastrophe of 1972 after having suffered the Flood of 1936.

Tropical storm Agnes caught everyone by surprise. "Rain heavy at times continuing today, ending by evening," the 8 P.M. weather report on June 21 came over the teletype for reprinting the next morning. With that forecast on the front page, the *Patriot* came out on Thursday, June 22. By 11 A.M., rising water forced the cancellation of the *Evening News*, and there was not another paper until the combined edition of June 28—the first time in 120 years that the *Patriot-News* missed publication. With $2.5 million in damages, its 10-unit Hoe Colormatic presses 28 feet under water, the *Patriot-News* was printed in Allentown, Chambersburg, and Lancaster until press room operation was resumed on July 12. The last of 1,200 soggy tons of newsprint was removed from the *Patriot-News* building on August 2.

The storm came out of the Caribbean into western Florida and northward, but it lost strength and veered out to sea off the Virginia Capes. In the Atlantic, it picked up moisture and moved back to hit Pennsylvania, carrying 28 trillion gallons of water.

Two unusual things happened. There was a rain squall that preceded and had nothing to do with Agnes, but it caused some flooding in New York State and raised the drainage into the Susquehanna. Then came Agnes, traveling at about 10 miles per hour, slower than usual. She meandered, unloading her ocean moisture as heavy rain. The western cold front that could have pushed Agnes back to sea was stalled by a pressure trap, while the upper air in the Atlantic hemmed Agnes in over Pennsylvania—a lethal combination.

Two inches of rain is considered a fairly heavy storm. Here is what Agnes dropped: Harrisburg, 13.3 inches; Williamsport, 11.94; Eagles

Mere, 9.42; Wilkes-Barre, 4.9; Huntingdon, 9.74; Altoona, 8.6, and Newport, 9.9.

The water table for the Harrisburg Area had been above normal since February 15, though snowfall for the winter was a below-average 34.6 inches. In March the rainfall was 3.43 inches below normal, but then in April it was 1.08 inches above and in May, 1.66 inches above. In the first 20 days of June, Harrisburg had 11 days of minimal rain. Then it happened.

On Wednesday, June 21, a record rainfall began, with 5.39 inches. This topped the 4.66 inches that fell May 31, 1889, to start the state-wide Johnstown Flood. The next day it poured 7.16 inches, a new all-time record. On June 23 there was 0.2 of an inch, and traces of rain the following two days. Harrisburg got better than 10 inches of rain above average.

The storm was unbelievably destructive because much of it hit below the 10 reservoirs built on the Upper Susquehanna Basin after the Flood of 1936. "We know that this storm was a very rare event. Statistically speaking, we would not expect it to recur again in 100 years. Actually, though, it could happen anytime," said Dr. James Rahn, the state climatologist.

The Susquehanna at Harrisburg on June 21 at 7 A.M. was 4.82 feet high, or only slightly above normal. As the rain continued, the two upper branches of the Susquehanna started pouring water down. The Mahantango, Sherman, Conodoguinet, Yellow Breeches, Paxton, Swatara, Conewago, and Cordorus creeks, as well as the picturesque Juniata River, feed into the Susquehanna between Selinsgrove and York. In high water, these overspilled, backed up, and became flood torrents themselves.

Here is how the river at Harrisburg progressed: June 21 at 7 A.M., 4.82 feet. June 22 at 7 A.M., 11.29; at 1 P.M., 15.63; at 7 P.M., 22.2, and at 9 P.M., 24.1. June 23 at 1 A.M., 27.0; at 3 A.M., 28.0; at 5:30 A.M., 29.23; at 7 A.M., 29.85; at noon, 31.4; at 3 P.M., 32.1, and at 7 P.M., 32.4. June 24 at 7 A.M., 32.7, at noon the high water mark of 32.8 feet, and at 7 P.M., 31.9. June 25 at 7 A.M., 29.95. And June 26 at 7 A.M., 23.19.

Harrisburg is 290.01 feet above sea level. The river slopes two feet per mile. Flooding is 17 feet above the 290-foot mark, with serious flooding at 22 feet above. The 1936 Flood crested at 29.23 feet (or, using the reading from the old gauge, 30.33 feet).

Here are the 1936 river levels as compared with the 1972 levels: Towanda, 25 feet and 33.25; Wilkes-Barre, 33.1 and 40.6; Sunbury, 34.65 and 35.79 and Williamsport, 33.57 and 34.75.

What happened is that Central and Northeastern Pennsylvania got the worst rain flood in American history.

There was 10 feet of water on Cameron St. as the Paxton Creek let loose. North of Reily St. to Third St. and south of the Harrisburg Hospital to Cameron St. all was flooded, touching 3,800 dwellings. West Shore communities, especially New Cumberland, were hit. Sewer backup damaged Camp Hill. Ground water flooding caused severe damage. The Enola Yard, Bethlehem Steel, Harrisburg Steel, and the Community College were under water. Harrisburg city government suffered $3 million in damages, while estimated overall destruction elsewhere was $5 million each in Steelton and Lykens; $4 million each in Middletown and Highspire, and $2.5 million each in Dauphin and Middle Paxton Township.

The Red Cross survey revealed in the Tri-County Area that 83 homes were destroyed, 3,507 suffered major damages and 2,131 minor damages. In addition, 61 mobile homes were destroyed and 449 had major damages. Some 616 small businesses were either destroyed or badly wrecked. Of Highspire's 990 taxable properties, 716 were damaged. On Steelton's West Side, all 310 homes were ruined. Three synagogues and many churches were damaged. There were 132 abandoned automobiles in Harrisburg alone, plus at least an equal number of flooded cars on dealer lots. Business damages went above $200 million in the Harrisburg Area. A conservative estimate is that it will take $25 million to restore Cameron St. and South Harrisburg.

The Governor's Mansion, only opened in 1968, received $500,000 in damages as water rose four feet on the first floor. Only 683 Pennsylvanians in the flood were insured for it, and the policy on the mansion lapsed the previous November. Gov. Milton J. Shapp became an evacuee on June 24, the day before his 60th birthday. While the Shapp family was rescued, a nearby block of houses on Second St. went up in flames from an explosion, while the firemen were kept out by the surrounding water.

President Nixon helicoptered into William Penn High School on June 24 to visit a rescue shelter. "He said Harrisburg was too beautiful a city to give up," reported Mayor Harold A. Swenson.

Rescue operations were remarkable. There were only six deaths from the flood in Dauphin County.

Harrisburg went into an emergency for two weeks. On Thursday, June 22, two days before high water, Mayor Swenson decided on using the Farm Show parking lot for mobile housing and he began signing $300,000 in City emergency purchasing orders. Public Works Director Houghton R. Hallock, a former West Pointer and retired colonel with the Army Corps of Engineers, requisitioned all available contractor equipment for the clean-up. Harrisburg stayed ahead, and the Mayor joked about sightseers: "It takes 400 National Guardsmen, 60 State Police and the entire Harrisburg Police Force to keep people out of Downtown Harrisburg who a week ago said it wasn't safe to go Downtown anymore." Swenson pushed himself so hard that on August 7 he was hospitalized for 18 days because of exhaustion.

The 21-community area of Wilkes-Barre was hit with flooding worse than Harrisburg's. Much of the Luzerne County flood plain was devastated. In all, Pennsylvania suffered at least $3 billion in damages, with a death toll of 51. Amazingly, Johnstown, with its world reputation, was stone dry.

The Midstate was unprepared for the Flood of 1972 because of its own lackadaisical attitude as well as its false assumption that a catastrophe like the Flood of 1936 could never happen again. It is only fair to acknowledge, however, that the 1972 Flood was the result of a completely untypical storm and was not a spring-thaw flood as virtually all had been in the past.

It cannot be logically explained why Harrisburgers were so nonchalant about floods. In its 188 years, Harrisburg has had 42 serious floods. Three of them occurred on St. Patrick's Day, in 1865, 1875, and 1936. There were two floods in 1886. And on Oct. 5, 1786, Harrisburg had the great "Pumpkin Flood," in which thousands of ripe pumpkins came bobbing down the river into the City.

Geographically, the Harrisburg Area is vulnerable to floods. The Susquehanna has 27,500 square miles of drainage, the 16th largest river basin in the nation. The average daily flow by Harrisburg is 23 billion gallons, and at the June 24 crest of the 1972 Flood it was 650 billion gallons.

William H. Shank, a Midstate engineer, in his 1969 study, *Great Floods of Pennsylvania*, said the river towns can expect a major flood every 25 years. He based this on the fact that the drainage basin is large, most streams flow in the same direction traveled by the prevailing storm centers, and, because the Commonwealth is more than half covered with forests, the Upstate tree-filled plateaus can hold snow until late spring and then suddenly release the water with the first warm spell.

The 1936 Flood was the result of the spring thaw and heavy rains. Across Pennsylvania it took 80 lives, caused $212.5 million in damage, knocked out 275 bridges, and chased 400,000 persons from their homes.

The Harrisburg Area was badly hit in 1936. Water covered 28 percent of the City, or 1,107 acres of its 3,916 land acres. At least 1,145 Harrisburg families fled their homes. From March 11 to 19 there was a steady rainfall of 3.41 inches. Though the weather report on March 11 forecast "little danger of flooding here at the present," the emergency lasted from March 14 to 21, with high water of 29.23 feet on March 19.

It was clear after 1936 that there should be river and flood plain protection and, by all means, control of the always dangerous Paxton Creek to safeguard Cameron St. and South Harrisburg. Midstate leadership, however, was oblivious to the situation and the public similarly was unconcerned. Army Engineer studies for South Harrisburg repeatedly were ignored.

The one positive development after 1936 was the DeHart Reservoir in Clark Valley, between Stony Mountain and Peter's Mountain. The new water source was tied into the original 1841 Harrisburg system, connected with the 1888 Reservoir Park.

Mayor John A. F. Hall directed the City during the 1936 Flood and backed a 25-year, $1.8 million bond issue, matched by federal funds, for the reservoir project. It was dedicated on Oct. 1, 1940, and named for long-time Uptown Councilman William T. DeHart. Clark Creek is one of 43 small streams feeding into the 6-billion-gallon, 4.5-mile lake behind the 105-foot dam, which was 5 feet above the 1972 outpour. The dam releases 16 million gallons of fresh mountain water daily to the City. After Jan. 23, 1948, Harrisburgers stopped using the Susquehanna totally, though during droughts the river is used as an emergency water supply. Amazingly enough, surrounding communities did not join Harrisburg to expand the DeHart project into an area-wide, secure water system. Ironically, two months after the 1972 Flood, Mechanicsburg and Upper Allen Township were critically short of water and restrictions were placed on its use.

Complacency after the 1972 Flood is not likely to be tolerated. That was too traumatic an experience to be forgotten.

Camp Hill, Camp Hill

. . . It's a Wonderful Town

The West Shore tends toward a blended suburban uniformity, except for Camp Hill. Every metropolitan area needs one community to pick on and mock. New York laughs at Brooklyn and San Francisco at Oakland. The Harrisburg Area has Camp Hill, as if it were a blue-nosed duchess.

The jokes flow unceasingly. "Jack Armstrong, the All-American Boy, is alive and hiding in Camp Hill, married, with 2½ children, a beagle and a self-propelled power mower." "If Edgar Guest had never lived, Camp Hill would have invented him." "Norman Rockwell is avant-

CAMP HILL

garde for Camp Hill." "Camp Hill is hoarding all the old copies of Whittaker Chambers' *Witness*."

Need a scapegoat and Camp Hill is it. At a public discussion in Steelton about absentee slum landlords, someone unfairly charged, "They all live in Camp Hill." When there was a dispute over fire protection, an East Pennsboro official described Camp Hill as "a town of 10-cent millionaires." Julian Bond spoke at the Community College in 1970, and afterwards with glee headed over to all-white Camp Hill for a party. When syndicated columnist Dick West spoke in Camp Hill, he jokingly referred to it as "the queen city of the west bank of the Susquehanna."

Camp Hillites themselves contribute much of the humor. Its newly hired borough manager in 1969 asked Council to relax its rule so that he could live out of town. He said he could not find "a decent place in which to live" under $20,000 in Camp Hill. Police Chief Andrew C. Janssen, a native of Scranton, came to Camp Hill in 1970 driving a used white Cadillac. He recognized the humor in the compliments he received; so when he traded it in, he got a used black Cadillac from a funeral director. In 1971 Borough Council signed a contract for bright orange Mercedes-Benz garbage trucks, first-class all the way.

Camp Hill's reputation as "God's little acre" is half earned and half a lefthanded compliment. The community had the foresight and smugness to have the only borough school district on the West Shore, to develop a 50-acre park in the 1930s before the population avalanche fell on suburbia, and to have its sewage treatment plant properly located outside the borough. In the past, its blend of arrogance, pride, and suburban hauteur peeved its neighbors, though folks did not deny that it was nice to have a Camp Hill mailing address even if one lived in Hampden, East Pennsboro, or Lower Allen townships.

Camp Hill no longer is the richest residential community in the Harrisburg Area, if it ever was. To the credit of Camp Hill, few of its residents ever wished it were. And yet, whenever others, or Camp Hillites themselves, get nasty about the borough, the myth of affluence is thrown around. "Even Mount Carmel has paved alleys and here in the most affluent, progressive community on the West Shore, we don't even have . . ." And so the conversation goes. Half of the talk about affluence is poppycock, but part of the enduring charm of Camp Hill is that every man supposedly has either $1 million or a $1 million mortgage.

In actuality, Camp Hill in many respects is bourgeois poor. Its tax rate is the highest in Cumberland County. Its school system, accustomed to thinking itself tops, no longer is, and furthermore is in financial difficulty. More urban today than suburban, Camp Hill suffers from municipal overload, such as rising crime and heavy traffic. Each year more of the upper incomes slip out of town, replaced by middle-income families who want a new high school but cannot afford it.

Now a crowded small town, Camp Hill's population grew in the 1960s by 1,372, so that the borough had 9,931 people in 1970. Lewis M. Sutton, postmaster for 20 years, was born in 1887 and was the oldest native. He remembered when Camp Hill had 191 persons in the 1890s. "It's clean and kept up well and people want to live here, but it's grown to be a different town from what it used to be," he commented before his death in 1971. "I can't say it's a very friendly place. It used to be friendly, though never to the extent that Steelton was, but now it isn't."

Camp Hill can be the most progressive community on the West Shore. It proved that in 1956 when it started the campaign for a library. The West Shore Public Library, opened Oct. 16, 1967, in Camp Hill, is the result of the borough's citizenry enticing cooperation from East Pennsboro, Hampden, Lemoyne, Lower Allen, and Wormleysburg—a step toward unity that is still eons away from realization in East Shore suburbia. Yet Camp Hill's stamp of approval can mean death to most projects. Knowing how its neighbors are envious, distrustful, and just plain hostile, Camp Hill must work in the most devious ways to accomplish cooperative action.

Surprising for a patio suburb, Camp Hill is a sports power. In 1953 its team finished fourth in the Little League World Series at Williamsport, setting a record for 17 runs against Little Rock. From 1968 to 1970, the Camp Hill Lions high school team played 25 undefeated football games, the longest stretch in Pennsylvania schoolboy sports. In the school year of 1970, the Lions were football champs and Eastern Pennsylvania Class B basketball champs, with Pete Kramer and Craig Roberts the heroes. The 6-foot-3 Kramer is the all-time leading basketball scorer of the Harrisburg Area. One notable Camp Hill figure is Bruce Brubaker, the world's professional fly-casting champion.

Camp Hill exudes Republicanism. Just about everything and everybody is Republican, possibly even the dogs and cats. In its first statewide election as a borough in 1887, Camp Hill showed its party staunchness in what was then Democratic Cumberland County. Its results for state treasurer: 37 Republican votes, 12 Democratic, and one Prohibition. Republican presidential candidates since 1932 have carried Camp Hill with ease. Alf Landon in 1936 received only 62 percent of its vote and Barry Goldwater in 1964, only 63 percent, but General Eisenhower in 1952 got almost all of it, 87 percent. Richard Nixon received 79 percent both in 1960 and 1972 and 72 percent in 1968.

In 1971 there was a slip in Camp Hill's Republican regularity, and the first Democrat since the 1930s was elected in the borough. H. C. Erickson, 70, had his name written in by a Republican friend, and won the post of assessor by a total vote of 1 to 0, because no other names were on the ballot. The job paid $2 an hour. "He's one of the cleanest Democrats I know," said Christian L. Seibert, a resident since 1915 and the founder of the borough park which bears his name.

Camp Hill Republicanism is not only regular, but aged. George N. Wade has been its state senator since 1940, the record in Pennsylvania history; Guy A. Kistler its state representative since 1960, and Samuel D. Williams its mayor from 1938 to 1942 and from 1954 on. Not one is a native of Camp Hill. Wade and Williams, long-time friends, were born in 1893, and Kistler in 1910.

With political conservatism goes a cultural conservatism, reflected by the hair controversy of 1970. While Harrisburg schools were making a difficult change to integration, the all-white Cedar Cliff, Red Land, and Camp Hill high schools battled the innocuous issue of long hair on boys. Three Camp Hill brothers were suspended after the School Board upheld the superintendent's ruling by a 7 to 1 vote. A Cedar Cliff case went to Cumberland County Court, where Judge Clinton R. Weidner determined, among other things, that the "plaintiff has violated the hair guidelines because he wants to and for no other reason." The judge stated in a popular decision: "The quality of education at Cedar Cliff High School has been tested and regarded here and elsewhere as one of the best. This is due to the dedication of the administration and board members to the cause of education and the youth of the area. Now, this lawsuit is proving that it takes the parent Monday morning quarterback longer to second guess the quarterback school directors than it does to play the game. And with more disastrous and far-reaching effects because, for the other quarterbacks there will be another game, but for the second-guessing parent, his child may not reach another game, having tasted the sweet wine of protest against regulations and having a come-late model in his father."

Judge Weidner found the long-haired youngsters and supportive parents to be extremists. "If and when the time arrives when the extremists are willing to serve, and able to be elected by majority vote, they should then serve, change the rules and others will abide with their rules," he said, carrying the issue of hairstyle regulations into constitutional legal theory.

Camp Hill's history goes back to the early 1730s, and in *Manor on the Market*, a pamphlet, local historian Robert Grant Crist describes the first land purchasers:

"Gathered in one saloon, the very first settlers would have made a memorable picture: Chartier, a Shawnee who joined the enemy; Montour, rings in his ears and his hair in braids, escorting the white wife he bought for 15 pounds; Tobias Hendricks, putatively Sephardic, with his black slave Cato; and Robert Whitehill, militant leader of a mob which overturned one government and fought in the streets for civil rights against another. Long-haired, black, trafficking with the enemy, demonstrating for civil rights—something seems familiar. However, the next 28 fit a pattern, too: hard at work on home improvement, spading the garden, mortgaged, sensitive about taxes, building schools and churches, joining committees, dependent on the market across the Susquehanna."

From 1851 to 1867 it was known as White Hall, after an academy there, but when it received a post office it took its name from the religious camp meeting, of all things. Camp Hill was incorporated as a borough on Nov. 10, 1885.

The famous Oyster's Point Hotel at 31st and Market Sts., a landmark since 1814, was razed in 1969. Built by Abraham Oyster, of Abbottstown, the hotel was located where, in those days, Trindle Spring Road joined the Carlisle Pike. Before the Battle of Gettysburg, the Confederates swung east down the Pike, had a brief skirmish at the hotel, lobbed shells through its woodshed, and then headed west on Trindle Road. Thus the hotel became "the high-water mark of the Confederacy." The late Col. Wilbur S. Nye, of Wormleysburg, tells in his Civil War history of the Harrisburg Area's "manifest reluctance" to fight the Rebels and how defending New York troops so disliked Camp Hill that they threw apple butter on people's walls and split open featherbeds just for the devil of it.

Until Prohibition, Camp Hill was notoriously wet. Tobias Hendricks had his tavern in the 1760s at 24th and Market Sts. It was here, later on, that the Rev. John Winebrenner supposedly founded the sect which became the Church of God. The Bigler family, of whom William Bigler became governor of Pennsylvania and John the governor of California on the same day in 1852, operated the Yellow Tavern.

It was not until the early 1950s and the rush to suburbia that Camp Hill became a special place, and almost a code word of praise or scorn. While there are still some Camp Hillites who get angry at the rebukes, the community actually is perhaps more self-critical and witty than any other in the Harrisburg Area. It is obviously not just another unidentifiable, rootless place when a resident can describe his vacation: "I didn't go anywhere. I spent my two weeks in Camp Hill enjoying it."

STEELTON

Good Old Steelton

. . . Little Mill Town
with a Big Name

"These were foreigners who came to America for gold and found sledgehammers," wrote Warren Eyster in his novel about his hometown of Steelton, *No Country For Old Men*. They came to "the steel mill stretched long and dark on the river edge."

The foreigners made Steelton one of the hardest-working, hardest-playing towns in America. Always a bit rundown, forever poor, Steelton earned a distinction with its overflowing self-pride that made it a special place for generations in Central Pennsylvania. Among its attributes:

1. Steelton is long on neighborliness, civic pride, and fun, and short on affluent pretentiousness.

2. Steelton has everybody. The sequence of neighborhoods started in the lower end with Croatians, whose names end in "ic," progressed north with Serbians ("ich"), Germans ("berg"), Slovenians ("ak"), Italians ("o"), Irish ("y"), Bulgarians ("eff"), and Macedonians

51

("off"). In 1969 the Pennsylvania Department of Education cited Steelton for its "rich and varied ethnic pattern." It is one of the most ethnically and racially, though not economically, integrated communities in the United States.

3. Academically, Steelton need not blush before any of its rivals in the Harrisburg Area.

4. Culturally, Eyster's novel remains the best literature ever produced in the region, while Will Pollard might be the finest poet. Pollard, a black and a street foreman with a pickax for the gas company, was president of the Pennsylvania Poetry Society. A poet for 35 years, he marked his thousandth poem in print in 1970, two years after he received a second prize in the National Book Awards for his *Where the Wind Lives*. Steelton also produces a fair share of folk artists and musicians.

5. And in sports, it always has been Steelton against the world. The smallest school in the Central Pennsylvania League with only 550 students, the Steelton-Highspire Steamrollers repeatedly topple the Goliaths of suburbia.

There is something refreshingly American about Steelton, an intangible that has to do with its still-strong grip on the tenets of family and home, friends and community. Outsiders scoff at first, while the Steeltonites cannot help wondering if elsewhere there is a correlation between the crumbling of many American values and the popularity of split-level housing developments, poolside cocktail parties, and affluent moms and dads in the social swing.

Downtown Steelton especially was ravaged by the 1972 Flood, and losses exceeded $5 million. Perhaps Steelton is a "dying community," as a Susquehanna University student wrote in a 1971 term paper. "Steelton is old and looks its age," he wrote. "The people are friendly amongst themselves because they have all been placed in the same plight." But maybe the word "enduring" is more accurate than "dying." As a Swarthmore student wrote in her term paper in 1970, "I know that many of my Catholic-school friends had a self-bemused but real and deep loyalty to Steelton."

Steelton was important enough to Eyster to inspire his creativity. It gave him something to react against, not the alienation or ennui that a faceless, noncommunity with high zoning restrictions provides. Eyster's angry novel, published by Random House, covers a period from 1889 to 1941 of the Lang, Pierce, Mijack, and Rowiger families in Bethel, his name for Steelton.

"They came here with hope, to build a new life, and then like the cowards and weaklings they are, they settled down and lived the same damn way they did in the old country," complains Mijack to his son Bart. "My own father did that, went back to the same rotten life he had fled. Oh, he lived a little better, a little better. That satisfied him."

The town, as Eyster saw it, was preoccupied by politics and sports.

Tad Stevens was the country boss. "Tad was one of their own kind, a friend by instinct, and they could talk and haggle with him. He would not pay the least attention to their opinions unless he agreed with them. . . . He was corrupt in the worst sense of Pennsylvania politics, where it was difficult to surpass previous corruption. . . . Every ounce of his lean, bony figure was proud of his reputation, the good and the corrupt, and many people were proud of him. He raked his tithe, doubled it in good years, did not deny it, and in turn could be trusted to do what really needed to be done."

Football—and after Eyster's era, basketball—was the passion. As Eyster saw it:

"The football coach was paid more than the superintendent of the school. . . . There was the pressure on the players of knowing that their fathers and brothers and friends were betting on every game. There were the football pools in every bar and poolroom, pools on picking the score, on total points, on the subtracted score, pools in every way that men could devise to gamble. There was the 'Player of the Week' award, and the sports banquets at which boys learned to taste fairly good liquor and lots of beer. And there were men under 25 years of age, slumped over bars with defeated eyes, talking of their gridiron victories . . . . It made human ambition center around becoming a football player and then a coach, or making a lucky business contact. It made children despise intelligence, made adults despise children who were trying to become intelligent."

In one memorable scene, Mrs. Malancic goes to the Saturday afternoon football game and screams to her son: "You play hard. You don't, I get your brothers beat hell out of you. You hear you lazy sonofabitch, you hear your mother?"

There is a dramatic exaggeration to Eyster as there was to Thomas Wolfe about his Asheville, N.C. But, strangely enough, Eyster arrives at what has proven to be a totally inaccurate conclusion:

"There was a prophecy of violence in the attitude of these people. They made victory too important and too ruthlessly sought. They could not accept victory, let alone defeat. They could not find sufficient expression for the dissatisfaction in their lives, and their eyes watched the field with the squint of hatred. . . . It was the wrath of men who were being choked by their own narrowness of mind, who were being imprisoned by the nature of their work in the steel mill, who needed to make a declaration of their existence before it was too late. They were dangerous because they did not understand themselves, nor their growing animosity toward life."

The very opposite seemingly is true. Steelton has little violence or self-destruction. Personal identity does not appear to be choked by narrowness of mind, but rather reinforced because much of the status and economic competition bedeviling the upper middle class elsewhere does not affect Steelton's blue-collar culture. Ambition among the young is strong.

Education thrives in Steelton. The borough accepted integration before the Supreme Court decision of 1954. Steelton was a leader in vocational-technical training and in the establishment of the Community College, where an unusually high percentage of its students excel in their studies. The 1957 merger with Highspire and the $2.5 million junior-senior high school gave the community a fine educational system —though, ironically, the school is built in Swatara Township and youngsters who live within yards of it are bused to classes in the Central Dauphin District. Culturally, there is no slack. The high school band, though one of the smallest in the Area, was the first to have summer camp. Music especially has always been regarded as important.

Steelton naturally has not stopped cheering for its athletic heroes. "Sports has helped hold this community together," said Dr. Harold T. Griffith, its outstanding school superintendent from 1950 to 1968. "The kids show tremendous desire, and for the size of our district our record is remarkable."

One of the great Steel-High melodramas took place in 1969. Against big, powerful Cedar Cliff, the Steamrollers held a magnificent goal-line stand for eight plays. Steel-High was ahead 18–13, and by the fifth play everyone from Allendale to Highland Park knew that the Steamroller line would not budge. An awesome silence descended upon the Cedar Cliff Stadium as the last repulse unfolded. A few weeks later, undefeated Steel-High went against the undefeated state champion, John Harris, and was thrashed by an embarrassing 49–0 score. As the weary, weeping players straggled off the fields, members of the school band spontaneously began to play the alma mater. The merciful consolation of it all and the pride in the face of being vanquished was almost Homeric. "You don't teach kids these things. They live them," a spectator said.

"Steelton," said Dr. Griffith in 1968, "is a much finer town than it usually is given credit for. It's a deep-rooted serious town. Many of its people are third-generation Americans and they're ambitious for their children. They know what school can do for them. The local tax support for our school is greater proportionally than many suburban districts, evidence of the concern education is given here. We send about 30 percent of our youngsters to college. That percentage is all right, but it will get better. We've always been accredited."

High school principal Max J. Katz, a native of Harrisburg, observed in 1969: "The family is still so well respected in this community that the school doesn't have to pick up much of its responsibilities, I mean like discipline, respect and haircuts."

Warren Eyster, an only child, was born in Halifax on Jan. 2, 1924, but was raised in Steelton by his grandparents, Mr. and Mrs. Samuel J. Orndorff, of 322 Locust St. "I took games too serious," he once wrote, "and although too small to be a big shot in sports, I have always liked them." He had little home life, spending much of his youth hanging around Front and Pine Sts. Everybody called him "Little Eyster."

He graduated from old Steelton High School in 1942, had a few jobs, such as a shears operator in the mill, and then went off to be a seaman on a destroyer in World War II. After the war, he attended the Harrisburg Academy and went through Gettysburg College in three years. He was part way through his master's degree program at the University of Virginia when he quit.

His first novel, *Far From the Customary Skies*, a navy story, received accolades from Adm. Chester W. Nimitz, James Agee, Nicholas Monsarrat, and William Inge. Bennett Cerf predicted Eyster "will be one of the next decade's most important writers."

He wrote his second novel, *No Country for Old Men*, in the early 1950s while living in Mexico with his Mexican wife and a daughter. He disappeared totally from the Steelton scene after that. "Warren was a quiet, unassuming boy, not particularly active in extracurricular activities, but friendly. He had a talent for minding his own business, if you can call that eccentric," his principal, Charles Eisenhart, recalled.

Though the canal went through what is Steelton, the town did not get started until 1866. It is one of the youngest communities in the immediate Harrisburg Area.

The Pennsylvania Steel Co. was formed on June 26, 1865, with an investment of $200,000. Harrisburgers—the Camerons, Hickoks, Calders, Kelkers, Haldemans, Boyds, Kunkels, and others—raised $24,-577 to buy 97 acres of land for the company. On Nov. 25, 1865, the steel company decided to settle in Steelton because of the transportation facilities and the nearness of the Cornwall orebank. On May 25, 1867, steel was produced—the first steel in the United States from a plant built specifically for that purpose.

The town initially was named Baldwin, for Matthias Baldwin of the

Baldwin Locomotive Works, who died in 1866. A post office was established in 1871. Because another town of Baldwin existed in Allegheny County, the post office was called simply "Steel-works." It was not until 1880 that the name Steelton was selected. By then its population had grown from six families in 1866 to 5,000 persons. In 1910 the population reached its height of 14,550. On July 1, 1916, Pennsylvania Steel was sold to the Bethlehem Steel Co., with the plant occupying 600 acres on a site four miles long.

Out of the little borough came the steel for the Niagara River Bridge, the Goteik Gorge Bridge in Burma, the Queensboro Bridge, the Harrahan Bridge at Memphis, the Peace Bridge linking Canada and the United States, and the most famous of them all, the Golden Gate Bridge.

The steel plant built the first public school in 1882. By 1898 there were 16 churches for the 9,230 residents who were of 33 nationalities. Barrooms lined Front St. Carl B. Shelley, born in 1893, tended bar at his father's Central Hotel on Saturday nights and taught Sunday school at St. John's Lutheran Church the following mornings. The 5-foot-3 Shelley, a typical Steelton roughneck with a quick wit and uncommonly fast mind, went on to be the district attorney of Dauphin County for 14 years, longer than anyone, and then a judge for 10 years.

A steelworker's life repeatedly was threatened with joblessness. Steelton endured a strike of 28 days in 1946, 42 days in 1949, 58 days in 1952, 34 days in 1956, and a record 116 days in 1959. "Pisibuk," meaning "put it on the book," or grocery store credit, became a way of existence in Steelton.

Immigrant laborers rode the rails or actually walked the tracks into Steelton. Many non-English-speaking families came with tags on their jackets for identification. The railroad station, which closed in the mid-1930s, was on the West Side, and it was from this station in 1861 that Abraham Lincoln in the middle of the night, to avoid possible assassins, departed from Harrisburg for his inaugural.

The unwritten history of America is in Steelton. Mato Verbos left Croatia as a draft-dodger in 1885 with his brother Lovro's passport. Three years later, Lovro used Mato's passport to emigrate. Lovro was not able to bring his wife to Steelton until 11 years later. The year after they were reunited, John Verbos was born, the Steelton postmaster from 1934 to 1965. Lovro Verbos worked in the mill for 9 cents an hour. When John quit school at 16, he went to work for 12 cents an hour. They worked 11 hours daylight and 13 hours nightside, with one Sunday off every two weeks and the other Sunday on a 24-hour shift.

Samuel Lehrman came from Russia in the 1890s. Though he had

rabbinical training, he started a grocery company business. His brothers Louis and Abraham Jacob came. From this beginning of *schwer arbeit* (hard work), *mahzel* (luck), and *mishpacha* (family unity) developed the amazing Lehrman clan, which now has the Rite Aid Corp. on the New York Stock Exchange, a janitorial supplies business, and an impressive growing wealth among not only Lehrmans but the family in-laws of Hurwitz, Grass, and Weinberg.

David Morrison came to Steelton from Poland. He started his shoe store in 1916, succeeded by his son, Al Morrison, the noted musician. Meanwhile, David's brother Hyman went to Harrisburg and founded the family that includes the internationally known contact lens specialist, Dr. Robert Jay Morrison, and his brother, Dr. Victor Morrison.

Mary Sachs, a native of Lithuania, came from Baltimore to Steelton, first as a stock girl in a store and then as a salesgirl at $6 a week. Her sister Sarah ran the Baltimore Bargain House on the West Side, while Mary went on to Harrisburg to find fame and fortune with her own store in 1918. Miss Sachs died in 1960.

Cornelius Dailey talked back to a British landlord in Ireland and ended up in the Steelton mill in 1869. Of his nine children who lived to adulthood, three became physicians, one a certified public accountant, and another a school principal. The family went on to produce dozens of more Daileys, including two more physicians and two dentists. And for 100 years, a Dailey has worked in the steel mill.

The Mulligan stew of people resulted in a mix of nationality churches: the Irish St. James, founded in 1866; the German St. John's, 1890s; the Croatian St. Mary's, 1898; the Slovene St. Peter's, 1909, and the Italian St. Ann's, plus the Serbian St. Nicholas. The major social forces were the Irish and Croatians. From 1900 to 1940, it was Irish territory north of Lincoln St.

"I'll tell you how times are changing," observed John Verbos in 1971. "You never hear 'Hunkie' said anymore. That used to get me mad. They called us 'Hunkies,' but we were Croatians, Serbs, and Slovenians and Slovaks, not Hungarians. Back in the old country, our crowd didn't like the ruling Hunkies at all. There never were many real Hunkies in Steelton."

Margaret Seaker in her Swarthmore paper, "The Fate of Ethnicity and a Pennsylvania Town," listed churches and family names: St. Mary's—Bahoric, Belsak, Furjanic, Kaponjak, Malesic; St. Peter's—Bratina, Gornik, Kastelic, Starisinic; St. Ann's—DeMarco, Falcone, Julian, Magaro, Spizzirri; St. James—Crist, Devlin, Gould, Reed; St. John's—Okum, Scheib, Soutner, Szabo. "The ethnic parishes with native priests and native languages provided a way for the immigrant to accustom himself, without becoming alienated and degraded," she wrote. The ethnic flavor is preserved to this day with St. Ann's monthly spaghetti dinner, St. Mary's famous dancing group, the Kola Club, and others.

Steelton had some of the most interesting nicknames for its characters, like Muck, Raz, Geep, Feesco, Tup, Popeye, Midnight, Boomie, Chinx, Peppy, Sata, Cacky, and Sleese.

The town divided up into many neighborhoods, with parishes, sports, and politics all playing a part. There was Chicken Hill, the Hollow, the Lower End, the Fothergill Playground Area, and the West Side. Once the West Side had a third of Steelton's population. Less than a mile long, from the old canal to the river, on the west side of Front St., the neighborhood originally was called Ewington. It thrived with as many as 3,000 persons until the Flood of 1936 almost made it a lost Atlantis. When the Flood of 1972 hit, the West Side had fewer than 1,000 persons, and it was wiped out again.

In its heyday, the West Side was virtually a self-contained community. It had grocery stores, a brewery, boarding houses, churches (including a Mennonite church), the West Side Hose Co. No. 3, a lumber yard, flour mill, coal yard, the Bessemer House hotel, the river for swimming, and the canal for ice skating. Much of the friendship was engendered at the Old Scratch House by the canal. "Scratching" meant you were not working that day at the mill, so you philosophized at the tavern.

"There is a 'certain something' you find on the West Side that does not exist in every community," Miss Mollie Mickey, a teacher at the old West Side Elementary, wrote for the 50th anniversary of the school in 1940. Dr. Fred Knuth, principal from 1935 to 1943, said it was the most enjoyable assignment he had in his career. "Once 13 boys were causing mischief on the way to school," he said. "I lined them up and started to paddle. I got no farther than the first one, the ringleader, when his dad burst in. He went right for his kid and started to wallop him twice as hard as I did. I never had such parental response anywhere as I had in the West Side."

Mary Sachs got her start on the West Side. Judge James Bowman's father and Judge Richard Wickersham's grandfather lived there. Warren Heller, the 1932 All-American halfback for Pitt, came off the West Side's sandlots. Heller and Duke Maronic, guard for the Philadelphia Eagles, are among the athletic greats out of Steelton. And the last man from Dauphin County to be electrocuted for murder was a West Sider, and he was convicted by a fellow Steeltonite, District Attorney Shelley.

Steelton has had a black community for generations. It had a black councilman at the turn of the century. While full integration was lacking, there was never total alienation between the races. At one time it was not unusual for white families to buy the homes of black families. In 1967 Steelton became the first Harrisburg municipality to have a black police chief, named Frederick Douglas, appropriately enough. Its great All-State basketball star of the mid-1960s was a black, Dennis Stewart.

If ethnic politics had applied, Steelton would be a stronghold of the Democratic Party. It did not, mainly because for many years, as the *Patriot* said in 1932, Thomas J. Nelley "carried the Steelton vote in his vest pocket." Nelley, a half-year younger than M. Harvey Taylor, was an Irish Catholic Democrat on Mayor John A. Fritchey's Harrisburg police force. In 1901 he moved to Steelton and took over the Halfway House, so named because it was the watering hole between Middletown and Harrisburg for the old canalboat crews. Nelley switched to the Republicans, became a dear friend of Taylor's, and rose to be county commissioner. Not only was the County Courthouse always well stocked with Steeltonian jobholders, but three judges came out of Nelley's district, Frank B. Wickersham, J. Paul Rupp, and Carl B. Shelley. Until Nelley's death in 1957, the GOP could count on Steelton. In fact, when John Verbos reorganized the Democratic Party in 1928, there were only 50 Democrats in town, most of them Irishmen from the Upper End.

Tom Nelley once had an argument with the late Earl V. Compton, a fine Harrisburg attorney. "What do you know about politics?" asked Nelley. Compton explained he had been involved for 12 years. "Well," replied Nelley, "I've had 37 years' experience and I know mighty little about it." The story is told that when Nelley was hospitalized, he sneaked out twice—once to go to New York for the World Series and the other time to cast his ballot.

Though Steelton is still Steelton, it changed radically during the 1960s. *No Country For Old Men* is what Warren Eyster entitled his book, but more than 15 percent of its male population is now over age 65. The population took a drastic drop of 24 percent in a decade, down to 8,556, so the town has fewer people now than it had in 1890. The company store has been gone for a long time. Many steelworkers commute to work. Contrary to Eyster and misinformed public opinion, academic standards are high. But on any given Friday night or Saturday afternoon in the fall, the Blue and Gray Steamrollers are as difficult to beat as any football team in all of Pennsylvania. They do it today with speed, rather than brawn, but the fighting spirit of Steelton has never changed.

PERRY COUNTY

Perry County

. . . Far from the Madding Crowd

"Perry County is rural America saved from urbanization. They have a different way of life up there," said Carroll F. "Dan" Purdy, the former district attorney now practicing law in Harrisburg. Purdy was speaking about "the folded hills of Perry County" to the Harrisburg Exchange Club on the county's 150th anniversary in 1970.

Perry County is indeed different. Its theme for its sesquicentennial, for example, was "Hoop Poles, Brains and Buckwheat Cakes," celebrating the county's superior quality hickory stems for barrel making, its human contributions, and its pancakes.

The county lies between the Blue Mountains and the Tuscaroras. Horse Valley, in the far western end, should really be in Juniata County. The county is 345,600 acres big, or slightly smaller than Cumberland County's 355,200 acres but bigger than Dauphin County's 332,800 acres.

It won independence from affluent Cumberland County on March 22,

1820, and is named after Oliver Hazard Perry, the naval hero of the War of 1812.

Perry Countians would feel crowded if the place exceeded 30,000 people. Its Civil War population was 22,793; in 1880 it was 27,500, and in 1970, 28,615. There is not a traffic light or parking meter in the county. It has only 11 policemen, and in 1970 had only six people in jail. Though only a half-hour's drive from Harrisburg, the county is still 63 percent forest and has fewer than 10,000 housing units. The 1970 Census listed one nonwhite family living there. There are no cities and only eight boroughs—Blain, Duncannon, Landisburg, Liverpool, Marysville, Millerstown, New Bloomfield, and Newport.

No one knows who came to Perry County first. The Bower family is one of the oldest. Christopher Bower and his oldest son Abraham came into the county in 1790 looking for limestone land with a limestone spring—limestone makes good whiskey. A German church was built in Loysville in 1794, and a jug of whiskey was awarded the man who split the first log. Bootlegging and moonshining were popular in the county for years. People still speak in awe of Perry County's "white lightning."

John Bower, a blacksmith on Manassa Road, is part of the legend of Perry County. He was born in 1814 and grew up with a still 40 feet from the house. John always enjoyed a whiskey each evening. One night he returned home to find a man from Landisburg with his wife. He chatted with the fellow and discovered that he liked hunting too. So John made a deal. Since his wife thought highly of the visitor, he would trade her for a shotgun and a watch. It was agreed. John later married again, had five children, and continued the Bower clan.

Some say Perry County is paradise because it has only seven lawyers. It does have about a dozen physicians, but some are retired. It does not have a hospital, television or radio station, or a college. It has only four high schools: Susquenita, Newport, Greenwood, and West Perry.

Perry County once was the land of the Indians and the buffalo, who liked living near the Juniata and the Susquehanna rivers. Even today it has one of the highest deer kills per square mile in the East.

The social statistics are interesting. Its divorce rate is higher than Philadelphia's or the West Shore's, but so is its marriage rate. It has few reported suicides, but the figures may be deceptive. Its mark for functional literacy is high, but until recently its school graduation record was low. It has an unusually high per capita death rate on the highways. In 1970, almost 21 percent of its families lived in poverty, and 38 percent of its houses had inadequate plumbing. Yet its death rate from ulcers of the stomach and duodenum in 1968 was exactly zero in comparison to rates more than five times greater in Dauphin and Cumberland counties.

The crime rate is ridiculously low. In 150 years only one fellow has been executed. Before the Civil War, John Weaver fed his wife arsenic in increasingly large doses. Weaver was hanged. His body today reposes beneath an old oak tree in the corner of the poorhouse land at Loysville.

What angers Perry Countians the most is "zealous game wardens enforcing the law." Untying game wardens from trees used to be a time-consuming occupation for public officials. Today the biggest headache is trying to collect nonsupport payments.

Fame has come out of Perry County. Gen. Ephraim Blaine was born in Blain and James G. Blaine's ancestors lived there. The ancestors of President Warren G. Harding, Vice-President Thomas R. Marshall, and Confederate Vice-President Alexander H. Stephens came from the county, as did the folks of Jane Addams and Harold Ickes. Two Pennsylvania governors came from Perry County: William Bigler and James Addams Beaver. Bigler was inaugurated the same day his brother, John, became governor of California. Alexander K. McClure, one of the founders of the Republican Party, came from Sherman's Valley.

Two Pennsylvania chief justices, John Bannister Gibson and Charles Alvin Jones, were from Perry County. Gibson's mother inherited a mule, a slave, and $1. She spent the dollar, shot the mule, and freed the slave, or so the story goes. Dr. Elizabeth Reifsnyder, the first woman medical missionary to China, came from Liverpool, and the colorful State Sen. Scott S. Leiby was from Marysville.

Joe Roddy, of New Bloomfield, ran the 1,500 meters in the 1896 Olympics. Billy Cox, perhaps the finest fielding third baseman ever, still lives in Newport. Judge William Woodrow Lipsitt spent nine wonderful boyhood years in Newport, the town that is home for David Mingle Myers, funeral director, furniture dealer, and the county's leading talker.

The Box Huckleberry near New Bloomfield is the oldest living plant in America. In 1968 a four-acre sanctuary for the 13,000-year-old plant was designated a National Natural Landmark. In comparison, the bristlecone pine of California is only 4,600 years old and the *Sequoia gigantea*, 3,200 years old. The nearby trilobite fossils date to the Paleozoic Age. As Ralph L. Barnett's 1910 poem, "To a Trilobite," puts it: "There's nothing that's high and nothing low,/There's nothing that's old or new;/There's nothing in race or age or time,/To separate me and you;/And it may be that all things, great and small,/From mammal to gastropod,/Are born to a common brotherhood,/In the infinite plan of God."

Perry County does have a different way of life, so far.

Railroading, Canaling and Dredging

... *Ways of Life in Days Gone By*

In the first 30 years of the century, the Harrisburg Area was one of the great railroading communities in America, with more railroaders, 12,000 to 14,000 of them, than even government employees.

In that golden age of railroading, 65 to 75 percent of the families in Enola and Rutherford had their wage-earners working for the railroad. West Fairview, Marysville, Lemoyne, New Cumberland, Middletown, Paxtang, and Oberlin were all good blue-collar railroad towns. A 1927 City street list shows that on the 600 block of Dauphin St. lived three engineers, a fireman, a car repairman, and a machinist, as well as a few railroad widows. The section from Forester St. north, between Third and Seventh Sts., was railroad family country. A railroader could buy a three-story brick duplex for $2,800 and raise his family within walking distance of work, church, school, stores and, most importantly, friends.

The railroaders of that era were men of simple joys and much pride.

ROCKVILLE BRIDGE

The pay was never much. Clerks' wages went from 16.9 cents an hour to 25 cents on Jan. 1, 1918 .The Wilson Administration in 1920 forced the railroads to cut back the 12-hour day to eight hours. The one-week vacation plan did not take effect until 1945. Paul S. Roberts, of Camp Hill, broke in for 10.9 cents an hour, 12 hours a day, seven days a week and no vacations in 1907, but he liked railroading so much he stayed with the Pennsy until 1963.

There was "railroader's coffee," which they said could cut through anything, even coal dust. A railroader would dilute the coffee four to one with spring water, and it still would be powerful enough to eat the bottom out of a tin cup. At the old coal wharf on the Main Line tracks near Verbeke St., a boilermaker was supposed to rinse out the pot once a week, but some weeks he forgot.

The wharfs in Harrisburg, Enola, and elsewhere along the line were demolished in the early 1960s. They were the symbols of old-time railroading. Crews of 12 worked shifts at these coaling stations. "You'd come out dusty," one said, "but you loved it."

The steam engines were the heart of the railroad. As late as 1949 the Pennsy had 2,490 steam locomotives, compared to 549 diesels and 268 electrics. "Old Goat," the last of the wood-burners, carried coal from Lykens to Harrisburg, making steam by burning half a tree trunk. Generations of Harrisburg children watched her choo-choo into town.

The coal wharf near Verbeke St. was more than 100 feet high, one of the town's largest structures. Freight trains with 60 to 80 tons of coal unloaded, and a two-way bucket system hauled the coal to the top of the wharf. The great "hand bombers"—the fireman-shoveled steam engines—would come aboard to be loaded by chute. The most magnificent of the iron horses, the K-4s, would take 33 to 35 tons to get them to Manhattan Transfer, which is the junction near Newark, N.J., where electric engines would take over for the pull through the tunnels to New York. John Dos Passos entitled his 1925 novel *Manhattan Transfer*.

Because of the mountains, it took more coal for the hand bombers going west than east. A good fireman could economize on coal use, too. "The fireman in those days was a price man," said one veteran. "There was no talk about featherbedding then. He'd hand-fire all the way. Sometimes it took a pair of men to do the job. When a man wasn't shoveling, he was keeping the fires clean."

Double-headers of K-4 engines would take the trains the 136 miles from Harrisburg to Altoona, and then another pair would carry on from Altoona to Pittsburgh. A snapper, or low-geared freight engine, often was needed to boost the bombers over Horseshoe Curve.

Freight steam engines were "hogs" and their crews, "hoggers." It was a matter of pride that passenger crews never were referred to in such charming terms. The old wharfs became almost useless about 1953, when the steam engines went their way.

The first electric train pulled into Harrisburg on Jan. 15, 1940, at 12:08 A.M., eight minutes ahead of schedule. The headline of the *Evening News* was: "Dream of Years Is Realized as First Electric Train Rolls into City Today." A crowd of 2,000 was at the station to greet train No. 25, the Metropolitan, with William O. Buck, of Herr St., the engineer. Buck was a railroader for 45 years, an engineer for 40 of them. His fireman was Emory A. Mundis, Sr., of Enola.

The Pennsy, which eventually had more miles of electrification than any other railroad in the nation, began planning for it in 1928. It spent almost $53 million and by 1935 had lines between New York, Philadelphia, Baltimore, and Washington electrified. From Paoli to Harrisburg was the last big stretch to do. The line west of the Enola Yards has never been electrified, because diesels are more efficient for the hilly terrain.

Train No. 25 opened the electric path to Philadelphia. Fifty-eight minutes after Buck brought his in, train No. 2 from Chicago, St. Louis, and Pittsburgh pulled out under electric power. It had come east to Harrisburg under steam, and Charles H. Gehr, engineer from Harrisburg, took it on to Philadelphia.

The Harrisburg Area has always been a transportation center. There were Indian trails here and then John Harris's ferry and trading post. The Pennsylvania Canal was authorized Feb. 25, 1826, to "advance the prosperity and elevate the character of Pennsylvania," in the words of Gov. John Andrew Shulze. On July 4 ground was broken not far from where the Forum and the Main Line are now, and the canal went into operation in March of 1828.

Harrisburg was the center of Pennsylvania's 900 miles of state-owned and 300 miles of privately owned canals. It was from Harrisburg that Charles Dickens took his famous canal trip to Pittsburgh in 1842, lasting from Friday night to Monday morning. The passenger fare from Philadelphia to Pittsburgh, with some railroad passage added to the canal service, was $7.

The canal system was a way of life from 1826 until November of 1900, when the last canalboat went through Harrisburg. After the winter freeze, the canal was never again used commercially.

Tough Irish, Slavs, and Negroes hand-dug the ditches for the wages of $9 a month, but it was usually Pennsylvania Germans who captained the boats. The work-day was long, the pay short, and the tempers often shorter.

"There will never again be a period in the travel history of this country quite as colorful or as unique as the canalboat era," writes William H. Shank. "The canalers were a hardy lot, and although certain rules and regulations existed about right of way on the canals, it was usually the canalboat with the toughest crews that cleared the locks first. It was at the locks that the most frequent bottlenecks occurred. Some of the competing packet boats literally raced each other from one lock to the next. The lock tender was supposed to decide, in the event two boats arrived at the same time, which was to be given preference, but usually the boat whose crew could lick the other, and often did, was on its way while the other waited."

Shank, a York engineer, has written on the Pennsylvania canals, railroads, highways, and floods. He is descended from an immigrant German ship carpenter who moved inland to Liverpool in the 1820s and built what is believed to be the first canalboat north of Harrisburg. His grandson, Shank's grandfather, worked on the Pennsylvania Railroad.

The Pennsylvania Canal through the center of the state lasted only 18 years without competition from the railroads. It is questionable how much the big canal, winding 320 miles, contributed to Pennsylvania's prosperity. It cost $101.6 million to build and maintain, and only $44 million was returned in revenue. The Commonwealth was happy to sell the canal to the Pennsy at bargain prices in 1857.

Harrisburg got railroad service as early as 1838, when the Cumberland Valley Railroad and an eastern line from Lancaster and Mt. Joy came into town. The Cumberland Valley built the first railroad bridge in these parts to get over the Susquehanna.

The Pennsy was chartered on April 13, 1846, and eight years later offered Philadelphia to Pittsburgh service. The Reading Railroad entered Harrisburg for the first time on Jan. 18, 1858, when it brought 1,000 passengers to the inauguration of Gov. William F. Packer. Though not as big as the Pennsy's Enola Yards, the Reading's Rutherford Yards at one time was classifying 5,500 freight cars daily.

The first barnlike railroad terminal was built in Harrisburg in 1837. The Pennsy began to use that station in 1849, and the famed general superintendent, John Edgar Thomson, had his office and staff here. The second station, from 1857 to 1887, had two great towers and wings, a House of Parliament type structure obviously symbolizing the new vigor of American industrialism. The current station was opened in 1887. Bigger than a football field, it is made of red brick and has eight double-window dormers and a slate roof. It is a monstrosity, sometimes called "Old Ugly"; yet, as Frank O'Connor in a short story once described such a structure, it is "beautiful in the way of buildings that have not been looked at too much."

The Reading Railroad built the most impressive depot, a marble, Gilded Age shrine that stood at Eighth and Market Sts. from 1904 to 1960, when it gave way to the new post office. The better of the two depots was not only ripped down, but a nondescript, bland post office building put in its place, another mark of regression in the architectural environment.

The smoke-belching Broadway Limited first sped into Harrisburg on June 15, 1902, the day that the competing New York Central launched its Twentieth Century Limited. While the Twentieth Century rolled through Albany, N.Y., on its way to Chicago, the Broadway Limited zoomed into Harrisburg for a three-minute layover.

Called the "Pennsylvania Special," Engine 395 had four cars and 52 travelers. Calvin C. Miller, a Harrisburger who worked 30 years for the railroad, was at the throttle. He took it the 84 miles across New Jersey in 88 minutes, and arrived at Harrisburg exactly on time. He steamed out of the City, headed over the new Rockville Bridge and then from the Cove, just north of Summerdale, got the train going at almost 100 miles an hour. The "Pennsylvania Special" arrived at Altoona at 8:30 P.M., exactly on time.

"So fast, indeed, did it go that the road crossing whistle seemed to come from the rear of the train instead of from the engine," a passenger observed. "The rush of air against the steam as it came from the whistle squeezed the sound and the noise resembled a wild, unearthly shriek that seemed to linger among the trees." The next day, at 8:35 A.M., the Broadway Limited reached Chicago, three minutes ahead of schedule. In just 20 hours, four hours less than previous trains, the Special had gone from Gotham to the Windy City.

The Broadway Limited was reduced to just coach service in 1967, the same year the Twentieth Century made her last New York to Chicago run. The following year, the Penn Central merger was effected, and 871 days later, on June 21, 1970, the nation's sixth largest company, losing $1 million a day, went bankrupt. By 1972, however, Pullman service was restored on the Broadway Limited and efforts were under way to attract more passengers.

The last mail cars on the trains ran through Harrisburg on April 30, 1971, ending 104 years of service. When Wilmer King, the retired Harrisburg postmaster, started as a road mail clerk in 1919, there were 400 men working the mail trains between New York and Pittsburgh. They would take the late business mail out of New York and sort by sections for Philadelphia, Lancaster, York, Harrisburg, and westward to Pittsburgh, so that most of it would be delivered within 24 hours.

Railroading never came close to being as dangerous as coal mining, but it has had spectacular accidents. Two of the recent bad ones were the Harrisburg Baseball Special, which went off the track in Steelton on July 28, 1962, killing 19 persons and injuring 102, and the freight collision at Herndon on March 12, 1972, in which four railroaders were killed in a 45-boxcar pile-up.

The Lochiel wreck of May 11, 1905, remains "the most horrible calamity in the railroad annals of Harrisburg," as the *Patriot* said that morning. It killed 23 and injured 146. Among the dead was Sam Shubert, 28, the founder of the Shubert theater empire and the older brother of Lee and Jake Shubert. He was in the sleeper of the westbound Cleveland and Cincinnati Express. Minutes after the train passed through Middletown, a small eastbound freight had an air-hose break at Lochiel and its cars were thrown to the other track. The 10-coach express hit the freight cars at 1:38 A.M. Two cars laden with dynamite exploded. Many of the victims, including the engineer, were burned to death instantly.

Sam Shubert was blasted free from the wreck. At first he thought he was only slightly injured, and he refused to be taken to the Harrisburg Hospital but took a room at the old Commonwealth Hotel instead. Charles Germer, a 17-year-old lad from Shipoke working at the Central Iron and Steel Co., was one of the first on the scene. He helped Shubert and later visited him at the hotel. Some 200 telegrams from all over the country came to Shubert wishing him well, but the next day his condition worsened and he died. The Shubert survivors gave Germer $100 in appreciation.

The Cleveland and Cincinnati Express was filled with notables of the day—and it is ironic that no Harrisburgers were killed and only five injured. J. W. Anderson, the Pittsburgh steel magnate, and his son were killed, as was Max Stettheimer, a New York garment manufacturer. Mrs. J. H. Tindell, the daughter of Sen. Philander C. Knox, was injured slightly, and Gov. Samuel W. Pennypacker had her taken to a room in the Governor's Mansion. Mrs. Albert J. Barr, of the *Pittsburgh Post* family and a relative of Mayor Joseph Barr, had her clothes burned off, as did her two daughters.

Paul G. Smith, later president judge of Dauphin County Court and once the football coach of old Central High, was at the time a member of the Bucknell University baseball team. The team was supposed to board the sleeper to get to Harrisburg, but it was too crowded. Smith and his teammates waited five hours for the next train, but they got to Harrisburg safely.

Carl Bartram Shelley, later district attorney and judge, was 11 and asleep in his dad's old Central Hotel in Steelton. The blast from the dynamite explosion knocked two windows out of the hotel, a mile away. Shelley's father prepared sandwiches and had his boy dash with them to the scene.

A temporary morgue was set up at 128 Chestnut St., but five victims never were identified. Inquiries came from as far away as Canada, families asking if missing persons, including absconding husbands, had been killed. Perhaps one famous missing New York lawyer was among the unidentified, but it will never be known.

A special Harrisburg memorial service was held at the Market Square Presbyterian Church. For the unknown dead, the honorary pallbearers were this town's leading citizens: Mayor E. Z. Gross, Vance McCormick, Judge George Kunkel, James Cameron, John Y. Boyd, and Spencer C. Gilbert.

The Pennsylvania Railroad bought a grave plot at the Paxtang Cemetery, and there they are buried. The tombstone, with the old PRR emblem on it, reads: "In reverence for the five unknown dead who departed this life in the railroad accident near Harrisburg, Pa., May 11, 1905. And in sympathy with unknown mourners, this stone is placed by the Pennsylvania Railroad Co."

Gone forever, like the canalboats and steam engines, are the Susquehanna coal-dredgers and barges, once described as: "Two hundred of the most unlovely craft in the world, grimy, battered barges, smoke-stained, open-deck, paddlewheel pushers, pump boats that look like a donkey engine on a raft." Between March and Thanksgiving Day, 300 men would be out, often from 6 A.M. to 5 P.M. The yearly haul could be as much as 500,000 tons of coal, worth $2 to $4 a ton. The business hit its peak in the 1920s, and the decline set in for good in the 1950s because of pollution control and less mining north of Amity Hall.

The Downey family, working out of Lochiel, had as many as 55 coal barges, five paddlewheel steamboats, and 12 dredges. The barges were 51 feet long and 10 feet wide, but only 20 inches deep. There were 20 competing fleets on the river. The Stroah family from Hardscrabble had five dredges.

The river navy was an eyesore and noisy, but it kept the river open and free of coal deposits and serviced Bethlehem Steel, the City, and other users of screened coal. In 1963 the enterprise passed into history. "It was a great life out there on the river," said Charlie Downey. "We loved it there, in the fresh air, away from the autos, chugging up and down and working real hard. It was more than a job. It was a way of life."

Spanning the Susquehanna

. . . From Old Camelback

to Interstates

The art of bridge-building across the Susquehanna is not what it used to be. Harrisburg once had distinctive old bridges. Today it has conventional, multilane, concrete spans.

Old Camelback was a shingle-roof, clapboard-side barn on nine piers and four abutments, but it was the pride of Harrisburg.

CAMEL BACK BRIDGE

"We crossed the Susquehanna River by a wooden bridge, roofed and covered in on all sides, and nearly a mile in length," wrote Charles Dickens in 1842. "It was profoundly dark, perplexed with great beams, crossing and recrossing at every possible angle, and through the broad chinks and crevices in the floor the rapid river gleamed far down below like a legion of eyes. We had no lamps, and as the horses stumbled and floundered through the place toward the distant speck of dying light, it seemed interminable. I really could not at first persuade myself, as we rumbled heavily on filling the bridge with hollow noises and as I held down my head to save it from the rafters above, that I was not in a painful dream, for I have often dreamed of toiling through such places and as often argued, even at the time, 'this cannot be reality.' "

Dickens was right in his *American Notes*. Old Camelback was not reality. It was romantic, even its odor.

The bridge was built in two sections, with the first stone laid Dec. 12, 1812. It was opened for tolls on Oct. 16, 1816, and was in business until March 2, 1902, when a flood demolished it. In its 85 years it was threatened repeatedly by floods and fires, but somehow endured. Harrisburgers loved the old thing. "As it grew old along with them," Marian Inglewood noted in her 1925 book, *Then and Now in Harrisburg*, "it came to fill a place in their affections peculiarly its own. Everyone pointed to it with a loyal-hearted pride that refused to see how ramshackled it was beginning to grow."

Theodore Burr, a New Englander who came here at age 40, was the designer. His work on the Susquehanna, Mohawk, Hudson, and Delaware rivers makes him one of America's great bridge builders. "It was the handicap of Theodore Burr that he did not have at command in his lifetime materials worthy of his genius for fabricating," wrote the late Dr. Hubertis M. Cummings, the historian from Camp Hill. What he had, however, was good enough for his sturdy arch, which lasted longer than Burr himself. At age 51 in 1822, he was dead. Burr was buried in an unknown grave, probably near Middletown.

Camelback made a fortune for its Front St. financiers. It cost $192,-138. Its toll in 1816 for a two-wheel vehicle with one horse was 32 cents. Eventually the price was raised to 37 cents, with horseback riders paying a 25-cent fee and pedestrians, 6¼ cents. Under the original 1809 legislation governing Old Camelback, the bridge was to be paid for and then made free, but what developed was "the privilege of perpetual toll"—so lucrative that special pens were built for livestock to enable the tolltakers to count heads accurately. The Commonwealth had $90,-000 worth of shares in the bridge, but sold out for $9,000 to the McCormicks, Camerons, and Haldemans.

The Confederates vowed to burn Camelback, as they did the Columbia-Wrightsville Bridge, the world's longest covered bridge. That is one reason why the Union insisted upon fighting Robert E. Lee's forces west of the river. Yet the Harrisburg owners charged the defending troops to cross the bridge to save it. A bill for $3,028.63 was submitted after the Battle of Gettysburg. When the Commonwealth paid, the bridge company doubled its annual dividend for 1863.

A rival to Camelback went up in 1889, the Walnut Street Bridge. In 1951 an engineer testified that "Old Shakey" should have a lifespan of 84 years, or through 1973. The Pennsylvania Department of Transportation announced that "Old Shakey" could topple into the Susquehanna if there were a heavy ice jam, and then just months later "Old Shakey" was lapped by the Flood of 1972 and to the joy of cheering onlookers magnificently endured again.

The 1902 Flood half-collapsed the eastern section of Old Camelback, while the rickety western section tottered. Thousands of Harrisburgers gathered at riverside to see the end. James McCormick, with the superb elan of the Harrisburg gentry, that night installed a searchlight at Front and Walnut Sts. so that the folks could see his profits crumbling.

With Old Camelback destroyed, residents used "Old Shakey" and the Rockville Railroad Bridge, then under construction. The Rockville Bridge, with 48 arches of 70-foot widths for a distance of 3,830 feet, is still the world's longest stone arch railroad bridge. To its south, by the Harrisburg Hospital, is the Cumberland Valley Railroad Bridge, originally built in 1835 as the world's first combined railroad and highway bridge, but never really used as a highway. Near it are the piers of the bridge, never built, for Andrew Carnegie's intended South Penn Railroad. And to the north of Rockville are the piers for what was the bridge of Simon Cameron's Northern Central Railroad. Still in use is the Clarks Ferry Bridge, which was another wooden bridge the Northerners believed threatened during the Confederate invasion. In 1925 it was reinforced with concrete for heavy, modern-day automobile use.

With the identification marker from Old Camelback imbedded in it for posterity, the Market Street Bridge was opened Feb. 27, 1904. Two of the old State Capitol's six great columns were placed at its Harrisburg entrance. In 1928 the bridge was widened and in 1962, at a cost of $1 million, it was redone with prestressed concrete. Finally in 1968, more work was done, much of it decorative, thanks to a campaign by the Civic Club. The six ornamental iron lanterns were cleaned, coated with a metallic paint, and given an eerie yellowish glow.

The Commonwealth purchased the stock of the Market Street Bridge in August of 1949 for $3.85 million, though a board of reviewers found the structure worth at least $100,000 less. The tolls came off on May 15, 1957, when at 9:30 A.M. Sammy Donowitz, a junk dealer from Cameron St., gave Gov. George M. Leader the last nickel to cross the bridge with a team of horses. The next man, Seth B. Keener, Jr., an insurance man, was waved on free.

The M. Harvey Taylor Bridge opened Jan. 24, 1952, and the John Harris Bridge—the expressway bridge always called the South Bridge— opened Jan. 22, 1960. Both of these are really extended highways, not traditional bridges, and the same is true of the George N. Wade Bridge on Interstate Route 81, opened in 1973.

The City's Mulberry Street Bridge, over the railroad tracks, opened Sept. 3, 1909, as the world's longest reinforced concrete highway via- duct. A wonder for its time, today it is a traffic-jam marvel.

The firm of Modjeski and Masters built the Market Street, Taylor, and South bridges. Frank M. Masters, Sr. became an employee of the famous Polish engineer, Ralph Modjeski, in 1905 and a partner in 1924. Modjeski died in 1940. Masters was honored in 1969 by the Smithsonian Institution as the "granddaddy in civil engineering," after his firm designed such bridges as the Ben Franklin, Walt Whitman, Quebec, Huey P. Long, the Ambassador, and the Mid-Hudson.

Bridge-building, Masters told the Smithsonian, should be "harmoni- ously blended durability, simplicity and grandeur." The grandeur must be emphasized, he asserted. But, of course, in so much modern bridge- building, the technician dominates the artist and there is little concern for grandeur.

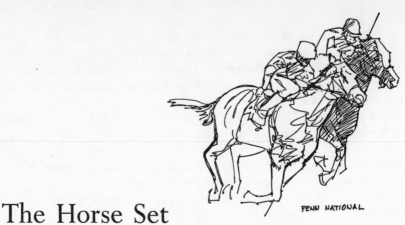

PENN NATIONAL

The Horse Set

. . . *Enthusiastic Equestrians*

Harrisburg has never been a one-horse town. The Pennsylvania National is in the triple crown of North American indoor horse shows. The Beaufort Hunt, the Harrisburg Horse Show, and the colorful Rose Tree Steeplechase at Wellsville are popular attractions. The harness horse industry is a multi-million-dollar business, and the standardbred sale in the fall is the nation's largest. Hanover Shoe Farms, Lana Lobell Farms, and Hempt Farms are among the world's greatest for raising trotters and pacers. There is always a good run for the ribbons at the Bloomsburg and Carlisle fairs, and there is even a West Shore Polo Club.

The $18 million Penn National Race Course at Grantville opened on Aug. 30, 1972, with Le Grand Jour, appropriately enough, winning the first race, paying $9.80, $5.60, and $4.20. Established by John J. Shumaker, Edward C. First, Jr., and Jack B. Gross, the Penn National quickly should become one of thoroughbred racing's most exciting tracks.

The climate and the wide-open, rolling limestone land made Central Pennsylvania excellent horse country. Before the era of the automobile, the gentry grew up with horses and had the space and the competitive spirit to breed them, show them, race them, and hunt with them. Love of horses caught on early and became part of the Midstate tradition.

This is old cavalry country. Predecessors of the 104th Cavalry—now the Governor's Troop—fought in the Civil War. In the mid-1930s, Col.

74

Jonathan M. Wainwright led the last cavalry march through Pennsylvania, taking 400 men and horses from Fort Myers, Va. to Indiantown Gap. When the procession reached the West Shore, Wainwright halted and called for the flag-bearers and buglers to lead the troops across the Market Street Bridge and into Downtown Harrisburg. It was a colorful invasion, a mix of Cecil B. DeMille with Douglas MacArthur. Actually, Capt. Albert H. Stackpole was riding with Wainwright, and the later hero of Corregidor was informed that Harrisburg is crazy about horses and parades with plenty of panache and jingoism.

Great horses and horsemen have come out of this part of Pennsylvania.

Lawrence B. Sheppard developed Adios Harry, Dean Hanover, and Bret Hanover at his Hanover Shoe Farms, a 2,300-acre campus for the greatest of American sulky horses. Adios Harry once held the world's record for the fastest mile race. Sheppard, who died at age 70 in 1968, was a leathery old fellow and a superb businessman, who himself drove Dean Hanover to a world's record.

Max Hempt is a remarkable horseman. At 6-foot-7, 275 pounds and in his 50s, he mallets his way through eight chukkers of polo. His 1,200-acre breeding farm in Silver Spring Township is the largest three-stud farm in the nation and the fifth largest breeding farm. A contractor by profession, Hempt has produced Harlan Dean, a Hambletonian winner; Stenographer, who set 11 world records, and together with Sheppard and Delvin Miller of Western Pennsylvania owned Adios (1955–1965), the sire of Harry and the greatest breeding stallion in racing history. Adios sired 79 horses who have won races in two minutes or less, and his off-spring have won more money than any other family in standardbreds or thoroughbreds, $19.4 million. The brothers Hickory Pride and Hickory Smoke are current great studs. Their progeny in 1971 won $3 million.

The late Bowman Brown, Sr. was another fine horseman. Brown, who lived in Camp Hill and had a breeding farm at Port Royal, founded the national weekly, the *Harness Horse*.

Ehrman B. Mitchell was one of the squires of the equestrian sport. The son of a lawyer, Mitchell went to Yale and then studied postgraduate agriculture at Rutgers. He returned to manage his family's estate along the Linglestown Road, while his wife, Alice, helped found the Harrisburg Symphony. In 1929 Mitchell and his friends, such as E. Z. Wallower, Dr. George R. Moffitt, Farley Gannett, Ray Shoemaker, Paul R. Gable, and Ross R. Rhoads, started the Beaufort Hunt, and in 1931, the Harrisburg Horse Show.

The Duke of Beaufort of Badminton, England made the original grant of Susquehanna Township to the Penns, acquired at no cost from the Indians. Beaufort became the recognized name for the plateau south of the Blue Mountains, and Mitchell called his place Beaufort Farms, now the name for a deluxe residential complex. The old Duke in the Midlands was anti-monarch during the Revolution. His was the world's most famous fox hunt and its colors were blue and buff, not royal scarlet. When Mitchell obtained permission to name his fox hunt Beaufort, he also adopted blue and buff. The Thanksgiving Day hunt is now held at the Hillsdale Farm in Londonderry Township, near Geyers Church. This 150-year-old farm goes back in the Gingrich family for generations. Dr. Rife Gingrich, master of the hounds for 15 years and proprietor, is the host for the fox chase.

The Harrisburg Horse Show is held at Belle-Nance Farms on the Linglestown Road the first Saturday of May. Farley Gannett, the noted engineer, was the first president, and Mitchell, who died in 1960, was the secretary for almost 30 years. The show is rated as one of the top one-day events in the East, recognized by the American Horse Show Association for qualifying points to riders headed to the Penn National and the Madison Square Garden National.

The famous Penn National, founded in 1945, grew out of shows given by the 104th Cavalry. Rare for Harrisburg, it started on borrowed money and more enthusiasm than pessimism, but in three years was an international contest. Today it is in a league with the Madison Square Garden show and the Royal Winter Fair in Toronto. Because the Farm Show Arena was built in 1931 as the largest building in the nation specifically for animals, the show is the biggest indoor equestrian competition in this hemisphere. There are at least a dozen other cities that would like to steal the Penn National from Harrisburg, but they cannot match the Farm Arena's seating and stabling facilities, nor the tradition and immense amount of effort Harrisburg has put into this extravaganza to make it the spectacular it is.

"It's getting as tough for a horse to get in the Penn National as it is for a kid to get into Harvard," said John R. Sterling, the unpaid secretary who shares responsibility for keeping the billing to about 1,000 horses. Sterling, a native of Linglestown, owns a 126-acre hay farm near Dover and is one of the most knowledgeable horsemen in the nation.

In mid-October, the Penn National brings some of the finest riders and most devoted lovers of horseflesh in the world to Harrisburg. The Olympic Gold Medal winner Bill Steinkraus for 20 years rode the United States colors in the international jumping. Col. Pierre Cavaille of France and the exciting Major Humberto Mariles Cortes of Mexico were among other famous riders to make the jumps here.

The Penn National is backed by the Harrisburg Kiwanis Club, and over the years has earned more than $260,000 for its Youth Fund, including $85,000 for Kamp Kiwanis.

"We've avoided making the show an in-group thing," said Sterling. "We've made it a public attraction, something that no matter how rich or poor a person is he can still feel part of the audience. We get horse lovers, of course, and fans who follow this sport as fans follow any sport, but we also get people who like it because it's a great spectator event and want to see what goes on."

The Penn National has had only five presidents: Franklin Moore, A. H. Stackpole, George Deubel, Carlos F. Bodwell, and Matthew M. Douglas, Jr. Bill Stackpole—always called "Bill" and never by his proper name of Albert—was president for 13 years and saw the show through its first quarter-century.

Stackpole was the younger of a pair of Harrisburg lieutenant generals. He was born in the City on June 28, 1897, two years after his brother, Edward J. Stackpole, Jr., who died at age 73 in 1967. They were the sons of the owner of the *Harrisburg Telegraph*. Bill, a columnist and city editor, became the editor and publisher after his father's death in 1936, while Ed became chief of the Telegraph Press and WHP radio and television. The Stackpole brothers were as fine gentlemen as Harrisburg ever had. Both went to Yale and both had distinguished careers in the two world wars. Ed was wounded three times in World War I and won the Distinguished Service Cross. Bill won the Bronze Star in World War II for special service with the Chinese Army. Both brothers also commanded the 104th Cavalry. In their avocations, Ed became an outstanding Civil War historian, while Bill was the horseman. From 1925 to his death on July 31, 1971, Bill lived in the Clarks Valley home of the late novelist Conrad Richter. His wife, Mary, is a Distinguished Daughter of Pennsylvania and one of the community's leading civic servants.

A memorial service was held at St. Stephen's Cathedral for Gen. A. H. Stackpole. As the Reporter At Large column said: "General Bill probably was the last to have the full respect of the patricians and plebeians alike. And so the lowly, as well as the cream of Harrisburg society, turned out to honor his memory. . . . His finest accomplishment was to be himself. With great self-assurance that didn't automatically come from social advantage, but from character, he lived a life that emphasized living and he welcomed people as they were." No horses were used for the last tribute to the old cavalryman. The Penn National is his living memorial.

Annals of Crime

. . . Three Famous Murder Cases

The 1920s and 1930s, though scarcely a violent era compared to today, was the period of the great American murder cases. Central Pennsylvania had four especially exciting ones: the Lamb's Gap double slaying, the Case of the Missing Body, the Babes in the Woods mystery, and the Hex murder. The first three will be traced here. Arthur H. Lewis, a former Harrisburger, thoroughly covered the York County hex murder of Nov. 28, 1928, in his book, *Hex*. This was the case of an old farmer, a self-proclaimed witch, who was bludgeoned to death by a young practitioner of witchcraft and his two teen-age accomplices.

The Ganster-Ellenberger murder at Lamb's Gap in Perry County on May 16, 1924, is one of the most celebrated cases in Pennsylvania crime. It was the murder of two persons with one bullet. It remains unsolved, although as recently as 1971 there was a deathbed confession in Harrisburg. It was not accepted, however, and the mystery continues.

Harry L. Ganster would have marked his 21st birthday that August 19. He was a senior at Marysville High School and was the assistant to the dean of Harrisburg photographers, Sam Kuhnert, then 33. The night of the murder, Ganster and his girl friend, Leah Ellenberger, were to have supper at the Kuhnerts, but Ganster passed Kuhnert on the river road and told him he had to go up to Lamb's Gap and pick flowers to decorate the platform for that night's baccalaureate service.

78

Ganster was planning to attend the Jefferson Medical School. The previous fall he worked eight hours a night after high school as a watchman to earn money. His photography also contributed to his savings. He was independent-minded and had the strange diet of drinking two to three quarts of milk daily, but not eating meat. He loved nature and often hiked in the Perry County mountains.

Miss Ellenberger, 22, was a school teacher at Hollidaysburg, but she often visited Marysville because her uncle lived near the Ganster family. The Sunday before her death she sang at the Marysville Methodist Church.

The mountains of Perry County for decades had been a hotbed for bootleg booze. With Prohibition, the moonshiners moved in by the battalions. Lamb's Gap is at the top of Blue Ridge Mountain, six miles west of Marysville. Kuhnert, the first of the aerial photographers, often saw the smoke from the stills floating up from the patches of green hemlocks below.

Ganster had taken pictures of bootleg stills, and the *Harrisburg Telegraph* printed one, foolishly crediting him as the photographer. Not long afterward he received a note: "If you ever come out again, you'll be a dead duck." Kuhnert told his assistant that the bootleggers meant what they said.

The Friday night of the baccalaureate (Ganster was to have graduated 13 days later on May 29) Harry and Leah drove up to Lamb's Gap for flowers. Nobody knew they were going there. About 6:45 P.M. they were murdered with a rifle that has never been found. Leah was at the steering wheel of the car, while Harry had his left foot on the running board. The bullet passed through his right arm and through his body and into the school teacher. Later that night when Ganster's father and Miss Ellenberger's uncle, George Albright, found them, they thought the pair was asleep. "What's going on here?" Joe Ganster shouted. He grabbed Harry's arm and then realized he was dead.

McCormick Scout Lodge was only 500 feet away from the scene. Fifteen Boy Scouts from Troop 13 of Boyd Memorial Hall were hiking and heard the shot. State police combed the mountain and later investigated all persons living at the foot of it, but came up with few leads.

One early theory of murder-suicide was soon discarded. It was suggested that a jealous husband shot Ganster, mistaking Leah for his wife, but that idea led nowhere.

"The dual murder is as much of a mystery today as it was when we started on the case," State Police Commissioner Lynn G. Adams said a week later. "Every theory thus far advanced has been run down without a favorable result. A moonshiner's feud was considered the logical solution but we have been unable to locate anything that would establish any reason for a moonshiner's killing the pair. If Ganster and Miss Ellenberger had walked near a still and the moonshiner had seen them, got his gun and walked to the top of the mountain and shot them, you would think that the man would be in such a hurry to get out of that section that he would at least leave some evidence behind where he had had his fire. But there is no such evidence around.

"On the other hand, if the shooting was for revenge, then the gunman must have seen the pair drive up the Perry County side of the mountain and followed them. But we couldn't find anything to show a man went up that side of the mountain. Certainly the murderer didn't know in advance that these young people intended going to the mountain, and if he were on the Cumberland County side when they started up the Perry County side, he could not have seen them. It looks to me like a long hard siege if the mystery is ever to be solved." And that is where the case remains.

WALNUT STREET

The Case of the Missing Body stirred excitement in 1929 because for 24 days the body of Verna L. Klink was hidden beneath an unusually heavy ice cover on the Susquehanna River. Had the body never been recovered, a first-degree murder charge would have been out of the question. And if the ice had so damaged the body that it could not be determined if it were a matter of murder or suicide, the entire case would have taken a different turn.

Miss Klink, 31, of S. Third St., operated Candyland, a confectionery, at 129 Walnut St. She had a reputation for making the best milkshakes in town. After a year and a half in the business, she wanted to buy the shop. She borrowed $1,700 from her mother in Mechanicsburg, withdrew about $1,000 of it from the bank, and on a moonlit Friday night, Jan. 25, 1929, went for a walk in River Park, near the Walnut Street Bridge, with Harry Bowman, a perfume salesman from Evergreen St.

Bowman, 39, a native of Halifax, was married but had a girl friend other than Verna living in a boarding house on Market St. His mother called him "Hon," and people remembered him as an enthusiastic amateur baseball player.

Bowman was arrested the following Monday on Market Square. He was taken to the State Police barracks, not permitted to see a lawyer, and was grilled for 18 hours until he confessed. "She was sweet on me," Bowman told the police. But a few days after the confession, Bowman reverted to his original story. He said that he and Verna had had a suicide pact and that at the last minute he became scared. The police asked how he managed to get almost $1,000 in his pocket.

Bowman had no lawyer; so Solomon Hurwitz, then only 22, was called into the case. Hurwitz was Phi Beta Kappa, president of the Dickinson Belles Lettres Society, an outstanding collegiate debator, and the top man two out of three years in his law school class. Until his death in 1968, Hurwitz headed one of the top law firms in the City, with Irwin Benjamin, Macey E. Klein, and I. Emanuel Meyers among his partners. But in 1929 this was Hurwitz's first murder case—first, that is, if the body could be found.

Prison Warden William W. Caldwell kept Bowman in jail, while Hurwitz filed habeas corpus proceedings with Judge William M. Hargest. The search for the body started immediately after Bowman was arrested. More than 6,000 persons crowded the riverside from Harrisburg to Middletown to look. Dauphin County and the owner of the candy store each offered $100 rewards. Meanwhile, on February 4, Judge Hargest granted writ of habeas corpus and authorities, for want of the body, charged Bowman with adultery and larceny.

The City paid men 50 cents an hour to find Miss Klink. On February

5 the cost went above $160, and Mayor George A. Hoverter called off the official search. The next day it was reported that Miss Klink had been seen alive on Market Square. And then on February 17, Michael Krzyzosiak and Boyd Crumlich, both of Steelton, found the body. Miss Klink was buried on February 20, the same day the coroner's jury found the cause of death to be murder. Dr. John Kreider, the father of the later President Judge Homer L. Kreider, was the coroner.

The dramatic trial was held before Judge Hargest during Holy Week. District Attorney Robert T. Fox, seeking his first murder conviction, was especially effective in his cross examination. Hurwitz, as the press reported, "made an eloquent attempt to save the life of the man who entrusted his fate to the young lawyer's ability." He argued that Bowman had made no plans to kill Miss Klink and that suicide could not be ruled out. He quoted law, the Bible and "The Rubáiyát of Omar Khayyam." A reporter wrote: "His voice rose and fell like that of an experienced actor. He strode up and down. His gestures were telling and well-timed. He was appealing to the sympathies of the jury and made a good job of it." Hurwitz said, "If killing Harry Bowman would bring Verna Klink back to life, I'd say kill him, but it won't. You know that."

On Good Friday, the jury of 10 men and two women came in with the verdict: guilty and life imprisonment. Hurwitz and Bowman were lucky, for that year seven Pennsylvanias before Bowman were executed and an eighth, a man from Schuylkill County, was executed at Rockview Penitentiary while the Bowman trial was taking place.

On Nov. 24, 1934, a Saturday, two caretakers on the James Cameron Estate on South Mountain near Pine Grove Furnace, south of Carlisle, discovered the bodies of three young girls. It was the Babes in the Woods mystery. The girls appeared to be sisters, and a professor at Dickinson College proved that they were by matching strands of hair.

The homicides touched off a national search. "We'll find out what killed these little girls even if the tax rate in this county has to be raised," said Cumberland County District Attorney Fred J. Templeton. Eventually, 28 states were in on the investigation, and the Babes in the Woods mystery was front page news for more than a week in the nation's largest newspapers.

The murdered girls were found on a blanket about 20 feet from the Pinchot Road, which goes through Michaux State Forest at Pine Grove Furnace. The oldest girl was between 12 and 16; the second, between 9 and 11, and the youngest, between 5 and 8. The three were found with the youngest cuddled in the arms of the oldest and the other lying near the side of the oldest. They were clad in new coats with fur collars, dresses of good quality, silk underwear, and even new shoes. Later it was determined that the girls were dressed after they were slain.

All three had light brown hair, freckles, and gray eyes. It had rained the Friday before, but neither the girls nor the blanket was wet. Found nearby was a black leather Gladstone suitcase, containing, among other things, a woman's size 18 dress, a doll with a broken arm, and a tube of toothpaste one-third used.

The Cumberland County coroner, Dr. Edward S. Haegele of Mechanicsburg, immediately took charge and worked all night on the case. It was quickly determined that the girls had been dead 42 to 72 hours before they were found and that they had had nothing to eat 18 hours prior to their slaying. It appeared that a car had parked about 60 feet away, and the slain girls were carried one by one to the spot. Dr. George R. Moffitt, Sr., of the Harrisburg Hospital, established that the girls did not die of carbon monoxide poisoning. He concluded they were put to death by strangulation or suffocation, perhaps by what he called a Japanese wide-band method which left no scars on the neck. Dr. Vance McCormick Rothrock, of Carlisle, found a dime-sized scar underneath the skin of the forehead of the oldest girl, and he said she had been knocked unconscious before she was murdered. There were no other signs of physical abuse.

Right after the newspapers broke the story of the discovery of the girls, a murder-suicide took place in Duncansville, eight miles from Altoona. A man with no money registered in a lodging, tried to pawn his eyeglasses for $1, gave a nonexistent address in Philadelphia, and then shot his alleged wife and himself. They were listed as Mr. and Mrs. J. C. Gardner.

A Philadelphian said Gardner was really Horace Hughes, 37, of San Francisco, once a Salvation Army officer. The woman was 21 and his intended wife. The children were his own, Geraldine, 15; Dorothy, 12. and the youngest, whatever her name, eight. A Harrisburg bus driver said he had had the family in his bus. The youngest girl's name was Jennie, he said. Shortly afterward, an abandoned 1929 blue Pontiac with California tags was found in McVeytown. Tourist cabin and rooming house operators in Langhorne, Gettysburg, Waynesboro, and Chambersburg made identifications. One said that a Mr. and Mrs. J. C. Malone, of Vallejo, Calif., checked in, telling him that they had left Vallejo on November 6 after voting for Upton Sinclair for governor. The interesting initials of "J.C." popped up more than once.

The names of hundreds of lost little girls were sent to Cumberland County and the State Police from all over the nation. At first it was believed that the victims might be a woman and her daughters from Boston, but they were located at Portage, Pa.

Finally, after four days, the deceased man was identified as Elmo J. Noakes, 32, a widower of Roseville, Calif., and a former Marine who had a steady job and was well respected in his hometown. The woman was his niece and housekeeper, Winifred Pierce, 18. Pictures of the children were sent to an aunt, and they were identified as Noakes's: Norma, 12; Dewella, 10, and Cordelia, 8.

Dorothy Thompson and other top reporters got the story and then hurried to Flemington, N.J., where the Lindbergh baby murder trial was taking place.

On December 1 in the Westminster Cemetery near Carlisle, 500 persons gathered in the rain for the burial of the children. American Legion Post 101, the cemetery, and the undertaker paid the costs. A monument was erected, with the inscription: "Sleep tender blossoms, folded so close/In slumber which broken shall be/By His gentle voice whispering low/'Little Children Come Unto Me.'" Three clergymen conducted the service. A few days later, Noakes and Miss Pierce were buried nearby.

Commissioner Lynn G. Adams of the State Police said the case was closed on December 29. He remarked that Noakes must have been mentally ill to cross the country in seven days and murder his children for no apparent reason. A motive is still lacking for the Babes in the Woods case.

HACC

Education

. . . Emphasis Replaces Apathy

Placing a premium on cultural stability rather than change, the Harrisburg Area traditionally acquiesced to education, instead of embracing it. The subject never received top billing until the 1950s, and then a surprising reversal occurred.

Harrisburg, though the state capital, was the last major city in Pennsylvania to get a college. Until the impetus of Sputnik in 1957, the Harrisburg Area sent fewer than 30 percent of its high school graduates on to higher education.

When Thaddeus Stevens made his immortal free education speech in the State House on April 11, 1835, much of his opposition came from the Harrisburg Area and other Germanic communities. Tax the people for education, he said, because even misers "in their very meanness" will be induced "to send their children to get the worth of their money." He knew that with Pennsylvania Germans the best defense of a public necessity like education is a good offense.

It is not that Harrisburgers were anti-education so much as that they were not pro-education.

Harrisburg was Pennsylvania's third school district, established April 11, 1827. By 1836 the City had four high schools, two each for the sexes. In 1867 it formed "union" high schools. Boys Union was on Walnut St. and then was moved to Chestnut St. until 1893. Girls Union was in the Fager Building, now the Chamber of Commerce, from 1836 to 1859 and then at the site of the Moose Hall on State St.

Though education was available, this was a town of dropouts. From 1827 to 1893 the City produced only 685 graduates, and 477 of them were girls.

In 1893 Central High was built at Capitol and Forster Sts. for $107,-430. It was coed until 1920 and then was Girls High until William Penn and John Harris opened in the fall of 1926. Meanwhile, Harrisburg Technical High School opened in 1904 in what is now City Hall. It cost $258,358, and it lasted through 1926. With Central and Tech, the City had real secondary education. In fact, suburban students paid tuition to attend these schools. The town's leadership came from them, but undoubtedly the most noted graduates nationally have been Pauline Frederick, the news commentator, from Central, and Jacques Barzun, the author and scholar, from old Tech. In his famous *Teacher in America*, Barzun writes, "I had the good fortune to come in contact with a fine group of high school teachers."

Barzun was born near Paris, the son of a literary scholar. In 1917 his father came to the United States on a diplomatic mission and in 1919 accepted an appointment at Lehigh University. "The Bethlehem schools were then in a poor state," Barzun has written. "A friend of his who was state superintendent of schools recommended Harrisburg, where I was tutored in U.S. history, civics and English literature before qualifying for entrance to Tech. I managed to get through in three terms (in the class of 1925, but graduating in 1924). It was a fine experience, during which I made half-a-dozen lifelong friends."

Mere academics were not enough. Football brought the fame to Central and Tech. Schoolboy football began in Harrisburg in 1887, and quickly the helmetless but hard-headed railroader boys earned a reputation. Central—known throughout the Commonwealth as Harrisburg High—was the "Capitolians" of blue and gray. From 1887 through 1917, Central was state football champion eight times. The school's record was 137 wins, 91 losses, and 18 ties. It beat old Tech 11 times and tied twice in 15 meetings. The Carlisle Indians did defeat Central five straight times, but the Indians used lads as old as 23. Tech outdid Central, at least in legend. Its overall record was 131 wins, 53 losses, and 11 ties. Four times its team was first in the state. The 1917 Tech Maroons beat Altoona 117 to 0; in 1918 Tech scored 597 points and surrendered only 10, and in 1919 Tech amassed 701 points and gave up just 12.

Among Pennsylvania's all-time great schoolboy football teams have been Central's 1893–1895 and 1898–1900 state champions; Tech's invincibles of 1917–1919 and 1922–1923; the John Harris undefeated teams of 1929–1931, and the ten Harris teams of the 1960s, when it dominated Midstate football with 105 wins, 3 ties, and only 8 losses.

William Penn opened on Sept. 7, 1926, and John Harris 13 days later. The City outdid itself with 30-year indebtedness to have a $1.7 million building for Uptown Harrisburg and a $1.3 million one for Allison Hill. The facilities may have exceeded the community's appetite for learning. "Harrisburg's educational spirit was so bad, starting right at home with the parents," said one teacher who taught at Central, Tech, and Penn, "that the kids had the incentive to study hard so they could get out of town someday." Even so, in their 45 years as separate high schools, they produced a fair share of scholars, including noted criminologist Marvin Wolfgang and nuclear physicist Charles Whitten from Penn, and political scientists Arnold A. Rogow and Paul Tillett, actress Nancy Wickwire, and biophysicist Jerome L. Rosenberg from Harris.

Both Penn and Harris were placed virtually on City line in L-shaped Harrisburg, with the railroad as the divider for the student body. Until 1940, youngsters from Paxtang went to Harris. They could walk to school, but now they are bused to Central Dauphin. Penbrook students could walk to Harris, if the neighborhood school argument was valid. Similarly, Susquehanna Township pupils, three blocks north of Penn, are bused to their district school. The same is true of some elementary and junior high school pupils. In the 1940s there was an attempt to get Susquehanna, especially the upper part of the then second-class township, into the City and the school system. The effort came too late. Had Harrisburg sold itself as a growing city when Penn and Harris opened in 1926, its residential area might be twice what it is, and there would have been no necessity in 1971 to merge Penn and Harris into Harrisburg High School.

Catholic secondary education began in 1918, two years after Bishop Philip R. McDevitt, a native of Philadelphia, came to Harrisburg. The original Catholic High was at Cathedral Hall on North St. In 1930 the new school at 22nd and Market Sts. was opened. Bishop McDevitt died in 1935 and was succeeded by the fifth bishop of the Harrisburg Diocese, George L. Leech, who on Oct. 6, 1957, changed the name of the twin-towered school to honor his predecessor.

Harrisburg suburban education is still too new and growing too fast for much history. The Central Dauphin District, the giant of the East Shore, was started in 1950; and the West Shore District, the giant of the other side of the Susquehanna, was founded in 1953. Today both Central Dauphin and the West Shore have larger budgets than their county governments. Central Dauphin already has more students than the Harrisburg City schools.

Playing a part in the story of Harrisburg Area education were two colleges that have passed from the scene. Irving Female College in Mechanicsburg lasted from 1857 to 1929, and Beckley College on Market Square survived from 1918 to 1933.

Irving was a private school named for Washington Irving, a trustee because he had given some books to the college. It was the first women's college in Pennsylvania to grant degrees in arts and sciences. It stressed music, dramatics, and tennis, and its motto was a stirring: "That our daughters may be as cornerstones, polished after the similitude of a palace." Interestingly enough, Irving had a "sub-freshman" program or accelerated course for advanced high school girls. The school closed after its president, Dr. Ernest E.Campbell, a noted Lutheran layman, died.

Charles R. Beckley was a 6-foot-4, 280-pound supersalesman from York County who boosted his enrollment to 1,000, or ten times what Irving College had. In all, he produced about 5,000 graduates, including Albert Williams of Plymouth, class of 1931, who took his only post-high school study there and went on to the presidency of IBM. Beckley was a two-year business school that taught engineering and aviation. Its chief died in 1929, and four years later Beckley College was succeeded by Thompson Institute.

The Central Pennsylvania Business School was founded in 1922 by William Henry Hartsock. In the Sixties it fell on hard times and was purchased in 1969 by Bart A. Milano, a former teacher and businessman from Wilmington, Del. He relocated the school on a nine-acre site in Summerdale, invested almost $1 million, and by the school's 50th anniversary in 1972 had one of the most thriving business schools with a campus and residence halls in the eastern United States.

There never seemed to be a compelling reason to start a college in Harrisburg. The old command sent its sons off to Yale, Princeton, and other name schools. For the less prosperous, there were many colleges nearby, such as Gettysburg, Dickinson, Elizabethtown, Lebanon Valley, Bucknell, Juniata, Franklin and Marshall, and the state-owned colleges like Penn State and Shippensburg.

Messiah College was founded in Harrisburg in 1909, but the following year the Brethren in Christ moved it to Grantham by the Yellow Breeches, just 12 miles from Downtown Harrisburg. From the mid-1930s there were night school classes in Harrisburg, and in 1951 the

Harrisburg Area Center for Higher Education was formed by Elizabeth-town, Lebanon Valley, Penn State, Temple, and the University of Penn-sylvania. Day school courses were offered in 1961, and three years later the program evolved into the University Center. Meanwhile, in 1966 Penn State moved into the old Olmsted Air Force Base complex at Middletown with its Capitol Campus upper-level school, combining ju-nior and senior years with postgraduate work. The Milton S. Hershey Medical Center took its first students in 1967. And quietly and effi-ciently the Dickinson Law School, founded in 1834 and the oldest in Pennsylvania, continued preparing attorneys. Suddenly at the end of the 1960s, the Harrisburg Area had blossomed into an educational variety garden, blessed by many events for which it could take little credit.

The Community College is the one institution that did not just fortui-tously happen. The Harrisburg School Board, with Carl B. Stoner, Sr. as president, was its key sponsor. With no money, no campus, and no college president, a board of trustees was organized on Feb. 27, 1964. Bruce E. Cooper, 40, its chairman, and James W. Evans, 35, its vice-chairman, sold the plan to 64 of the 85 school districts in the Tri-County Area. Its key board members kept with the project, Mrs. Helen Swope, Mrs. Spencer G. Nauman, John Matsko, James Rowland, Stearl Sponaugle, William Davis, James R. Doran, Jacob Snyder, and Robert Rudenbdall. Dr. Clyde E. Blocker, a railroader's son and a young pro-fessor in Texas, was selected president. City Council turned over 155 acres of Wildwood Park for $1. And, somehow, perhaps because the politicians were never seriously enough interested in education to be for or against it, Harrisburg Area Community College was launched as Pennsylvania's first community college, with classes beginning Sept. 21, 1964 at the old Naval Reserve Center. The first class of 181 students graduated in 1966, with 110 of them accepted for transfer by other colleges. Accreditation came ahead of schedule in 1967, and on that September 26 the new Wildwood Campus opened.

From nothing, HACC went to a $4.2 million budget for 1972–73, assets of $13 million, and a student body of 4,300.

For the Harrisburg Area, the postwar emphasis on education has been fantastic. In no other aspect of public affairs has there been such a marked improvement: a community college, a medical center, an upper-level college, thriving business schools, a burgeoning suburban educa-tional system, and a City school district with the risky challenge of tackling what has been the most difficult social assignment since Thad-deus Stevens's day, integrated education. Prior to 1950, not one of these developments could have been predicted.

BARNARD
STATUARY

Capitol Statuary

. . . *Barnard and Republican*
Politicos

    Nothing quite reflects the preoccupation with politics in the capital city of Pennsylvania than its statuary. Matching the two bridges named for contemporary Republican politicians are eight statues to Republicans, not one to a Democrat. The biggest, most modern, and only interesting statue to an individual, however, is nonpartisan, the 18-foot bronze of William Penn in the State Museum.

There are also 28 nudes, jokingly referred to as the symbols of the Pennsylvania taxpayers. The Barnard nudes at the front of the Capitol account for 27 of them, and high atop the dome is Miss Penn.

The Barnard nudes remain the most exciting and controversial. When they were unveiled on Oct. 4, 1911, six years after the dedication of the Capitol, public opinion was split. They face down Harrisburg's State St., church row. Letters poured into the *Patriot* debating the subject of whether the marble figures should be draped or undraped. "Pagan Versus Christian Art," one letter tabbed the argument. With a theory not entirely correct, the writer said the pagans went for nakedness and the Christians for figleaves. He added that truly great art can withstand drapes—look at the *Discus Thrower*.

George Grey Barnard made his plaster models of the figures in his Paris studio, at a cost of $68,000 in 1905 currency. In France, Barnard had men, women, and children pose naked. But, anticipating the noise in Harrisburg, Barnard and his 15 assistants quickly added figleaves to the gentlemen in the final soft Italian marble statuary.

"I would put pajamas on Venus if it would save the cause of art," Barnard was quoted as saying.

Fifty years later Sen. Israel Stiefel, a Philadelphia Democrat, submitted legislation to have the Barnard statuary removed from its prime position and placed in an enclosed mall. The figures do need protection from the wind, rain, freezing and thawing, but Stiefel declared, "I do not believe this is the place for these figures. You need 10 interpreters in order to explain what these figures mean. I do not know. I doubt whether the children know, and thousands upon thousands of them visit the Capitol each year, each week and each day."

Two years later, in 1963, Stiefel was joined by two Democrats and a Republican in urging the removal of the nudes and their replacement with statues of Abraham Lincoln and Thomas Jefferson. "A good many visitors to the Capitol, especially school children, must be shocked and amazed at this example of meaningless art," exclaimed Pittsburgh's Democratic Sen. John Devlin.

What was meaningless yet shocking to the senators was not to Theodore Roosevelt when he saw the work. "I recognize in the foreground two symbols which are supremely contrasted," he said. "One is humanity pausing, dominated by the influence of past error. The other is humanity advancing, inspired by the gospel of work and brotherhood." Essentially the Rough Rider was correct. The 17 figures on the left, as you face the Capitol, represent "Laws Unbroken," while the 10 figures on the right, or south, are "Broken Laws."

Barnard's son, Monroe Grey Barnard, an engineer and inventor, visited Harrisburg at the age of 64 in 1968. He asserted that his father was not an early-day sensualist, but rather more of a Bellefonte Calvinistic Presbyterian.

"Father was a purist and a believer in nature," he said. "I never heard him tell even the mildest off-color story. He never swore, though when things got real bad he would say 'damn,' but in a quiet voice. He didn't even smoke. He was adamant about there being no odor of tobacco in his home. I've heard it say that geniuses have extra strong senses for sound, taste, for odor. Father certainly did. And I'll tell you another of his puristic principles. He never allowed any man other than himself or me upstairs. The upstairs were for his wife and two daughters. Not even workmen to repair the roof could go upstairs. They had to get ladders and get to the roof from the outside. So when I hear that the man who did the Barnard statues must have had a dirty mind, I laugh. And, of course, it is laughable when these statues are attacked as being a bad influence on children."

Monroe Barnard was accompanied by his son, Alston Monroe Barnard, the proprietor of a New York direct-mail advertising firm. "The blood runs thin and I have barely enough artistic talent to sign my own name," said Alston, though he did study opera and was a church tenor soloist.

The Harrisburg assignment was Barnard's masterpiece, and before he died in 1938 he instructed that he be buried at the Harrisburg Cemetery to be as near his work as possible. It was a job for which he was shortchanged. He expected $700,000 and received $180,000. The sculptor was not in on the Capitol Graft Scandal. In fact, that is one of the reasons his fee was shaved. While at the time it was the largest sculpture commission ever paid in the United States, the Commonwealth came close to throwing the work out. It took a Columbia University professor and the director of the Metropolitan Museum of Art to convince the politicians that they were getting work by a genius "at bricklayer's prices."

Barnard was born May 24, 1863, in Bellefonte, but was raised in Illinois where he became enthusiastic about the subject of Lincoln. He was a student of Rodin in Paris, and later himself was a teacher of Jacob Epstein.

His 13-foot *People's Lincoln* was as controversial as his Harrisburg nudes. "I wish to look into his soul and not into his face," said Barnard, so he made him a naturalistic, relaxed, patient-looking man, with sloping shoulders and baggy trousers. Robert Todd Lincoln, the president's son and a romantic about his father, thought the Barnard Lincoln was "monstrous." The Taft family purchased it for Cincinnati, and replicas were made after World War I to send abroad, though one now stands in Louisville, Ky. Meanwhile, Augustin Saint-Gaudens made a romantic Lincoln, and the argument was on. Teddy Roosevelt, Ida Tarbell, William Howard Taft, the *Philadelphia North American*, and George Bernard Shaw favored Barnard. A sloppily dressed Lincoln would feel at home near Parliament, which has the "worst dressed men in the country," joked Shaw. Robert Todd Lincoln, the *New York Times*, and most of the then conservative art, architectural, and sculptural associations and magazines favored Saint-Gaudens. The Barnard Lincoln eventually was sent to Manchester, where the *Guardian* called it "a regal gift." None was sent to France, and what happened to the one for Russia no one knows.

Barnard had a work in the famous 1913 Armory Show in New York.

He was quite a businessman. He paid $2,000 for two acres at Washington Heights in New York and in 1911 built a $20,000 museum. He sold this museum and its treasures to John Rockefeller II in 1936 for $650,000, and Rockefeller had the Cloisters built. Then Barnard constructed his "monastery," containing sixth-century cloister items, and later sold these pieces to the Philadelphia Museum.

He once was bicycling through France and saw a farmer's field with uneven furrows. On a hunch, he paid the farmer $4,000 to dig up the field. He was right that Huguenots of the 16th and 17th centuries had buried medieval masterpieces there. He uncovered a nine-foot marble retable with the stations of the cross on it. He sold it to the Boston Museum for $65,000 and built a magnificent New York home for his wife, the daughter of the writer of *Monroe's Reader*, a rival to *McGuffey's Reader*.

"I'll never forget Father's last words to me," said his son. "He said, 'I don't know if there is an hereafter, but if there is, we'll all meet again. And if there isn't, we'll still meet again.' "

Barnard came to Harrisburg for the unveiling of his nudes. It took 18 railroad cars to bring them to town. Harrisburg made a great day of the ceremony, even though the art was controversial. A chorus of 400 children, looking straight into the nudes, sang a song written especially for the occasion entitled "Barnard." He was called "the Michelangelo of modern times." Attorney General John C. Bell, Sr., the father of the Supreme Court chief justice of later years, asserted, "Barnard's statues will make our Capitol and its citadel, like the Acropolis, a Mecca of Art." Former Gov. Samuel W. Pennypacker, a patron of the arts, observed that the iron and coal state was improving its tastes. "It is a harbinger of the better and more accurate judgment which the future is sure to give," he said. And the program was closed, as it had been opened, by a message from the Rev. Dr. Joseph H. Barnard of Bellefonte. The Presbyterian minister said he was proud of the nudes and his son.

Miss Penn is so skimpily attired that she would count as a controversial nude if she were at eye level, but she is 91 yards over the Barnards atop the dome. She went up there on May 25, 1905. She is 14 feet 6 inches tall and weighs about two tons. The gold ball she stands on is four feet high. She faces west, with her right arm extended, palm down. The arm has a bad joint where she was hit by lightning in the early 1950s. In her left hand, she holds a "garlanded mace," or the staff of statehood representing government and benediction.

"The statue has no other significance than the symbolic embodiment of the Commonwealth of Pennsylvania," wrote sculptor Roland Hinton Perry in 1937 after he had been questioned about the matter for more than 30 years.

Strictly speaking, she has no name. "Miss Penn" is only the commonly accepted nickname. And she is not a model or symbol of William Penn's daughter, Letitia, who became a married woman anyway.

There are no myths about the 23-karat, gold-plated sweetheart, unfortunately. Unlike the obelisk at Penn State, which contains an assortment of all the rocks found in the Commonwealth and which is supposed to crumble the day an undefiled coed passes by, Miss Penn is not expected to topple from the dome the day a virtuous public official sets foot in the Capitol.

There is no truth to the repeated story that a girl committed suicide by jumping off Miss Penn, either from outside the Capitol or from just below her inside the rotunda. Capitol correspondents swore that bats lived inside the dome below Miss Penn. They said they once saw a bat swirling in the Senate chamber. That was right after the seal barked.

The bronze, 3,800-pound *William Penn* in the state Museum was done by Janet deCoux of Gibsonia. The $82,100 statue was cast in Mexico City. At 18 feet, the tallest statue in Harrisburg, it went up in 1964 and provoked newspaper criticism, not in Harrisburg but in Pittsburgh. DeCoux's Penn was described as "Frankenstein's monster," with "huge, flat feet and ridiculously long-fingered hands. He wears stockings, breeches, a waistcoat and a long overcoat, unbuttoned. His head is bent slightly forward and his left arm is crooked across his breast. He seems to be holding something symbolic in that hand, but it's impossible to tell what." Miss DeCoux specifically avoided a "Quaker Oats Penn," or the rotund, jolly, handshaking idiot famous as the Penn by Alexander Calder on Philadelphia's City Hall. Since 1964, no complaints have been heard about Miss DeCoux's sculpture, which is the lone individual statue of artistic inspiration in the Capital City.

Artistic is everything that *Stalwart Youth* is not. This 12-foot-high marble lad went up at the Dauphin County Courthouse in 1943. Facing the West Shore, the youth has 13 arrows in his left hand and is shown crushing the master of evil. He is supposed to symbolize man's ultimate victory over the power of evil and injustice, but as propagandistic art he is justly ignored.

Among the other pieces of statuary in the City are the elk at Reservoir Park, the war eagles, the Mexican War statue, and the fireman and soldier statues in River Park. The elk was erected in 1906 in honor of Meade D. Detweiler, a Front St. lawyer who was national president of the Benevolent and Protective Order of Elks. The war eagles were placed on the pylons at the Capitol end of the Soldiers and Sailors Memorial Bridge in August of 1930. The bridge is invariably referred to as the State Street Bridge, and the war eagles are not important. The Mexican War statue in Capitol Park dates back to the late 1840s. The fireman was given by the Volunteer Fire Department in the City in memory of eight men who paid the supreme sacrifice. The over-the-top soldier, or the "Lest We Forget" soldier, honors all war dead prior to World War I. The pedestal of this statue is composed of rocks taken from the foot of Round Top at Gettysburg.

And then there is the Obelisk, a bother when it was built and a bother when it became a nuisance to automobile traffic.

It cost the citizens, Dauphin County, and the Commonwealth $73,-600. The Washington Monument, finished nine years later, cost $87,-000, but is 555.5 feet high to Harrisburg's 110 feet.

Following the Civil War, Harrisburgers decided to have a memorial obelisk, rather than an ornamental mausoleum or a bronze statue of a Union veteran holding a flag. The idea, of course, was stolen from the Washington Monument, begun in 1847 and representing the "abstract perfection," and perhaps the virility, of George Washington.

To raise funds for the Obelisk, Harrisburgers held a bazaar in the rotunda of the old Capitol from September 24 to October 3, 1866. Miss Virginia Cameron, daughter of Sen. Simon Cameron, was chairman of a committee that included Mrs. Andrew G. Curtin. Old Simon attended the bazaar, and like a king of politicians put $5 bills on each table he passed. Gen. Ben Butler showed up and donated $10. The two candidates for governor, John White Geary and Hiester Clymer, each made a contribution. And money was sent in by President Grant, Gen. George Meade, Mrs. Stephen A. Douglas, and Tom Scott of the Pennsylvania

Railroad. In all, the committee raised $8,337 of its proposed $15,000 budget.

The committee rejected sites of Harris Park, Harrisburg Cemetery, Camp Curtin, Allison Hill, Market Square, and Capitol Hill. Instead, ground was broken on Oct. 23, 1867, at Second and State Sts. The cornerstone was laid April 10, 1869, and work continued until the committee ran out of money and the Obelisk stood at 62 feet. In typical fashion, the idealistic Harrisburgers became practical. They secured county and state funds, and the monument was finished on Nov. 4, 1876.

As early as 1903 there were complaints that the Obelisk was misplaced. The WPA during the Depression was supposed to remove it, but did not. In 1949 the City put a striped metal guard around it, and in 1957 a campaign was launched to move the Obelisk. Mayor Nolan L. Ziegler suggested that it should be on the river front. That idea was rejected, and so were others. On Columbus Day of 1959 a ceremony was held for the Obelisk's departure. On Lincoln's Birthday of 1960 the topstone on the Obelisk was placed at its new site on Division St.

In the heyday of Pennsylvania Republicanism, Harrisburg's statuary went Republican. A nondescript but popular Abraham Lincoln went up in the old State Museum. Attentive young admirers over the decades have rubbed Lincoln's bronze left boot shiny. The equestrian John F. Hartranft was placed in front of the Capitol on May 12, 1899, and later was removed to the south wing of the building. General Hartranft was a hero at Antietam, Fredericksburg, and Bull Run, and was awarded the Congressional Medal of Honor. A native of Norristown, he was an able soldier but only an average governor during his two terms, 1873 to 1878. Hartranft was a political associate of Boss Matt Quay, and that got him his posthumous statue.

Republicans had the four statues in the rotunda, outside the legislative chambers, reserved for party heroes. Civil War Governor Curtin certainly deserved the honor. But George Tener Oliver was only U.S. Senator from 1909 to 1917, and Brig. Gen. Thomas J. Stewart, who died in 1917, was only state adjutant general. The statue to Quay is rascality rewarded. Quay made his distant relative Samuel W. Pennypacker governor, and once in office Pennypacker saw to it that there was a $20,000 statue to the late lamented Quay. In the marble of the rotunda are the words of Penn about his Holy Experiment, and over the Quay statue, to the delight of thousands of visitors, are the 18th and 19th words in the quotation, "My God."

Curtin is honored also at the 100-foot-square Camp Curtin State Park at Sixth and Woodbine Sts. His statue there was dedicated on Oct.

19, 1922: "In memory of more than 300,000 soldiers of the Civil War, the flower of the nation's youth and the maturity of her manhood, who passed into and out of this camp to the field of battle. A united country enjoys the fruits of their victory for liberty and union."

The Boies Penrose statue is at the foot of Capitol Park, welcoming the just and the unjust. Penrose, a 300-pound bachelor from Philadelphia, served two years in the State House, 10 years in the State Senate, and then from 1897 until his death, Dec. 31, 1921, was a U.S. senator. At one sitting he could devour three steaks and drink a quart of liquor. One of his most gargantuan feats was to throw a 48-hour continuous party at Harrisburg's Lochiel Hotel and be the last legislator standing. Though U.S. senator longer than any Pennsylvanian in history, Penrose's public service record is nil.

In the late 1920s, when the Democrats had a total of 22 state legislators, Republicans voted the statue to Penrose. It was dedicated on Sept. 23, 1930, and a crowd of 3,000 Republicans gathered. Gov. John S. Fisher apologized that Penrose's "active career unhappily fell in a period when vilification of public men by speech and pen and pencil conveyed to the public, who were unacquainted with the victim, a distorted conception of every quality of person or character." The Republican gubernatorial candidate, the independent Gifford Pinchot, made it a point not to attend the ceremony. Vance McCormick instructed his newspapers to give full coverage to the event, but to run no picture of the statue of a man he considered "Machiavellian."

For years there was an untrue rumor that enemies of Penrose gathered on New Year's Eve, the anniversary of Penrose's death, to defecate on the statue. When Democrat George M. Leader was governor, he jokingly suggested putting the Penrose statue in the middle of the Susquehanna so Harrisburg could have an extra lane of traffic at the Third and Walnut Sts. intersection.

On the day of the Penrose statue unveiling, Richard J. Beamish, later of Harrisburg and a Pinchot politician but then a reporter for the old *Philadelphia Record*, broke a fabulous story, picked from the brains of a Philadelphia judge, he said. It seems that near the end of President McKinley's first term in 1900, McKinley's health turned poor. A urinalysis was made at the University of Pennsylvania Hospital, and Dr. Charles B. Penrose, the senator's brother, saw the report. McKinley had Bright's disease, or so Charles told Boies. McKinley's vice-president, Garret A. Hobart of New Jersey, had died in 1899; so there was a vacancy on the 1900 GOP ticket. Senator Penrose figured McKinley would never live through a second term, but he must run anyway. For vice-president, he decided upon Gov. Theodore Roosevelt of New

York. Mark Hanna in Ohio hated Roosevelt, and it was Hanna who in 1899 had blocked Penrose's associate, Matt Quay, from regaining his Senate seat. So, in revenge, Penrose engineered the placement of Roosevelt's name on the ticket, even though the reformer was not a personal favorite of his. The scheme worked, though not quite as Penrose expected. McKinley and Roosevelt were elected in a landslide, but on Sept. 6, 1901, McKinley was shot at Buffalo and died eight days later. The dead president's funeral train passed through Harrisburg, Roosevelt entered the White House, and Hanna's influence on policy was terminated.

However accurate the Beamish story may be, had Penrose not approved Roosevelt for the ticket that would have been the end of the New Yorker.

The Capitol has a long tradition of immortalizing in oil its governors, lieutenant governors, treasurers, auditors-general, and secretaries of the Commonwealth. For some reason, the attorneys general get only prosaic photographs of themselves on the walls of the Justice Department. What is strange about the tradition is that the Commonwealth is not the least concerned as to whether or not the hero had a criminal record.

When former Auditor General Thomas Z. Minehart had his portrait unveiling in October of 1971, he laughed when he was told that one of the Republican faces on the wall ended up in jail and at least two others should have. "Listen, one of my Democrats up there was lucky he missed jail," he said. The Minehart portrait was done by Harrisburg's Betty Snow.

The Capitol has interesting, but not great, pictorial art done by Edwin Austin Abbey, W. B. Van Ingen, and Violet Oakley. The finest mural work is in the Finance Building, done in 1939. Eugene Francis Savage was a professor of painting at Yale, and his work depicting highly muscular, expressive people tells the story of a laboring Pennsylvania. The bald, the blind, and the woebegone are Savage's subjects. There are scenes of miners at their backbreaking toil, of crippled old men being comforted in a hospital, and even one of a Pennsylvanian being tossed into jail. This is not the exaltation, the ceremonial, and the bombastic that interested Miss Oakley or Edwin Abbey.

The Forum's 1931 art is decorative. Its ceiling has pictures of soaring legs and arms, depicting astronomy, including the Ptolemaic, Copernican, and Keplerian theories. Its seven wall maps in the auditorium are brilliant in their originality, but its world is out of date—no Vietnam, no Indonesia, still a Republic of China, and the Union Jack in areas of the world the British long since have evacuated.

The State Museum, for years denied an adequate art budget, owns no

Andrew Wyeth, Mary Cassatt, Gilbert Stuart, Thomas Eakin, nor Edward Hicks. The most famous work in its collection is by Charles Willson Peale, Lloyd Mifflin, and Horace Pippin.

The most renowned painting in the Capital City is the State Museum's *Battle of Gettysburg*, done between 1866 and 1870 and purchased for $25,000. It is a brawling monstrosity, 33 feet in length and 16 feet 9 inches in height, by Peter Frederick Rothermel of Nescopeck.

Rothermel had the largest mural until Vincent Maragliotti, of Scarsdale, N.Y., came up with his *Pennsylvania Panorama*, 90 feet by 24, for the State Museum rotunda. Born in 1888, Maragliotti had done work for the Education and Finance buildings. His gigantic panorama unfortunately is pedestrian art, despite its $115,000 price tag, and is not half as interesting as Rothermel's mural.

Though the famous George Grey Barnard was successful in Harrisburg, the equally famous Carl Milles was not. William Gehron, of Williamsport and New York, was the architect for the Finance Building and got Milles to do the six bronze doors. Milles is a Walt Whitman singing of the inherent virtue and strength of the Pennsylvania people. His doors are of men working in the glass, oil, steel, and anthracite industries and on the farm. On these now weather-beaten doors, Milles scratched in comments: "Too beautiful to destroy, the virgin Pennsylvania"; "Lord told us to create, not destroy," and an example of his Swedish humor, "The crow thinks it strange that the big strong boy's freedom (a horse) is depending on a rope."

Milles lived from 1875 to 1955. A student of Rodin, he became an artist who could produce "genuine sculptural grandeur," in the words of the *New York Times*. He had "the rare power to clothe abstract ideas—youth, love, motherhood, patriotism—in specific and vital images." He came to this country in 1929, did art for St. Paul, Des Moines, St. Louis, Kansas City, New York, and elsewhere, as well as Harrisburg, and then returned to Stockholm, where his Millesgarden is now a national museum.

Gehron influenced the Commonwealth to pay Milles $5,000 to make models of at least 40 figures for two fountains for what was to be the "People's Court" between the Forum and the Finance Building. Milles in 1946 did these models, such as *Pioneer's Wife, Animal Acrobat*, and *William Penn with the Negro Angel*, but the Commonwealth let the project lapse. Milles took some of the models back to Sweden, and in what should have been the "People's Court" went an air-conditioning plant.

The author tracked the Milles story down in January of 1968, asking what the Department of Property and Supplies had done with the models Milles had given the Commonwealth. A retired workman for the department reported that the Milles models were removed from the basement of the Capitol and destroyed at Wildwood Dump in 1953. "Strangest things you ever saw," he said. "All kinds of animals and things. I looked them over because they caught my interest, but we were told to get rid of them. I'm sure the boss never knew what he was throwing out."

A local architect wrote to me:

"In the fall of 1948 my wife and I visited Carl Milles at his studio in Cranbook, Mich. He seemed particularly interested to see us since we were from Harrisburg, and his feeling then was that his project for the People's Court was not quite dead. He warned us, with a smile, that because of his advancing years, it was urgent to start work soon if it was going to be realized. During our conversation, he told us that he had been amused at a meeting he had had with the then Governor Martin and was puzzled by the governor's attitude and a remark he made, 'Are fountains necessary?'

"He told us that he had been requested to change the lettering on beer steins by the Pennsylvania Dutch figures to read 'Milk,' and was disappointed at the criticism of his figures of Benjamin Franklin. He had shown him fishing. As a boy he had admired Franklin and read considerably about his life, and as he said, 'I knew he liked fish.' The board felt that this pose was not dignified and might be a discredit to Franklin's memory and preferred one more statesmanlike in character.

"During our visit Mr. Milles showed us many models and casts of the figures he was planning to use in his then proposed work, 'The Fountains of Faith,' to be located in a cemetery in Falls Church, Va. This work has since been completed, and a Pennsylvanian on a visit there might get some idea of the proposed—but never realized—project he had in mind for Harrisburg."

SUNDAY PAINTERS

Les Beaux Arts

... *Painting and Crafts Thrive*

By the 1970s, culture outdistanced railroading in the Harrisburg Area. There were more art exhibits than there were daily passenger trains going through the City.

The fastest growing art forms in the 1960s and 1970s were painting and the crafts. In addition to a number of studios and galleries that were founded, such as the Camp Hill Art Gallery, both the Harrisburg Art Association and the Mechanicsburg Art Club at long last acquired homes. And the William Penn Memorial Museum opened on Oct. 13, 1965, with an important Wyeth family exhibit.

The Harrisburg Area has yet to produce a major American artist, but there is now opportunity for talent to emerge. After all, John Sloan came from Lock Haven and Franz Kline from Wilkes-Barre.

The Art Association wandered for 38 years until it opened a home of its own at 21 N. Front St. on Nov. 7, 1964. The association was founded in 1927, an outgrowth of the Independent Sketch Club of Walt Huber, Alden Turner, Harold Booth, Earl Johnston, and Nick Ruggieri. Only Ruggieri was around to see the new art center. He alone worked with the association as it progressed from a studio in a cigar factory, to lofts and cellars, and a long stay in an alley garret at 414 Spring St.

The Findlay Mansion was secured in 1964. The building, at least 160 years old, was the home of Gov. William Findlay, 1817–1820, and was last occupied by the Hoffer family. The association made its decision to purchase it, with Will Brown, an executive at Pomeroy's, as president. Theodore Arms, Edward C. Michener, and Mrs. Maurice Shaffer led the fund drive. Architects Milford Patterson and William Eppleman directed the remodeling of the building.

To launch its opening, the association established four galleries: The Vance C. McCormick Gallery, after one of the early presidents; the M. Louise Aughinbaugh Gallery; the Annie M. Rodearmel German Gallery, and the Founders Gallery. John Bowman Delaney and Michener contributed studio rooms. Among the families honored as founders were the McCormicks, Camerons, Kirbys, Gilberts, McFarlands, McCreaths, Masterses, Hickoks, Wallowers, Burkholders, and Bradys.

The Art Association has two traditional public events, the Bal Masqué and the Art Auction.

The Bal Masqué, in mid-February, was started in 1938 by Huber, Turner, Ruggieri, Michener, and Johnston, who was the cartoonist for the *Patriot*. It was held at the Harrisburg Country Club, then was moved to the West Shore Country Club, and finally discontinued. In the early 1950s, it was resumed when Franklin Moore of the Penn-Harris Hotel donated the ballroom for the event. It has been a lively affair ever since, but none was more exciting than in 1963 when its theme was the circus and the honored guest was Mrs. Mary Barnum Bush Hauck, one of the original members of the association. The 20th Bal Masqué was held in 1971.

The auction has gone on for years, with Peter Cryano Wambach and Shim Lehrman as the recent auctioneers. Wambach and Lehrman similarly host the Bal Masqué. In 1971 at the Penn-Harris, 368 works by 70 local artists were auctioned for $4,500.

Ruggieri, the dean of Harrisburg artists, for 30 years has been the art director of the *Patriot-News*. In May of 1971, for the 100th anniversary of Bowman's department store, Ruggieri presented his most popular show, 42 watercolor portraits of the City. "This is a beautiful city, colorful and individualistic," he said at the public reception. "There are a million pictures to be painted of it. Its beauty and fascination are everywhere, if people would only look." There was courage in his remarks, for he had recently come through some serious eye operations.

The most noted of the association's founders was the late Walt Huber. Son of a Chambersburg grocer and born May 11, 1886, he went to Drexel Institute and the Philadelphia Academy of Fine Arts and in his youth was a sports cartoonist for the Philadelphia and Washington newspapers. From 1909 to 1954 he was the art director at McFarland Press. He was a founder of the Seven Lively Artists, a teacher to young artists like Ruggieri, and the political cartoonist for McCormick's *Patriot*.

Huber was a natural caricaturist, so good that he never worked from photographs. His political cartooning at times ranked with the nation's best. When the *Patriot* uncovered the fact that its rival, the *Telegraph*, reaped $1.3 million in 12 years on federal, state, and county printing contracts, Huber portrayed the *Telegraph* as a happy hog stuffing itself from pots of dollars. Vance McCormick ran it with glee, as he did most Huber cartoons, at the top of page 1, three columns wide, on Nov. 4, 1912.

Huber never had the opportunity to do a comic strip, as he hoped, and his political cartooning today is forgotten. His serious painting, however, remains in demand by local collectors. For years he had his studio on the fifth floor of the old Antlers Bar on Walnut St., next to the old county prison. From 1931 to 1954 he turned his summer retreat, the Stone Jug, near Lewisberry, into a mecca for local artists and students.

He died Oct. 7, 1961, and is buried in Paxtang Cemetery. A prodigious worker, he did so many sketches, watercolors, and oils that every now and then another turns up on the Harrisburg market and is quickly grabbed for prices triple what Huber dared ask. In fact, Huber sold few works; he preferred to give them away.

T. Alden Turner was Huber's close friend. The son of a machinist, he grew up at Swatara and Crescent Sts. He went to John Harris High School, but never had any formal art instruction. He was the kind who had a natural talent for a multiplicity of things: wood cuts, etchings, photography, pottery, wrought iron, and especially watercolor. He was even a superb magician, pleasing Huber's love of fantasy.

As a young man he worked as an artist at the Telegraph Press with Ruggieri, Ray Snow, Moe Fenical, and the father of Hain Wolf, Joe Wolf. In later life he made it by free-lancing, and many of the Armstrong Cork national advertisements were his. "Al had empathy with people, a real love of people," recalled Michener. "He was the type who enjoyed life a great deal. He never made much money, but he used his talents to the fullest and he had a million friends."

Turner had a studio near Huber's Stone Jug in Lewisberry. He taught at the Art Association, and on Sept. 3, 1950 at the age of 45 he died of cancer. He was married to a colonel's daughter. She survived him, remarried, and became an invalid. In an act of mercy, her second husband in 1967 committed murder-suicide. Two years later a local bank, administering the estate, disposed of the Turner paintings by auction. In addition to Turner's own work, there were paintings by Huber and John Richard Flanagan, the York artist who illustrated the stories of the insidious Fu Manchu.

The Seven Lively Artists were formed in the mid-1950s, with Walt Huber as one of the founders. The group was devised as a means for afternoon and weekend painting jaunts for artists who wanted to do serious work in addition to their commercial art. There is no formal structure to the organization, no dues, no bylaws, and not even a permanent membership. Usually it has had 12 to 14 artists, and invariably they have been among the best and most active in the Harrisburg Area. Among the senior members are Cal Bange, Robert W. Bartlett, Earl Blust, Karl Foster, Charles Krone, Bob Lackhove, Don Lenker, the brothers George and Meade Logan, George Morrow, and William Rohrbeck. Lackhove was an iceman who suffered a heart attack, became a Sunday painter, and developed into a skilled artist.

Among the noted contemporary local artists have been Ira Dean, Richard Elliott, Gene Gulluni, Charles Hidley, Wanda Macomber, Edith Socolow, Maya Schock, portrait painter Betty Snow, Charles Speers, Barbara Lehrman Weinberg, and Mrs. Ivan Erb Lenker and her architect-artist sons, Edward and Donald Lenker.

Ned Smith and Bob Bates are the two artists known nationally. Smith, of Halifax RD, is one of the top dozen outdoor artists, featured by the American Museum of Natural History and leading magazines. A native of Millersburg, he has free-lanced for 15 years and done very well. "I'm not really an artist, if you mean skylight, smock and beret," he said. "I'm an outdoor artist because I love the outdoors more than art. I just plain refuse to do portraits, horses or dogs." Bates similarly is off the beaten track, a free-lancer for 20 years and hidden in the thicket of Dillsburg RD. He and his wife, escapees from commercial art, are superb printmakers, signing their work "Pierce Bates."

The Mechanicsburg Art Club was formed in 1954, with Harry Kirk as its first president. In 1961 the club got a studio in what was once a grocery store on York St. Finally in 1971, under President David Keefer, the club with 170 members bought a barn three miles west of Mechanicsburg, which it remodeled and gave its first art exhibit on Dec. 5, 1971. Supported by the Seven Lively Artists, the Mechanicsburg Club is one of the most exciting new cultural developments in the Harrisburg Area.

The Harrisburg Chapter of the Pennsylvania Guild of Craftsmen was founded Sept. 27, 1944, eight months after the Guild was started in Philadelphia. Among its early leaders were William Hilton, C. Valentine Kirby, Miss Ann Mueller, William Rohrbeck, John Butler, Mrs.

Donald Royal, and Miss Mary Douglass. Rohrbeck went on to be local president and then state president. The late Dr. Vincent C. Shepps, a noted state geologist who died in 1967 at age 38, is the other Harrisburger to hold both offices. The Guild's first studio was in the dungeon basement of the old State Museum, and in 1948 moved to quarters in Penbrook.

Charles Gohn and Averill Shepps are among the top craftsmen in Pennsylvania. Gohn was a World War II welder at Bethlehem Steel, then a washing machine repairman until he started a picture-framing business in 1953 on Haehnlen St., off 13th and Derry Sts. In 1959 Gohn opened a gallery and quickly became a leading metal sculptor. His work is now sold from Provincetown to Florida, and demand exceeds what he can supply. Mrs. Shepps grew up in Fitchburg, Mass., graduated *magna cum laude* in geology from Smith College, and learned crafts from her late husband, a skilled silversmith. She is now Central Pennsylvania's finest enamelist, a metal sculptor. And a past president of the Harrisburg Craftsmen.

The artists and craftsmen, among others, were instrumental in starting the Harrisburg Area Arts Festival during Memorial Day weekend at the State Museum. The Harrisburg Branch of the American Association of University Women in 1962 and 1963 sponsored single evening festivals at the Forum. For years before that, Mary Hauck directed folk festivals. In 1968 the festival idea was resumed, in cooperation with the State Museum and the new Pennsylvania Council for the Arts. Though it rained the first four days of the six-day event, the festival was a success.

Ted McKay, veteran Community Theater actor, was the director of the first festival. He was succeeded by Peter M. Carnahan, the Community Theater director. In 1970 and 1971 Mrs. Shepps and Richard M. Vanier, a silversmith and president of the Craftsmen's Guild, were directors. The fifth annual festival in 1972 had as co-chairman Mrs. Barbara Sherman and George H. Ebner, both board members of the Harrisburg Symphony Association.

The most famous of Harrisburg's own sculpture is Giuseppe Donato's *Dance of Eternal Spring*. In 1971, in the 33rd year of the J. Horace McFarland Rose Garden at the Polyclinic Hospital, the City removed the Donato nymphs to Italian Lake, as the hospital converted the rose garden into a parking lot. It was then discovered that the model for the 1909 piece of sculpture was living at Homeland.

Madeline Stokes, who died in 1972, was born Amanda Straw in Fishing Creek Valley in 1875. At age 18 she attended business school in Philadelphia, went on to do vaudeville tableaux, and then became one of the most famous artist models of her day. She was 5-foot-4, had a perfect figure, and remained a top-flight model until age 39. George Gibbs did her as a cover girl in June of 1905 for the *Delineator* and the *Metropolitan* magazines. J. L. G. Ferris drew her as Martha Washington for the *Ladies' Home Journal*. N. C. Wyeth, Robert Henri, and John Sloan painted her. Violet Oakley used Madeline as a model for murals, and one hangs in the Governor's Reception Room. Alexander Calder II used her for the Sun Dial in Fairmount Park. She danced clad in nothing but lard for $5 a night at the New York Roof Garden. She was simply one of the most beautiful women in America.

In 1909 Milton S. Hershey made a $2,000 down payment on a $3,100 verbal agreement to Donato to provide a sculpture for a garden fountain. Donato, a native of Italy working in Philadelphia, hired Madeline Stokes to portray three dancing bacchantes, or "three Venuses flinging aloft their grapes and a baby girl," as the work was sarcastically described.

The common myth in Hershey is that the chocolate king was disgusted with the nudity of Donato's work. Not so. He was disgusted with Donato's final bill for $30,000. "I wouldn't pay $10 for his entire studio," snorted the Dutchman, and the statuary remained at the Hershey railroad station in crates for two years.

Donato took Hershey to Dauphin County Court. "I don't want it because every time I looked at it I would get mad," said Hershey, meaning angry at the pricetag. "Besides, I have another fountain now, anyway. Who made it? I don't know. I bought it from Bethlehem Steel." The jury awarded Donato $23,931.25. Said the sculptor, "Every artist should make a contract before he does a stroke of work for any single rich man. They don't know enough about art to be able to deal fairly with artists."

In 1920 Hershey gave the nymphs to Harrisburg, which by then had recovered from its shock over the Barnard nudes at the Capitol. Until 1938 the statuary was at Reservoir Park, and Miss Stokes herself was forgotten. With the founding of the Rose Garden, the nymphs went to the Polyclinic, where it became a tradition at the School of Nursing for the seniors the night before September graduation to climb the statue and adorn the three maidens with lingerie. It was said that the trio of frolicking Venuses symbolize ecstatic nurses who entrap interns into pledges of marriage.

On July 16, 1971, with Madeline Stokes on hand, the Donato statue was transferred to the middle of Italian Lake, awaiting a new legend to evolve.

COMMUNITY THEATRE

Harrisburg Theater

. . . Its Death Greatly Exaggerated

The reputation the Harrisburg Area has for being the graveyard of theater is indelibly established, though not strictly accurate.

It is true that actor Joe Jefferson died in Harrisburg, literally. But it is Joe Jefferson, Sr. who is buried in the Harrisburg Cemetery, and he was not the immortal trouper his grandson was.

It is true that John O'Hara wryly remarked in a novel that all Harrisburgers want are "the proven plays of William Shakespeare," but the fact is that local theater-goers demand just about everything but Shakespeare, proven or unproven.

Similarly, it is true that the late Robert T. Seymour observed that only 3 percent of the metropolitan Harrisburg populace had any interest in and loyalty for the theater.

And, lastly, it is true that the Arena House Theater was a noble attempt at in-town professional theater, but it failed within four years.

Yet the Midstate's antitheater reputation is undeserved. In some respects, the Harrisburg Area has done amazingly well. Admittedly, the enthusiasm for theater has yet to be enjoyed by more than a minority of citizens, but the interest that exists is genuine and enduring. They used to say in show business, "If it goes over in Harrisburg, it'll go over anywhere," or "If you get a laugh in Harrisburg, you must be funny." Well, such unastute remarks have been made about many other American towns too.

The Harrisburg Community Theater started in 1926 and today is one of the oldest amateur playhouses in the nation. Its paid director, scene designer, and theater school director are recognized professionals. Year after year HCT does six shows a season. Folks yawn at some, but the productions and public acceptance of most are high. For a rip-roaring musical classic with local talent, like *Guys and Dolls,* or an occasional premiere, like *I, Elizabeth Otis,* HCT can bubble with excitement.

There is an intimacy to a community theater like Harrisburg's. Neighbors work onstage and backstage. Some of them have been professional or have had more training or experience than many touring pros. HCT is capable of doing gripping performances of such plays as *Death of a Salesman, A Man for All Seasons,* and *The Diary of Anne Frank,* and quality productions of big-time Broadway musicals like *Fiddler on the Roof,* which in October of 1971 set a local record by running 24 performances and drawing 11,514 people. The 40-member cast put 14,000 man-hours into the show to make it a hit, artistically and financially.

In April of 1971, HCT did *Anna Karenina,* with Anne Alsedek in the title role. This was a venture few theaters in the nation would even want to attempt. Furthermore, it was a local effort, as director Peter M. Carnahan spent two years studying and writing to transcribe the 200,000-word novel for the stage. Justice was done to the action and insights of the broad Tolstoyan epic. As the *Evening News* stated: "It worked. Not without imperfections but ofttimes brilliant, it worked."

There is a long tradition of summer theater in the Harrisburg Area, which at Allenberry, Mount Gretna, and Totem Pole in Caledonia State Park is more commercial than artistic, but that is what it is designed to be, and it has never claimed otherwise. It is a lively evening's entertainment. It has its place, and it has required considerable business and theatrical skill to make it competitive against a flood of leisure-time alternatives. Footlight Ranch Dinner Theater in Wellsville is winter stock.

Hershey Community Theater books touring shows, usually with the star system. This offering is an attraction, especially in an era when there is less travel to New York and Philadelphia to see theater.

In addition, the Area often is crowded with amateur groups, such as the Little Theater of Mechanicsburg and the Players Repertory Company. Performers also organize shows for special occasions. During the Harrisburg 8 trial in the winter of 1972, a group of HCT actors and others did *The Trial of the Catonsville Nine* in churches and colleges with great response.

A theater-goer can be amply accommodated in the Harrisburg Area. Anyone interested in working avocationally in theater, onstage or backstage, can find the opportunity. Local theater is not only an art form and entertainment medium, but a social activity as well. "The Community Theater reflects the community in that it is serious and not 'theatrical,' " Carnahan once observed. "I can see where we might lack the youthful excitement of some community theaters, but we have a deep and genuine appreciation of theater. The phony glamour of the theater doesn't go over here, and you might notice the little things at the Community Theater. The people don't call each other 'darling,' for example."

An eager student can get his start, either as a youngster in community theater or as an apprentice in stock. Bob Seymour started the HCT Theater School in the mid-1950s, the Junior League sustained it in 1959, and the annual spring Drama Festival for junior and senior high schoolers was begun in 1961, a competitive event that has encouraged much better school drama across Central Pennsylvania. Arriminta Gully, a native Harrisburger who for five years was director of the York Little Theater, has headed the HCT Theater School since 1959.

A number of old troupers came out of Harrisburg, including Billy Welch (1850–1877), a minstrel boy in *Dem Golden Slippers*. Jasper Deeter (1893–1972), of Mechanicsburg, played Smithers in the original Eugene O'Neill production of *The Emperor Jones* and talked O'Neill into breaking the New York color barrier in 1920 by putting a black in the title role. Deeter went on to found the famous Hedgerow Theater near Media. His sister, Dr. Ruth Deeter, was Harrisburg's first woman doctor, an osteopath, and was one of the founders of HCT. Donald M. Oenslager, a native Harrisburger, became a top Broadway scene designer with hits like *Born Yesterday* and *Of Mice and Men.*

HCT gave actress Nancy Wickwire, director Carman Capalbo, and musician Jack Holmes their starts. Margot Moser, of Colonial Park, was the first American to play the lead in New York's *My Fair Lady.* Shelley Berman, John Stratton, Eileen Brennan, Ruth Maynard, Arthur Storch, and John McMartin were pros at Allenberry. From Gretna came Charlton Heston, Robert Lansing, and Leonard Frey. Sada Thompson, Sandy Dennis, Keir Dullea, and Lee Ann Meriwether played Totem Pole early in their careers.

The first local theater was in September of 1796, when the Harrisburg Company of Comedians gave *Prisoner At Large* in the Washington House, on the southeast corner of Market Square.

In 1804 John Durang, of the York Area, rented a converted storehouse on Front St. to present excerpts of Shakespeare, as well as dance, acrobatics, horsemanship, puppets, circus routine, pantomime, tragedy, comedy, and whatever else delighted his audience. Durang (1768–1822) was the first Shakespearean actor to play the Pennsylvania Dutch country, and he could do a show in German when there was the demand. "We had crowded houses every night at 50 cents for the box and 25 for the gallery and very little expense," he wrote in his diary. At his tour's end, he splurged with a fireworks display for his Harrisburg friends.

Durang's wife, Mary, is buried in Harrisburg. His son, Ferdinand, won fame because in 1812 he was in a Baltimore tavern and heard Francis Scott Key recite a poem. While Key did his poetry, Ferdinand Durang took a volume of music, put his flute to his lips, and plagiarized the tune for "The Star-Spangled Banner." This is the explanation for the oft-told story of a Harrisburger's supplying the music for the national anthem.

Harrisburg's first auditorium came in 1822, when Shakespeare Hall was constructed in a hotel on Locust St. Five years later a near-riot occurred in the 600-seat hall when an actor named Tancred announced to the audience that his fellow actors were jealous of him and were trying to ruin the show. In the ensuing melée, Tancred was wounded by a sword, and the theater was closed. The first real theater, Brant's Hall on Market St., was not built until 1856.

The Grand Opera House opened in 1873 at Third and Walnut Sts. Though hardly "grand" and certainly not an "opera house," the five-story building served Harrisburg well. Mrs. J. N. Deeter, the mother of Jasper Deeter, gave the first concert. When raucous state political conventions were not being held, the illustrious of the theatrical world

performed, including Sir Henry Irving, Edwin Booth, the Drews, Frank
Bangs, Richard Mansfield, Billy Birch, and Joe Jefferson, Jr. On Feb. 1,
1907, just a decade after the State Capitol fire, the Opera House burned
to the ground. A gas explosion in the cellar started the early-morning
fire that quickly routed 22 tenants in 10 nearby buildings. It was probably the City's most dangerous fire, destroying $500,000 worth of prop-
erty. The Opera House was valued at $350,000, but was on the City's
tax books for only $101,139. For 10 years the site was vacant, and in
1919 the Penn-Harris Hotel was completed.

The Lyceum at 212 Locust St. opened in 1903 for "high-class attractions," such as *Princess of Kensington* and *Raffles*. The Majestic opened
at 323 Walnut St. in 1908 for theater and vaudeville, and that same
year the Hippodrome at 333 Market St. opened as the first motion
picture house, as well as a palace for vaudeville. Soon after such movie
houses as the Bijou, Lyric, Victoria, Photoplay, and Regent were in
operation.

William A. "Ike" Davis went to work at the Majestic in 1912 and
remained in Harrisburg show business for 50 years. He remembered the
Colonial Theater, opened in 1912, having three vaudeville shows daily
and the Orpheum's having two, while the Majestic played legitimate
theater. Working the lights, Davis saw the Barrymores, Will Rogers,
and even Albert Hole, the boy soprano of Britain. *Uncle Tom's Cabin*
played Harrisburg three times one season. For a production of *Ben Hur*,
eight horses and two chariots were gotten on stage. D. W. Griffith's *The
Birth of a Nation* was not permitted in Lancaster, because of its nasty
portrayal of Thaddeus Stevens; so it played a week in Harrisburg and a
30-piece orchestra was hired to accompany the silent film. Douglas
Fairbanks played the Orpheum for the week of Oct. 20, 1924, in *The
Thief of Bagdad*. Soon after that, however, touring American melodrama was over, and vaudeville expired in the mid-1930s.

The State Theater, Harrisburg's largest, went up in 1926 after the
Orpheum was demolished at that site. The Forum in the State Education Building opened in 1931, and the Senate Theater opened in 1938
in what had been a fish market with a turkish bath upstairs.

The Community Theater was launched in April of 1926 when nine
members of the American Association of University Women met in the
basement of the Public Library. Under the leadership of Mrs. Robert
Peters, Mrs. Donald Brinser, and Dr. George Ashley, rehearsals were
held in the ballroom of the Farley Gannett mansion at Second and
Division Sts. The Majestic was secured free of charge, and on Monday
night, May 11, *Dover Road,* the three-act comedy by A. A. Milne, was
presented before an audience of 1,500. The production was a success

"as evidenced by the applause during and between the acts," wrote a *Patriot* reviewer.

The Community Theater was organized officially the following Monday at the Civic Club. Mrs. Peters was named president. On the board of directors were Mrs. J. E. B. Cunningham, Mrs. John Oenslager, Mrs. C. Valentine Kirby, Miss Mary Rodney, Ehrman B. Mitchell, C. E. Zorger, William M. Harclerode, and Dr. Ashley.

Miss Adele Eichler, who directed *Dover Road*, became the first director. She had been with the Copley Players of Boston, and in 1926 was head of drama at Irving College in Mechanicsburg. HCT had two plays in the spring of 1927, and then that fall began its first full season. In all, Miss Eichler directed 24 plays before she left in June of 1930, succeeded by Gordon Ruffin, a former stock player who had worked Harrisburg. Ruffin stayed only for the 1930 season.

Plays such as *Pygmalion, He Who Gets Slapped*, and *Hay Fever* were done in the assembly room of City Hall, the Chestnut Street Auditorium, and Fahnestock Hall at Second and Locust Sts. Rehearsals were held wherever space could be found, in warehouses, basements, and even a cigar factory. Among the performers in those early days were Kitty Meikle, Frank Menaker, Ted McKay, Abe Derr, Eleanor Henschen, and Tim Conway.

Henning Cunningham Nelms, a graduate of the Yale School of Drama, was HCT director from 1931 through 1936, boosting membership to more than 1,100 and using the old Jewish Community Center to do *The Lower Depths, Anna Christie, The Plough and the Stars*, and the first musical, *The Mikado*, in the 1935 season. Nelms was a detective story writer on the side, under the pseudonym of Hake Talbot.

Alfred Rowe, an Englishman, took charge from 1936 through 1942. *The Petrified Forest, Peer Gynt, The Front Page, Our Town*, and *Ah, Wilderness!* were under his direction. On Sunday, Dec. 7, 1941, a group of HCT members met to plan a campaign for a theater building. All was canceled the next day as the nation went to war.

Charles F. Coghlan directed for three years, and then departed to establish Gretna Playhouse. Richard North Gage, another graduate of the Yale Drama School, came in 1946, founded Allenberry Playhouse while he was at HCT, and left in 1950 to devote full time to it. Karl Genus succeeded Gage, and had the honor of directing *Harvey* on Nov. 3, 1951, in the new $150,000 HCT Theater, just outside City Line in Susquehanna Township. The sets were by the new scene designer, Jerry Giddings, a native of Boston, who remained with HCT for more than two decades and 140 productions.

Harley Swift, Louis Snyder, and others spearheaded the theater building campaign, with the slogan "Help Get the HCT Out of the Stable." At the time, the theater was meeting at 411 Spring St., once a horse stable. Though it was an achievement to get the theater, the building has never been fully satisfactory and the mortgage continues to be a drain on the HCT budget.

Bob Seymour, a young man out of the Cleveland Playhouse, arrived in 1952 and stayed at HCT for nine years and 63 productions. Personable and energetic, Seymour drove the theater to artistic heights but ended up losing money at the rate of $5,000 a year for his last two seasons. Membership dipped, and Seymour's worst mistake was to air-condition the theater for what never materialized as a regular summer fare of musicals. Yet Seymour was successful and popular. He started the tradition of big musicals, and did some excellent ones in *The King and I, Guys and Dolls*, and *Finian's Rainbow*. Productions like *Detective Story, Darkness at Noon*, and *The Diary of Anne Frank* were community theater at its best. Seymour even broke the color barrier in Harrisburg art, no mean feat. Four and a half years after he left Harrisburg, he was dead at age 47.

HCT's reputation was so high that its board of directors received 75 applications to succeed Seymour. Studious Peter M. Carnahan, 30, a graduate of Amherst and director of the community theater in Mobile, Ala., was named. Among the first orders of business was an emergency fund campaign, headed by Stanley Miller and Hasbrouck Wright under HCT president John Millar. The drive raised $18,000, enough to pay overdue local taxes and keep the theater operational.

Carnahan stayed a record 11 years. Among his 71 productions from 1961 to 1972 were: *The Visit, Kiss Me Kate, The Man Who Came to Dinner, My Fair Lady, Death of a Salesman, The Sound of Music, Cat on a Hot Tin Roof, A Man for All Seasons, Camelot, How to Succeed in Business Without Really Trying, South Pacific, Cactus Flower, The Prime of Miss Jean Brodie, Fiddler on the Roof*, and his own script of *Anna Karenina*. Carnahan departed in August of 1972, replaced by Olan "Kit" Carson, 41, a native of Charleroi who headed little theaters in Tacoma and Phoenix. In two months only, Carson staged his first hit, *1776*.

Mount Gretna's picturesque Chautauqua auditorium, seating 1,200, opened July 4, 1899. Gretna between the world wars had summer stock. In 1945 Gene Otto, Sr., who ran the old Madrid Ballroom, acquired the park concession at Gretna and hired Charles F. Coghlan to reorganize the theater. Coghlan was the son of the famous British actress, Rose Coghlan, who for a quarter of a century was a leading lady on the American stage. He became an actor at age 10 and went on the boards with the Barrymores, Eddie Cantor, Pearl White, Eddie Foy, Marie Dressler, and others. He played the role of John Wilkes Booth in vaudeville and was in some of D. W. Griffith's silent films. In all, Coghlan was in theater for 66 years, the last 25 of them at Gretna. He retired in 1969 and died three years later.

Dick Gage joined Allenberry proprietor Charles A. B. Heinze to form the Allenberry Playhouse in 1949. The two launched the nation's longest summer stock season, from April to November, or "thirty weeks without a grant," in Gage's words. A superb organizer and talent finder, Gage made the playhouse thrive. Only 5-foot-5 and 115 pounds, he claimed, "I can't do any other kind of work, you know. I'm a basket case outside the theater." In exactly 50 years in show business, he directed more than 700 productions. He died at age 72 just three days before his 1972 Allenberry season closed. For many years his able assistant was Betti Endrizzi, a native Harrisburger who holds the local stage record by playing more than 250 roles in her career.

Totem Pole was founded by Karl Genus in the early 1950s. Genus was the third consecutive Community Theater director to start summer stock while still at HCT. In 1953, William Putch, a Carnegie Tech graduate, succeeded Genus. On Nov. 11, 1969, an arsonist burned the playhouse to the ground. It was on the north side of Route 30, directly above the hillside locale of Thaddeus Stevens' iron furnace which the Confederates burned 106 years earlier. With the help of Chambersburg neighbors and support from friends like Dick Gage, Putch built a new $140,000 theater to seat 400. In the summer of 1971 Totem Pole had a sellout run of *Hello, Dolly*, starring Jean Stapleton—the celebrated Edith Bunker in the television hit series, "All in the Family," and the wife of Bill Putch.

Arena House had excitement in its short life from Nov. 12, 1964, when it opened with the musical *Riverwind*, until April 29, 1968, when it abruptly closed in midrun of *The Mousetrap*. The theater-in-the-round at 21 N. Second St., an abandoned store, was backed by Ted Freedman, Sidney Finkelstein, and Martin L. Murray, among others, plus director Tom Ross Prather.

Prather, 27, was born on a Colorado ranch. He was advised by Actors Equity against coming to Harrisburg. At the time there were only 40 winter stocks in the nation, and the chances of success were estimated at one in fifty. Said optimistic Freedman, "We all knew this was a cultural desert, and I think we victimized ourselves by our stylized thinking."

For its 300 performances the first season, Arena House needed 20,-000 customers in its 185-seat back room. It got 15,665. After a loss of

$3,000 the first year, Arena House earned $1,300 the second. In the third year, it lost between $11,000 and $13,000. "We're not old, not venerable and not on a sound financial footing," said Murray, an architect, as the venture was turned into the nonprofit Central Pennsylvania Foundation for the Dramatic Arts. Mainly because of labor costs, the budget climbed from $45,000 to $90,000 the fourth year. "Mounting debts and general lack of interest" were the reasons given for its closing after 41 productions.

Arena House was surprisingly good theater, though it had to rely on Broadway material in an era of declining quality. It had at least two top regular professionals, Bruce Hall and Bob Wait, and its productions of *Riverwind, The Country Girl, Who's Afraid of Virginia Woolf?, Rashomon,* and *Stop the World, I Want to Get Off* were excellent. It received attention, but not enough support. Yet it was soaring theatrical costs, rather than public apathy, that doomed Arena House.

The original production of *My Wife and I* was its great adventure. Written by Bill Mahoney, then in radio in Carlisle, the musical melodrama played both the spring and fall at Arena House, attracting more than 5,000 persons. Prather and Mahoney, with local backing, decided to risk it on off-Broadway. In 1961, Bob Seymour, after leaving HCT, had had that unhappy experience with *Poppa Is Home,* a play by Dr. Monroe Schneier of Middletown.

My Wife and I opened in New York on Oct. 10, 1966, and was murdered by the critics. The *Times* said, "Only the perversely sophisticated and the incredibly innocent will be able to find much fun in the limp string of stituation-comedy clichés." I was with the critics that night on W. 55th St. and agreed that much of *My Wife and I* was banal; yet I disagreed that it lacked basic entertainment value.

I wrote four days later:

"As Harrisburg exaggerates the value of what its natives think is its good small-city living and the envious wholesomeness of its family-centered life, New York exaggerates its sophistication. Harrisburg tends to make conservatism a virtue, when often it is the Area's most besetting sin. New York makes a flair of being cosmopolitan, of being precious about its artistic tastes and of having a debonair approach toward life—and all the while it pushes you in the subway, reeks with a gaudy materialism and insults sensitivity and intelligence with much of its meretricious art."

The closing of *My Wife and I* seemed to foretell the eventual demise of Arena House Theater. But it did not mean the end of Harrisburg theater. That continues, with more glorious triumphs and pratfalls to come.

Music, Music, Music

. . . *Stirring the Harrisburg Soul*

Louis Moreau Gottschalk, America's first great pianist, was unfortunately booked for a recital in Harrisburg at the same time Robert E. Lee was trying to capture the town. "Too obstinate Stakosch [his manager], why in the world did he make us come to Harrisburg," wrote Gottschalk in his diary, after he boarded a crowded train to escape and gave his seat to an unappreciative young lady who ignored his gallantry.

The following March 28, 1864, the dashing, aristocratic Gottschalk, age 35, was back in Harrisburg. The concert was held in the old courthouse. "The audience is charming," he wrote. "I observe in it some of those rose and lily complexions of which our ladies have the privilege, and which I denounce to the artists who follow me, as being those which trouble the soul while you are playing. They make you play false notes, and give a suppressed sigh every time that your imagination evokes their charming images. The hotel is excellent." Gottschalk, from New Orleans, was difficult to please, but he liked Harrisburg.

Jenny Lind, the "Swedish nightingale" on P. T. Barnum's 1851 tour, packed Grace Methodist Church when it was located where the Federal Building is today.

Pablo Casals as a young man played at the Orpheum Theater on Jan. 22, 1925. "Harrisburg last night for the first time heard the master cellist, Pablo Casals, and Harrisburg waxed enthusiastic before his first number ended and reached the superlative of enthusiasm long before the program closed," the *Patriot* reported. Tickets to hear Casals were as inexpensive as $1.38.

116

Gregor Piatigorsky, another master cellist, received a similar enthusiastic reception under the most adverse conditions. He was guest of the Harrisburg Symphony on March 17, 1936. The great 1936 Flood had almost reached the City. In fact, it rained 1.24 inches that day, the heaviest of the week's downpour. But the Forum was filled, and Piatigorsky was cheered after he played works by Mozart and Haydn.

Many of the world's finest artists have been guests of the Wednesday Club Concert Association. In the era before 1960, when booking fees were reasonable, Harrisburg could afford the best: Kirsten Flagstad, Jascha Heifetz, Marian Anderson, Artur Rubinstein, Sergei Rachmaninov, Lawrence Tibbett, John Charles Thomas, Dorothy Kirsten, Thomas L. Thomas, Helen Traubel, Robert Merrill, Blanche Thebom, Isaac Stern, Ezio Pinza, Roberta Peters, Jerome Hines, and Eileen Farrell.

In 1972, the Junior League sponsored Van Cliburn at the Hershey Community Theater. All 1,904 seats were presold, plus 30 more seats in the orchestra pit and 150 more on stage. Cliburn responded with five encores.

The tops in musical entertainment played Harrisburg. Crowds of 2,000 mobbed the old Madrid Palestra Ballroom between 1926 and 1951 to hear Paul Whiteman, Duke Ellington, Cab Calloway, Bob Crosby, the Dorsey brothers and, the favorite, Glen Gray and his Casa Loma Orchestra.

Cal Turner in the *Evening News* of June 20, 1966, covered the closing of the Hershey Starlight Ballroom:

"Snug in the tattered shadows of the maples that lace the lip of the sunken garden, it looks like a woman's hatbox with the ribbon peeling away. Or cake somebody forgot to eat. But inside it's different. Different altogether. Even in the brash daylight there's an inkling that time is hung up in a far corner on a broken crutch. The floors squeak. And the doors, like unadorned buttons, give an inch to the wind.

"This is the Hershey Starlight Ballroom. Once all of Central Pennsylvania danced here. The big names with the big bands set up shop, sweethearts in evening gowns sipped soda and gay young blades, their herringbone and starched shirts punctuated with bow ties, slipped into the Big Apple.

"Rudy Vallee, Shep Fields, Hal Kemp, Whiteman, Lombardo, Red Nichols, Sammy Kaye. The names read like a bucketful of yesterday. And the bucket's upside down. Last week a rock 'n' roll combo moved into the bandshell. And for an era, the lights went out.

" 'Yes, an era has passed,' said Cy Little, promotion director at the

Ballroom since 1949. 'And I'm sorry, because signs of its revival are not too clear.'

"Little was sitting in his office at the Arena. He talked about the big band days. 'We've had them all,' he said quietly, scanning a fact sheet. 'And on Aug. 23, 1947, Vaughan Monroe grossed over $10,000. The crowd totaled 6,945. The biggest night we have a record of. We had to turn them away.'

"Staring at a poster announcing a combo for next week, Little told about how when the big bands were 'in' everything was formal. 'Neckties and coats,' he said. 'And I think in the Thirties, the tickets went for 75 to 85 cents.'"

For some of the talent, Harrisburg was almost home. Jimmy and Tommy Dorsey were born in Shenandoah and grew up in Lansford. Jimmy, the clarinetist, was the older by 18 months. Tommy was the bigger, the stronger, and the more emotional, with an immense talent and a trombone whose warm, silken, sensuous tone has not been heard since. The two took their music and their individualism so seriously that after a Madrid Ballroom performance one night they got into a fraternal fistfight on Chestnut St. that was broken up by the police. After 1935, they were apart for 18 years and then reunited to make the film, *The Fabulous Dorseys.* For its Harrisburg premiere at the old Loew's in 1947, Jimmy and Tommy returned to town for the last time. Tommy died at age 51 on Nov. 26, 1956, and Jimmy followed at age 53 on June 12, 1957.

Lester R. Brown, the son of a school band director, was born in Reinerton in Schuylkill County and grew up in Williamstown, Port Carbon, and Lykens. With "My Dreams Are Getting Better All the Time" and "Sentimental Journey," Les Brown and his Band of Renown quickly became headliners. Until he settled in California, Les often was booked in the Harrisburg Area. "Probably more than any other leader of the big band era, Les Brown has it really made in every way," George T. Simon wrote in *The Big Bands.*

Fred Waring and His Pennsylvanians undoubtedly have been the top all-time local pop attraction. Waring, born in Tyrone on June 9, 1900, attended Penn State for three years and made his public debut in Altoona. He started on radio in 1933, and has had a national reputation since. A hard driver, an admitted perfectionist, and something of a smiling martinet, Waring invariably pleases full houses at Hershey on his regular visits. He is now a millionaire squire living on an estate he calls Shawnee-on-the-Delaware.

Music is the Harrisburg Area's forte. Though it is the most precise of the arts, it is the cultural form with the most variety. There are more complementary and competing local organizations in music than there are in any other artistic endeavor.

The Wednesday Club of Harrisburg is the grandmother of all art groups. It was founded in 1881, second only to the music club of Tonawanda, N.Y., as the oldest in the nation. It began that fall at the home of Miss Mira L. Dock as a cooking club. "After some discussion, it was decided to not continue as a cooking club but to emphasize music," as the records of the club report. Miss Sara Fleming became the president, and the first official meeting was held May 17, 1882, at the home of Miss Dock. The original meetings were held on Wednesdays at 10 A.M. Today the club meets at the Civic Club but usually not on Wednesdays.

The Wednesday Club Concert Association was founded by the parent organization in 1937, and it has been the most successful box-office cultural organization since. From 1959 to the present, it has had Forum sellouts—on Tuesday nights—for its concert seasons of guest artists, a record unduplicated in the annals of the struggling Harrisburg arts.

The Harrisburg Choral Society came along in 1895 and, with a few exceptions, has had spring and Christmas concerts ever since. The singing of sacred music traditionally has been of major importance in Harrisburg, perhaps the art most accomplished and most widely appreciated. The Choral Society founders were the early church-going Germans, Scotch-Irish, English, Welsh, and Irish, including the first families of Harrisburg. "Neatly everybody of any consequence in town was in it then. It was the center of entertainment for many," recalled Thompson S. Martin, an attorney in 1967 who had sung in the society in 1905. A modern de Tocqueville scanning the early rosters of all cultural organizations, not just the Choral Society's, would find Martin's point documented. Harrisburg was much more egalitarian in its cultural participation prior to 1920 and even up to 1945 than it has been since World War II.

The Choral Society was directed by W. W. Gilchrist, who commuted from Philadelphia. He was succeeded in 1908 by Prof. Edwin J. De-Cevee, director of the Harrisburg Conservatory of Music. A giant in Harrisburg music, DeCevee also headed music at Dickinson College and directed it at Zion Lutheran Church for 20 years until his death in 1918.

Donald Clapper has been the director since 1956, and he has brought into town such guest artists as William Warfield, Richard Cross, Basil Rathbone, and Cyril Ritchard. Clapper, minister of music at Pine Street Presbyterian Church and a native of Altoona, is among the excellent musicians attracted to Harrisburg Area churches in the postwar era.

Among the other fine musical groups are the Hershey Community Chorus and the prize-winning Barbershop and Sweet Adeline choruses. Messiah College at Grantham is noted for its music and presents a spring concert, while Lebanon Valley College for decades has specialized in music education.

Combined with the tradition of fine choral music has been that of organ music. The Harrisburg Area has produced some of the nation's top church organists. Historic Peace Church in Hampden Township uses an original 1807 Conrad Doll pipe organ. St. Matthew's Lutheran Church in Hanover has the largest church organ in America. It has 236 ranks and 12,809 pipes, bigger than the 235-rank organ in Boston's Christian Science Mother Church or the 222-rank organ at New York's Riverside Church. The Forum organ has 68 ranks, Grace Methodist Church organ 65 ranks, and Pine Street Church organ 57 ranks, or equal to Radio City Music Hall's 58-rank organ but not the size of the Wanamaker organ in Philadelphia of 469 ranks and 30,067 pipes or the Atlantic City Convention Hall organ of 455 ranks and 33,112 pipes.

The Harrisburg Symphony gave its first concert at the new William Penn High School auditorium on March 19, 1931. Under the direction of George King Raudenbush, the orchestra struck up the band with Gluck's Overture to *Iphigenia in Aulus*. The rest of the program included Schubert's Symphony No. 8 in B Minor, the "Unfinished," works by Schumann and Fauré, some Slavonic dances by Dvorak, and Sibelius' *Finlandia*.

From that concert forth, the Symphony never missed a date. It survived the 1936 Flood, World War II, the dreadful era of the 1950s when nearly everybody was enraptured by television, and even the tight dollar of the early 1970s.

Mrs. Alice DeCevee Mitchell (later Mrs. Fred Morgan), as much as anyone, founded the orchestra. The daughter of Professor DeCevee, she attended the Juilliard School and met Jacques Jolas, a distinguished pianist. She and Jolas got the orchestra movement started, with cooperation from the J. H. Troup Music House and a small group of interested women that included Mrs. James M. Cameron, Mrs. Daniel L. Hunt, Mrs. Vance McCormick, Miss Mary B. Robinson, Miss Mary Worley, Mrs. Charles Stroh, and Mrs. Mary Barnum Bush Hauck. A few thousand dollars were raised, and the year after the first concert the parent Symphony Association was formed. Mrs. Arthur H. Hull was president and Mrs. McCormick, vice president, with Mrs. Hull serving 14 years. Meanwhile, the orchestra was organized with George W. Updegrove, violinist, and Dr. E. I. Shirk, trumpeter, as officers.

In recent years, the late Robertson C. Cameron and Robert L.

Ritchey headed the Symphony Association, with Mrs. Lillian Gallagher Smith as the treasurer for 13 years. What Mrs. Morgan started, the indefatigable Mrs. Smith kept going. Mrs. Hauck, meanwhile, purchased two of the best seats in the Forum for 42 years of concerts. A piano teacher and a descendant of P. T. Barnum, Mary Hauck is the only person to be active in the creation of the Symphony, the Art Association, and the Community Theater.

Jolas brought the 34-year-old Raudenbush to town as the first conductor. A fascinating figure, Raudenbush was "tall and thin, with a thinking face, steel-gray eyes and highly, highly sensitive," in the words of one feminine admirer. A violinist, he was quite continental, and it was almost impossible to detect that he was born of Pennsylvania Dutch heritage, in Jersey Shore of all places. He had been the youngest American regimental sergeant-major in World War I and had been a newspaper editor, a labor organizer, and even the manager of a fishing fleet out of New Orleans. But Raudenbush had learned music under Damrosch, Walter, and Toscanini, and he knew what he was about. He stayed for 20 years.

The first rehearsals were held on the third floor of the Troup music store, and an orchestra office was set up in the old Patriot-News Building on Market Square. Though some musicians were recruited from Lancaster, York, and Lebanon, local talent remained the backbone of the orchestra. The late M. Lee Goldsmith, the furniture merchant, not only was one of the patrons but also one of the violinists. A small and sparkling gentleman, Goldsmith had played for President Theodore Roosevelt at the 1906 Capitol dedication. At one concert, an extra note was hit at the end of a piece. "Was that you?" a member of the Symphony Association asked Goldsmith afterwards. "Couldn't have been me," laughed Goldsmith. "I finished two bars ahead of everybody else."

Among the early figures in the orchestra were D. Harold Jauss, Noah Klauss, C. Eugene Erb, and the late Salvadore Colangelo. Erb, a trumpeter and later tympanist, for decades was the orchestra manager. Colangelo, a clarinetist from Italy, played for the silent movies at the Majestic, was the last conductor of the Commonwealth Band, and was a charter member of the orchestra, in which his son and daughter later played. One of the most beloved men in Harrisburg music, Colangelo died in 1969.

Jauss at age 26 in the orchestra's fourth season became the concertmaster, and he went on to hold the first chair for almost 40 years. A lifelong dedicated classical musician, he studied at the Curtis Institute of Music, played under Leopold Stokowski, took lessons in New York from Leopold Auer, the teacher of Jascha Heifetz, and returned for a career in Harrisburg. He has played with the orchestras in York, Reading, and Lancaster and at the Bach festival in Bethlehem with his 1730 Joseph Guarnarius (Del Gesu) violin and 1910 James Tubbs bow.

Klauss, a native of Lebanon and raised in Hershey, was a violinist and assistant conductor until 1967. For almost a half-century he composed music, and for 31 years he taught at Elizabethtown High School. In 1952 Klauss founded the Harrisburg Youth Orchestra, and he directed it for 16 years. The Youth Orchestra has sent more than 50 of its students on to the Harrisburg Symphony and to orchestras across the nation.

Though the second oldest orchestra in Pennsylvania, in point of continuous service, the Harrisburg Symphony has had only two directors.

George King Raudenbush departed in 1949, and Mrs. Morgan hurried to New York to sign Edwin McArthur, who has been director ever since. Under McArthur's leadership, the orchestra not only grew, but added the youth concerts in 1951, the Youth Symphony in 1952, guest appearances by visiting foreign orchestras, and the Autumn Rhapsody Ball, a social event for patrons.

McArthur has been one of the most knowledgeable men in American music. Born in Denver in 1907, the son of a Congregational minister, he was a precocious musician who at age 18 went to New York with $60 in his pocket to begin his career. An exceptional accompanist, he played for Ezio Pinza, Richard Crooks, and John Charles Thomas, and for 28 years was a friend and associate of Kirsten Flagstad, about whom he wrote a book in 1965, *Flagstad, A Personal Memoir*. McArthur conducted the Chicago Opera Company's *Lohengrin* for Flagstad, and then made guest appearances with many of the nation's major orchestras. For 23 years he was music director of the summertime St. Louis Municipal Opera. In recent years McArthur moved from New York City to be a professor at the Eastman School in Rochester.

The strangest experience in McArthur's long career occurred when he was accompanist for Florence Foster Jenkins, the deluded soprano whose father once represented Wilkes-Barre in the Pennsylvania Legislature. McArthur, who was succeeded by Cosme McMoon, with whom he is sometimes confused, eventually was fired when Miss Jenkins caught him giggling. "She usually sang at least a half a tone flat," he wrote. "Curiously, when singing a cadenza where of necessity she had to go very high, she often went half a tone sharp. I cannot recall any song or even an individual phrase in which she consistently adhered to the required pitch." Before her death at age 76 in 1944, this entertaining lady cleared $6,000 in a sellout Carnegie Hall concert. At one of her recitals, Cole Porter pounded his cane up and down on the floor between his knees, exclaiming, "I can't stand it. I can't stand it." Edward Canby wrote of her: "Her music had a subtle ghastliness that defies description." Her recording of "Like a Bird I Am Singing" verifies Canby's judgment that "it is an infinite gift to sing as well as a Flagstad; it is hardly less an accomplishment to sing as badly as a Jenkins." Edwin McArthur had the privilege of working with both extremes.

The Hershey Orchestra Society was founded in 1969 by Dr. Bryce L. Munger, chairman of anatomy at the Hershey Medical Center and one of a number of physicians there with an interest in music. The society started with chamber music, but it quickly expanded to a performing group of 65. The following year, 1970, Mrs. Fred Ratowsky started a Sunday afternoon chamber music series at the Art Association, filling the gallery with music lovers.

The Harrisburg Civic Opera Association is another new endeavor, making its debut on May 16, 1970, with *La Boheme* at the State Museum. It too is an example of the quantity and quality of musical talent available in the Harrisburg Area. Its director is Kenneth L. Landis, minister of music at Market Square Presbyterian Church.

A remarkable part of Harrisburg's past has been its many fine brass bands and dance bands.

The community once had the Municipal Band, the Good Will Fire Company Band, the West End Band, the Knights Templar Band, the Tall Cedars Band, the famous Steelton Band, and even the Methodist Sunday School Band. The most renowned was the Commonwealth Band, from 1888 to 1943. When the Commonwealth became the Moose Band, it gave its treasury of $3,781.43 to the City for the Ralph Feldser Band Shell at Reservoir Park. Feldser was a noted Harrisburg trumpet player who in 1938 was killed in an auto accident on a snowy night returning from New York, where he had gone to secure work for his local members of the American Federation of Musicians.

Today Harrisburg has the American Legion Post 27 Band, the Moose Band, and the New Cumberland Band. The Legion Band, founded in 1920, grew out of the old Eighth Pennsylvania Infantry Regimental Band of the National Guard. From 1923 to 1965 the late Luther W. Hose was the narrator of the band. C. Eugene Erb was its director for more than a decade. The Moose Band was founded in 1943 and the New Cumberland Band in 1947. In addition, there are the Zembo Concert Band, founded in 1906, and the Oriental Band of Zembo, 1954. The Westshoremen Drum and Bugle Corps, originally out of Wormleysburg, won a national title after World War II and paraded down Broadway with General MacArthur. In 1959 it merged with the Bonnie Scots of Millersburg, took headquarters in Mechanics-burg, and regained its distinction as one of the top five corps in Pennsyl-vania.

Such a variety of bands has made Harrisburg an excellent training ground for young musicians. At one time in the mid-1960s, the major service bands had 11 Harrisburg Area men, including five with the Marine Band. Except for "drummers who can read music," talent is readily available, said Randall Evertts, a railroader, tenor saxophonist, and a charter member of the New Cumberland Band.

Just as the Area had a flowering of rock groups and folksingers in the late 1960s, in the 1920s and 1930s it had an unusual number of dance bands. "Even in the tough times, folks would put away the pennies so they could go out dancing. Some thought it was the most important thing in life," recalled the hat merchant who had a group called "Gwil Heller and His Playboys."

The dance halls required as many as a dozen bands to keep the customers happy. Among the many ballrooms were the Madrid, Willa Villa, Casino Dancing Academy, the Colliseum, and Summerdale. Some of the Harrisburgers who had bands were Dan Gregory, Ted Brow-nagle, Red McCarthy, Howard Gale, Don Peebles, and C. Lloyd Major. Mayor Nolan Ziegler as a young man played banjo for both Gregory and Major. The musician who had the most exciting career was John Brown, an Uptown black, who went with Louis Armstrong and Dizzy Gillespie and made six movies with Pearl Bailey, Nat King Cole, and Armstrong.

"Remember this," said Lloyd Major before his death in 1970, "the audience in those days heard orchestra after orchestra, night after night. People then were much better judges of live music than people are today. They had much more exposure to it. And because they knew what they wanted, orchestras had to be good." Major, a violinist and charter member of the Harrisburg Symphony, broke up his band in the mid-1940s. "We all thought that the big bands were going to blossom after the repeal of Prohibition," he said, "but the return of booze killed the big bands. When there wasn't drink, people came to dance. Now they started going out for drink and not strictly dancing, and in came the combos and out went the big bands."

Mitch Grand was the one musician who survived for almost 50 years as a full-time professional. A pianist, occasional composer, bachelor, and devotee of mystery stories, Grand for nearly a quarter-century has been the Arena organist for the Hershey Bears. In his perch atop the rink, Grand holds the mark for playing more music to more people than anyone else in the history of the community.

CAPITOL

Central Pennsylvania Politics

. . . Regularity and Republicanism

Shortly after the Revolutionary War, the rebellious Central Pennsylvania citizenry exchanged their delight in exciting politics for the security of supine politics. It was a choice in accord with their pleasant environment and their Germanic temperament. From Gettysburg to Hershey, among the rural and urbane, the educated and uneducated, the preoccupation became, not politics, but business and the contentments of *"kinder, kuche, und kirche,"* or children, kitchen, and church.

125

Though Harrisburg has been the seat of state government since 1812, it has no love of competitive, pluralistic, adventurous politics.

Harrisburgers and their neighbors enjoy a highly private society, more self-satisfied than disturbed by social inadequacies. Community problems usually are attacked privately, by committees of citizens independent of politicians. Pressure and political solutions are last resorts. Similarly, the reforming spirit never took hold. With infrequent threats of radicalism, equal rights for blacks, social experimentation, or disturbance of the status quo, few outward social controls were needed. For the majority of citizens, a greater personal freedom existed than any activist or libertarian could provide.

To love politics is to appreciate change, action, and controversy. And to have genuine democratic politics is to have a vibrant two-party system. But as a Harrisburger once quipped, "The two-party system is all right, except that you feel lousy on Sunday morning."

So the Harrisburg Area opted for sameness, stability, and rectitude in its public life.

"See how little and tight his mouth gets when he thinks about politics," says Janice about her husband in John Updike's *Rabbit Redux*, his 1971 novel about nearby Reading. "I don't think about politics," exclaims Harry Angstrom. "That's one of my Goddam precious American rights, not to think about politics."

An almost steady economic prosperity reduced class antagonisms, usually a fuel for the fires of politics, and helped create a burgeoning middle class—mostly now harbored in suburbia. The priorities of this majority have been: common decency within orthodox morality, unoppressive and good-natured hometown leadership, the sanctity of contract and property, and, in general, the doctrines of the Puritan Ethic. Though there is much that is admirable in such principles, the price paid politically has been mediocrity, cronyism, some anti-intellectualism and much anti-culturalism, virtually no innovation, and a steadfast refusal to modernize government to adjust to urban necessities.

In his 1971 political novel about Central Pennsylvania, *Lafayette's Pigeons*, Cole Atwood of York wrote: "In Lafayette County, an officeholder's chances of reelection are in direct proportion to what he has done while in office. If he has been progressive, aggressive and accomplished much, made many changes, instituted reforms and abolished costly or inefficient practices, his chances of reelection are extremely small. If he has done little or nothing, his chances of reelection loom extremely large."

Machiavelli said it is better to be impetuous than cautious, but Midstate politicians reversed his dictum.

The politicians, hesitant to stray from the simplistic and superficial, run intellectually at the lowest gear. Theirs is the soft politics of status. Seeking election on the basis of their public identity, not public programs, they cultivate friends and not issues. They enter politics with no ego-demands, no self-esteem demanding gratification through public service. Rather, they want to fit in, as a clerk in a corporation, and they desire to be no more than a ripple in the concentric circles of political give-and-take.

It is not a coincidence that the most successful of Central Pennsylvania politicians—the Camerons, Ed Beidleman, Harve Taylor, and George Wade—have been coordinators of party activity and reflectors of community attitudes, not innovators and certainly not mavericks. It is no accident, either, that Midstate politicians have no impact on national affairs, or that their local political system does not propel them into prominence. Harrisburg Area boys do not make it big in Washington. No one expects another president from Central Pennsylvania, as James Buchanan was, or even another Pennsylvania senator, as William Maclay was. No one even expects, at home or in Washington, a Central Pennsylvania voice on any controversial subject; in ten years none was heard on Vietnam. The tepid, pedestrian politics carries right into the State Legislature, where the eight assemblymen and two senators for decades have been neither a power bloc nor individually distinguished for any programs or ideas.

With one ear to majority opinion and the other to the needs of special clients, the Central Pennsylvania politician has been a foot soldier in the ranks of what Edwin A. Van Valkenburg, the old Philadelphia editor, called "commercialized Republicanism."

The lone exception in 125 years has been Thaddeus Stevens, who represented Gettysburg in the State Legislature and Lancaster County in Congress. "It is easy to protect the interests of the rich and powerful," he said, "but it is a great labor to protect the interests of the poor and downtrodden. It is the eternal labor of Sisyphus forever to be renewed." Stevens passed from the scene in 1868, and he left no disciples.

The late political scientist Paul Tillett, a 1941 graduate of John Harris High School, had a familiarity with Harrisburg Area politicians and noted in his study, *The Political Vocation*: "Politicians are important to the system, but it is easy to overestimate their capacity to achieve reform. They are competitors for place and power, not the architects of the policy. They will more likely respond to, than suggest, far-reaching changes in their environment."

One-party politics has had a deadening effect on Central Pennsylvania public life. Ever since the Civil War, Republicanism has been more than politics; it has been a way of life. It thrives not so much because the party leads the people, as it mirrors them—in many admirable traits, but also by braying the fears of taxation and participatory democracy. Almost to the point of Toryism, the leadership usually has maintained a militant noncommitment to anything other than what is advantageous to its patrons and party functionaries. Reasonably honest and decidedly patriotic, the Central Pennsylvania GOP has a reputability that is almost unbeatable, coupled with the support of the most pervasive conservatism of any metropolitan area in Pennsylvania.

"I'm not talking as a Republican. I'm speaking as a human being," Rep. Blaine C. Hocker of Oberlin exclaimed in the State Legislature in 1965 when there was a debate over juvenile detention centers. The remark brought an immediate laugh, and was reprinted on the editorial page of the *Wall Street Journal*.

Negativism has dominated. The Midstate legislators voted against Thad Stevens' free schooling in 1835. One of their contemporary neglects was to do little about the development of the Susquehanna River basin, though it was the largest uncontrolled basin in the East and always threatened serious flooding. Oddly enough, Central Pennsylvania politicians have never been much for log-rolling. Public works, with the exception of highways, seldom received much attention. In its entire history, Dauphin County never constructed a public library. Concern is evident, however, in the distribution of state rental property, much of it to favored landlords and amounting to almost $3 million a year in Dauphin County alone.

As the Harrisburg Area is over-Republican by assimilation, acculturation, and osmosis—increasingly so from City line into suburbia—it is correspondingly under-Democratic. Midstate Democrats since Woodrow Wilson's era have been aimless, leaderless, and often obsequious. With the exception of George M. Leader's York County, they even neglected to build on the politics of Franklin D. Roosevelt and John F. Kennedy. The result is that few persons vote Democratic locally, so much as they vote anti-Republican. With such a predictable limp opposition, Central Pennsylvania Republicans save their energies for primary elections, where challengers fight fratricidally, usually to get farther to the right than the incumbents.

When Marlin E. Olmsted bowed out of Congress in 1912, the Democratic House speaker, Champ Clark, paid his respects by saying, "As the Harrisburg District always sends a Republican to Congress, I wish he had not determined to retire."

The degree of Republicanism that existed for decades is astounding. In 1930 of Dauphin County's 65,892 registered voters, only 7,519 were

Democrats, and just 1,581 of these lived in the City. The County and City row offices stayed under Republican control even during the New Deal. The first Democratic judge was not elected until 1961. In all the mayorality elections from 1916 through 1963, the Republican machine won easily, sometimes by as many as 18,000 votes. The Derry Township Board of Supervisors got its first Democrat ever in 1971, the same year the Penbrook Council broke a 22-year Democratic drought. In many Central Pennsylvania communities, the executive, the council, and the school board are controlled exclusively by Republicans. The congressional and legislative representation is Republican, and Republicans dominate appointed boards and authorities. Cumberland County Courthouse has been Republican since 1938 and Dauphin County since beyond memory, though by law there must be a minority commissioner, often a weak Democrat elected deliberately by Republican ticket-splitters.

There are four reasons for Republican hegemony. The first is the citizenry's reverential attitude toward the GOP and conservatism. The second is patronage, which is the Republican organization's obsession and the one thing it practices liberally. Third, the GOP kept the black vote and most of the workingman vote, despite FDR and Barry Goldwater. Today as these old standbys crumble, the advantage is more than made up with new suburban white Republican conversions. And, lastly, there has been fraud, though not on the order of magnitude of that of the big cities.

Fraudulent voting long was a part of the election scene. In 1947 the Second Precinct of the Seventh Ward turned in a 400–0 vote, only to be outdone by the Fifth Precinct, which had 976 votes for 953 registered voters; the Election Board settled for 894 votes. In 1961 the FBI investigated after four teen-agers voted, an adult admitted voting in both Harrisburg and Lewisburg, and 15 percent of the tally in a Seventh Ward precinct was called "ineligible." In 1963 Charles A. Franklin, known as "Nibs," the masterful wardleader, engineered such fine tuning in the Sixth of the Seventh that 12 winners for nine different offices received exactly 627 votes, the 16 losers got between 52 and 54 votes, and four Constitutional amendments were rejected by almost the exact vote. In 1965 Gov. William W. Scranton conceded there was "immoral" conduct in a Harrisburg election. In 1969 the League of Women Voters found 380 phantom voters in three precincts, after the courthouse uncovered 119 dead souls in five precincts. And in 1970 the Post Office returned as "undeliverable" 43 percent of the voter letters the League sent to Harrisburg and Steelton. "Perfection is not expected by citizens, but vigilance is," the League told the County Commissioners.

The gentle art of fraud often was not employed so much to help Republicans defeat Democrats as to keep the Republican machine safe from Republican challengers. Renegades always knew that popularity was not enough.

Until recently, white Anglo-Saxon Protestantism was a major part of the political situation. No non-WASP candidate for president or U.S. senator has ever received the Central Pennsylvania vote. John F. Kennedy lost every precinct in Cumberland County in 1960 and carried only 18 of the 145 districts in Dauphin County. Every elected mayor of Harrisburg has been a WASP, and 40 of 42 Dauphin County judges have been WASPs too. Every Congressman for Dauphin County has been a WASP. Cumberland County, in a district with Adams and York counties, has had one Catholic congressman, James M. Quigley, a lawyer and a capable representative who lasted only three terms until he was swept out as part of the Kennedy ticket. Central Pennsylvania has been WASP four times longer than Moscow has been Communist.

In the mid-1960s change came, and the stability Harrisburgers desired in their politics disappeared. In 1964 in the Republican primary, unknown William B. Lentz upset State Sen. M. Harvey Taylor. In 1966, unendorsed George W. Gekas, 36, was barred from a local GOP rally, but won a seat in the General Assembly. In 1967, Albert H. Straub won a disputed mayoralty primary over Paul "Tim" Doutrich by a mere 64 votes, and then, though he had a Republican registration lead of 18,055, defeated a young Democrat, John M. Lynch, by the narrow margin of 1,095 votes.

To the spoils belonged the victor. Straub, an insurance man, proceeded to be one of the finest mayors Harrisburg ever had, but to his detriment. He ordered an audit, only to learn of thousands of missing parking tickets, phantom signatures on invoices and unpaid bills, violations of the state purchasing code, duplicated payments for goods and services, and mispayments and undercharges. Nobody ever went to jail, but the police chief pleaded guilty to the larceny of 19,599 unaccounted traffic tickets, two police lieutenants were convicted for U.S. income tax evasion, and a councilman, two City Hall officials, and two businessmen stood trial on indictments of conspiracy to defraud the City, but were declared innocent. "A mere error of judgment or departure from sound discretion is not a crime," said the judge.

Straub, meanwhile, supported a new City charter, and Lynch ran first on the ticket for Study Commission. James W. Evans, past president of the School Board, headed the commission, and the strong mayor-council form of government was approved by the voters on May 20, 1969, by 6,614 to 4,665. "We have reached a new day, and I hope the politicians in this City see this point too," said Straub. "The outcome of issues vital to the City no longer are solely the matter of judgment of precinct leaders."

Because of the new government, Straub was forced into a special election in 1969, the very year when there was turmoil in the streets and schools. In the closest election in City history, Harold A. Swenson won, 8,753 votes to 8,703. "He came from nowhere to cap the mayorship in one of the great upsets of modern Pennsylvania politics," said the *Patriot*. "He won that fight without staff and without adequate funds. And it took a two-thirds ticket splitting to make him the winner." He also did it by keeping his supporters in the background, so voters would not think they were voting Democratic.

Swenson, 42, a native of Brooklyn and the lanky son of an immigrant Norwegian, was a Capitol bureaucrat for eight years until he and his wife, Elsie, started a Downtown travel agency. He had never run for elective office in his life, and suddenly he was the first non-Republican mayor of Harrisburg in 57 years. A low-profile, moderate Democrat, he appointed a 43-year-old, civic-minded enthusiast from an old Harrisburg family, Francis B. Haas, Jr., as his solicitor. Together with a capable staff they started on the problems Straub himself had listed as "a civic spiderweb spun from rising costs, complacency, lack of imagination"—housing, public safety, recreation, trash disposal, fire protection, traffic, parking, redevelopment, and transportation. Midway in the Swenson Administration, Hurricane Agnes hit, submerging a third of the City and making every problem worse.

Crisis today is not unexpected for any metropolitan area in the United States, but there is evidence that Harrisburg has at least begun a renaissance. The interest in politics has picked up, and from Harrisburg it could seep out across Central Pennsylvania and stir into being a new era of excitement.

The Harrises

. . . *Pioneer and Founder*

The river was named for the Indians, the City for a Yorkshire brewer, and the County for a French dauphin who did not live beyond childhood. Yet the place considered itself Pennsylvania German for decades.

HARRIS MANSION

John Harris the Elder, the pioneer, was born in Yorkshire, England, about 1673. He was a brewer and went to London, where undoubtedly he read William Penn's advertisements for a settlement "upon the river of Susquehannagh."

With 16 guineas in his pocket, Harris migrated to Philadelphia and took a job grading streets. In 1698 he was one of the rowdies who protested the disenfranchisement of persons owning less than 50 pounds' worth of property. In 1705 Harris secured a license to get land, and sometime between then and 1718 he arrived in the Indian wilderness of Harrisburg.

There were about 300 settlers and 50 houses along the banks of the Susquehanna when Harris arrived. A trader, real estate agent, and ferryboat proprietor, Harris built his first dwelling and storehouse near Front and Paxton Sts. Harris saved the riverbank by settling there, and this is probably why the railroad did not lay its tracks adjacent to the river. At Harris Ferry, the pioneer was well liked and highly respected, by both white settlers and Indians, and he prospered.

The famous mulberry tree story was told, not by Harris, but by one of his grandchildren, Robert Harris, a local banker and congressman. A band of Indians returning from the south stopped and demanded rum. When Harris refused, the Indians carried him to a mulberry tree in River Park and prepared to burn him. Harris' black slave, Hercules, escaped to the West Shore, rounded up some Shawnees, and saved the old pioneer. Today Hercules is buried near Harris and a Harris daughter in the park.

It is only speculation that Harris may have married an Indian girl at one time, but it is fact that he married Esther Say, a native of Yorkshire too and the niece of Edward Shippen, the first mayor of Philadelphia. The Harrises had four sons and two daughters.

The pioneer died in December of 1748, leaving behind an estate of 800 acres that is now most of central Harrisburg. A few years after his death, his widow married William McChesney and went to live on the West Shore—the first Harrisburger to move from town to suburbia. She died in 1757 and is buried at Silver Spring.

John Harris II, the founder of the City, was born at Harris Ferry probably in October of 1727, the third child and the oldest son of the pioneer. He succeeded his father in operating the ferry and the fur trade, and he developed orchards and farms. During the Indian wars, he made his post into a stockade. "He was as honest a man as ever broke bread," said Parson Elder.

He vigorously supported the Revolution, giving 3,000 pounds to help the cause. Well before the Declaration of Independence was written—

which he read to Harrisburgers from his front porch—his son, John Harris III, age 24, was killed at the Battle of Quebec on December 31, 1775.

Harris II planned the City with his son-in-law, William Maclay, laying out 207 quarter-acre lots between the river, Mulberry, Fourth, and South Sts., on April 14, 1785. He kept 20 lots for himself, plus the property he already occupied. After his death, his executors added another 114 lots. Harris also started the first school in 1784. It became the Harrisburg Academy in 1804, the tenth oldest independent school in the nation.

Harris died on July 29, 1791, and was buried in Paxton Church Cemetery.

He married twice. He wed Elizabeth McClure of Paxtang in 1749; she died in 1764. That same year he married Mary Read of Hanover Township. He had 5 children by his first wife and 10 by his second. Among them were David, who served in the Revolution as a major and became a banker and an associate county judge; Mary, who wed Maclay, the first U.S. senator from Pennsylvania, and two-term Cong. Robert Harris.

A sister of Harris II, Esther, married Harrisburg's frontier physician, Dr. William Plunket. They had nine children, a daughter of whom married Samuel Maclay, brother of William Maclay and also a U.S. senator.

For a time, Harrisburg was known as Louisbourg, after the ill-fated King Louis XVI of France. But Harris II insisted it be named in memory of his father, which eventually the State Legislature officially approved on February 1, 1808.

Harris II also helped organize Dauphin County, which was created from part of Lancaster County on March 4, 1785. In gratitude to the French for support in the Revolution, the County was named for the Dauphin, Louis François Xavier of France, who was just 4 years old at the time. The Dauphin, however, died at age 9 on June 4, 1789, and was succeeded by his younger brother, Louis Charles, who had been born 23 days after Dauphin County was formed. Louis' parents, King Louis XVI and Marie Antoinette, were guillotined, and he either died in prison at age 10 or was smuggled out by royalists to disappear from history.

Harrisburg, in the meantime, was incorporated as a borough with fewer than 500 people on April 13, 1791. It received its charter as a city on March 19, 1860, when it had a population of about 13,000.

John Harris II is the important man in Harrisburg history, because before his death he conveyed by deed "Four acres and 13 perches to be held in trust until the Legislature sees fit to use it" as the site for the capitol. The Legislature moved from Philadelphia to Lancaster in 1799, and then in February of 1810 selected Harrisburg to be the capital city, beginning in 1812.

There are no portraits of either of the two Harrises, but the second Harris was described as having good teeth, brown hair turned gray, a light beard, and a healthy appearance.

John Harris II built his impressive mansion on Front St. in 1766. It is possible that President Washington slept there on Oct. 3, 1794, as he journeyed through Harrisburg to quell the Whiskey Rebellion. Simon Cameron later owned the mansion, and it was given by his heirs in 1941 to the Historical Society of Dauphin County. The mansion is the second oldest house in Harrisburg, predated only by the Elder Mansion at 2426 Ellerslie St., just off Derry St. The latter was built by Parson John Elder of Paxton Presbyterian Church in the 1740s. The oldest house in Dauphin County is the Peter Allen House near Dauphin, built about 1726.

The Historical Society celebrated its 100th anniversary in 1969, and at ceremonies at the mansion, John B. Pearson, an attorney, read the minutes from the first meeting. Pearson is the great-great-great-grandson of Harris II and the grandson of Judge John J. Pearson, the local Civil War judge. Other descendants of the City's founder are William Pearson, Henry and Hugh Hamilton, Spencer G. Hall, and Mrs. William L. Yeager.

The Irascible Maclay

. . . Commoner with Vision

Fractious and caustic, William Maclay is the most underrated figure to come from Harrisburg. A case could be made that he is Central Pennsylvania's most important historical personage.

He and his father-in-law, John Harris II, laid out the City of Harrisburg in 1785 and by deed conveyed "Four acres and 13 perches to be held in trust until the Legislature sees fit to use it," thus setting the stage for Harrisburg to be the state capital, its singular distinction.

Maclay was Pennsylvania's first U.S. senator, and he is credited with two lasting achievements. He and Thomas Jefferson established the first loyal political opposition, which meant the founding of the Democratic Party. Historian Charles A. Beard called him "the original Jeffersonian Democrat." And, secondly, as a great commoner, it was Maclay who successfully fought attempts to call the president of the United States by any other title.

Maclay was a surveyor, soldier, lawyer, state and national politician, a judge, and, unexpectedly, a splendid writer. His journal, or diary of the first two years of the U.S. Senate, is the most widely read and important book ever written by a Harrisburger.

MACLAY HOUSE

It is remarkable so little is known about Maclay, for he was a fascinating character. In his own day, particularly, he was underrated, and after he died on April 16, 1804, his obituary made only page three of the *Oracle* of Dauphin, which neglected to mention his major achievements and merely praised him as "beloved and venerated," a man with a "superior mind" who had "firmness and integrity."

Had the Maclay descendants outside of Pennsylvania permitted his journal to be published before 1880, the sharp and disputatious gentleman might not have been lost in the historical past.

The journal is a minor masterpiece by a man who, Beard said, was a great writer because he had a discerning eye and an irascible temperament.

Here is an excerpt for March 4, 1790: "Dined with the President of the United States. It was a dinner of dignity. All the senators were present, and the Vice President. I looked often around the company to find the happiest faces. Wisdom, forgive me if I wrong thee, but I thought folly and happiness most nearly allied. The President seemed to bear in his countenance a settled aspect of melancholy. No cheering ray of convivial sunshine broke through the cloudy gloom of settled seriousness. At every interval of eating or drinking he played on the table with a fork or knife, like a drumstick. Next to him, on his right, sat Bonny Johnny Adams, ever and anon mantling his visage with the most unmeaning simper that ever dimpled the face of folly."

Maclay was two years younger than Washington, but he was disturbed by the President's "lax appearance," "cadaverous complexion," and "hollow, indistinct voice." He did not care for Washington's playing cards for moderately high stakes, riding to the hounds, wine-bibbing, and "occasional hilarity over champagne." Washington was a big man, but Maclay at six-foot-three had an inch or two over him. Even though the first president was the hero of the Revolution that Maclay supported and probably was the foremost world figure of the day, the Harrisburger was only modestly respectful.

"It was a great dinner, all in the taste of high life," he wrote of another presidential function. "I consider it as a part of my duty as a senator to submit to it, and am glad it is over." He and Robert Morris of Philadelphia were the first Pennsylvanians in the U.S. Senate, but Maclay, anything but a self-indulging man, disliked public frills and equated the life of being a senator with that of pushing a wheelbarrow.

Vice-President Adams, in particular, angered Maclay. "His pride, obstinacy and folly are equal to his vanity," wrote Maclay.

In the great debate over the title of the president, the Harrisburger topped the little giant from Boston.

Vice-President Adams said, "The President must be himself something that includes all the dignities of the diplomatic corps and something greater still. What will the common people of foreign countries, what will the sailors and soldiers, say, 'George Washington, President of the United States'? They will despise him to all eternity. This is all nonsense to the philosopher, but so is all government whatever."

Wrote Maclay: "The above I recollect with great precision, but he said 50 more things, equally injudicious, which I do not think worth minuting. . . . Having experienced relief by the interference of sundry members, I had determined not to say another word, but this new leaf appeared so absurd I could not help some animadversions on it. I rose. 'Mr. President, the Constitution of the United States has designated our Chief Magistrate by the appellation of the President of the United States of America. This is his title of office, nor can we alter, add to or diminish it without infringing the Constitution. . . . As to what the common people, soldiers and sailors of foreign countries may think of us, I do not think it imports us much. Perhaps the less they think, or have occasion to think of us, the better.' "

The U.S. Senate met in New York, and on May 11, 1789, President Washington gave an extra theater ticket of his to Senator Maclay. It was Washington's first appearance as president at a theater, and it also was the debut of the first theater critic from Harrisburg.

Wrote Maclay: "The President, Governor of the State, foreign ministers, Senators from New Hampshire, Connecticut, Pennsylvania and South Carolina, and some ladies were in the same box. The play was the 'School for Scandal.' I never liked it; indeed, I think it an indecent representation before ladies of character and virtue. . . . The house greatly crowded, and I thought the players acted well; but I wish we had seen the 'Conscious Lovers,' or some one that inculcated more prudential manners."

Like a typical critic, Maclay got his ticket free and then went out and panned the show.

Maclay was "an apostle of agrarian simplicity," in Beard's words, a believer in frugality of government, states' rights, the glory of Pennsylvania, and personal humility. The vanity he thought he saw everywhere and in everybody angered him, and his own rheumatism contributed to make him dour and difficult.

On Jan. 26, 1791, he made an entry on the "Cures of Rheumatism":

"1. A teaspoonful of the flour of brimstone taken every morning before breakfast. General St. Clair and Mr. Milligan both relieved by it. Note, they are both Scotchmen.

2. Asafoetida [a gum resin of a plant] laid on burning coals and held to the nose. Mr. Todd greatly relieved by this.

3. Cider in which a hot iron has been quenched. This has relieved many, though cider is to many people very hurtful in that disorder."

Maclay was born on the frontier in Franklin County on July 20, 1737, and came to Harrisburg as a young man after he helped plan the town of Sunbury. He married Mary Harris, the eldest daughter of John Harris II, and they had nine children.

In his first of two years in the U.S. Senate, he offered 100 free acres for the U.S. capitol in Harrisburg. His actual proposal of Aug. 25, 1789 suggested the national capital be Harrisburg, Wrightsville, Carlisle, Reading, Germantown, or Yorktown. He voted against the final choice of the Potomac site.

Almost everyone was glad to see Maclay depart from the U.S. Senate in 1791. He returned to Harrisburg and built his mansion with its huge rectangular stairwell and limestone walls at Front and South Sts. Maclay was succeeded in the Senate in later years by his brother, Samuel Maclay of Sunbury, who was less objectionable but also less capable. They are the only brother combination ever to serve in the U.S. Senate from Pennsylvania.

From being a U.S. Senator, William Maclay willingly humbled himself to be a state legislator—a trip down the ladder that no Pennsylvania politician since has accepted. As a legislator, Maclay fought for Harrisburg to be the state capital. In his lifetime, he failed. As early as 1795 the State House voted to remove the capital from Philadelphia to Carlisle, but the State Senate blocked it. Then in 1799 Lancaster became the capital, as Philadelphia was suddenly deprived of the distinction of being both the national and state capitals. At last on February 21, 1810, Gov. Simon Snyder signed legislation, passed by the House 57–28 and the Senate 20–9, to make Harrisburg the capital as of October, 1812. Other choices were Northumberland, Reading, Carlisle Columbia, Bellefonte, Lancaster, and Philadelphia. A last-minute attempt was made to substitute Sunbury for Harrisburg, but the House beat that down, 62–25.

From 1812 to 1821, the Legislature met in the old courthouse on Market St. The new $275,000 capitol opened January 3, 1822, and the dream of William Maclay was fulfilled.

The old gentleman served in the State Legislature briefly. As a private citizen he helped found the Harrisburg Public Library in September of 1795. At his death at age 70 in 1804, he was a county judge. He was buried in Paxtang Cemetery.

PRESIDENTIAL
CONVENTION
— ʊ —
The Whig Convention of
Dec. 1839 met in this
church and nominated
Wm. Henry Harrison for
president. John Tyler
for vice-president.
Popularized as "Tippe-
canoe and Tyler Too,"
they were elected, 1840

ZION LUTHERAN
HISTORICAL SIGN

The Whig Convention

. . . Harrison, Tyler, and

Harrisburg Too

Harrisburg is the smallest town in the nation ever to play host to a national presidential convention of a major political party. The Whig Party, predecessor to the Republican Party, nominated William Henry Harrison at Zion Lutheran Church in early December of 1839.

Harrisburg, strangely enough, was a logical place to have the Whig convention, because in 1839 it was centrally located in a nation of 26 states and 17 million people. Then only a borough, Harrisburg had a population of but 6,000, but it was in the process of growing larger in size, expanding its northern boundary from North to Maclay St. The town had good rail and canal transportation, as well as friendly hotels with ample supplies of Old Highspire and Old Monongahela for the thirsty politicos.

Harrisburg also had a new hall that could seat the 254 delegates and accompanying hangers-on. Zion Lutheran Church was completed in November of 1839. The sanctuary was not yet dedicated, and this is why the Whigs, with all their deals and schemes, could move in for their December 4–7 convention. While the present stained glass windows

140

were not there, the pews were, though they were not padded in 1839. Zion Lutheran, one of the City's most famous churches, goes back to 1787, when it was founded with Salem Reformed Church. It formed its own congregation in 1795, built at its present site on Fourth St. in 1814 before there was a railroad, and then rebuilt in 1839 after a fire destroyed the original building. The new church was the biggest hall in town.

Political conventions were in their infancy in 1839. It had only been in 1822 that Democrats in Lancaster County called for a national convention to select candidates. The first such national convention was held in Baltimore in September of 1831 by the short-lived Anti-Mason Party, which put up losers William Wirt of Virginia for president and Amos Ellmaker of Pennsylvania for vice-president. Ellmaker, of Lancaster County, had been a Dauphin County judge when he was 28 years old in 1815–1816. The Democrats in the following May of 1832 held a national convention, also in Baltimore, and its candidates, Andrew Jackson and Martin Van Buren, went on to defeat the Whigs' Henry Clay of Kentucky and John Sergeant, the Pennsylvanian who was the great-grandfather of Harrisburg's Cong. John C. Kunkel. Wirt and Ellmaker finished a weak third.

The 1839 convention was held almost a year before the election, because in those days it was difficult to get candidates known. States also had their election days at different times of the year, though most of them voted in November. Maine held its election in September, while Pennsylvania and Indiana held theirs in October.

The Whig Party was a strange amalgamation of talented men and outrageous political hacks. Its biggest names were Daniel Webster and Henry Clay. Essentially, it was a party of such diverse interests that the only thing which held it together was opposition to the dominant Democratic Party. It had support throughout Central Pennsylvania, though it was still the minority party.

The Whigs elected two presidents, both generals, Harrison and Zachary Taylor, both of whom died in office. In Pennsylvania, the Whigs elected two governors, William F. Johnston and James Pollock. Most of its candidates were doomed to be runners-up, and the party occasionally was referred to as the "Whippables."

The *Harrisburg Telegraph*, founded in 1831, favored the Whigs. It gave the convention front-page coverage, describing the meetings thus: "All was courtesy, suavity and good feeling." The *Pennsylvania Reporter*, predecessor of the *Patriot*, was a Democratic journal; so it was antagonistic and placed its stories on page three.

It was Henry Clay's convention to win, but he had to do so on the first ballot. Like all the principal contestants in those days, Clay himself did not attend the convention, but his cousin, Cassius Clay, was there. The party pros did not want Clay, however. State Sen. Charles B. Penrose of Carlisle got the unit rule passed, and this and other machinations kept the Clay men from scoring.

On the first ballot it was: Clay, 103 votes; Harrison, 91, and Gen. Winfield Scott, 57. After a 24-hour intermission and more balloting, it ended up Harrison, 148; Clay, 90, and Scott, 16. The New York State boss, Thurlow Weed, threw his bloc of votes to Harrison. Clay was in a boarding house in Washington, drinking freely, when he heard the sad news. "My friends are not worth the powder and shot it would take to kill them," he barked. As he knew, he was sacrificed, for the Whigs did not necessarily want the best man—Clay undoubtedly was that—but a sure winner.

Clay went into the convention with a plurality of delegates, but not of states, and that is why the unit rule hurt him severely. He should have foreseen seven months earlier when the Whigs approved Harrisburg as the convention site that the power of such anti-Clay men as Penrose and State Rep. Thaddeus Stevens would be increased.

After Daniel Webster turned down the nomination, the Whigs chose for vice-president delegate John Tyler, a former senator and governor of Virginia. Harrison, at age 68, became the nation's oldest elected president, but he lasted exactly one month in office and died of pneumonia. Tyler took over and was thoroughly inadequate. In fact, the rest of his career was downhill. He died as a member of the Confederate Congress, a foe of the nation he once served as president.

The Harrison-Tyler ticket produced the robust slogan, "Tippecanoe and Tyler Too" (Harrison in 1811 had won the Indian Battle of Tippecanoe). It tied in with the log-cabin hoopla that was used to make Harrison appear a homespun candidate. Henry Clay had been much poorer than Harrison, who at the time of the Harrisburg convention was living in a 22-room mansion in North Bend, Ohio. Webster complained that he was sorry he had not been born in a log cabin as his brothers and sisters had. Clay snapped that if Harrison were given a pension and a barrel of cider, he would have been more than pleased not to run for president, but retire to a log cabin.

"Keep the ball rolling" was a lasting slogan that came out of the 1840 campaign. Some young Whigs from Pittsburgh traveled with a papier-mâché ball which they kept rolling to get larger. It was a great stunt to promote Harrison, who won narrowly in Pennsylvania, but he had to take 18 other states to make it to the White House.

FAMOUS BOOTBLACK STAND

Capitol Graft

. . . Per Foot and by the Pound

"By jove, Governor, these are handsome doors," said President Theodore Roosevelt as he walked through the six-inch-thick portals and into the new Capitol on a rainy Oct. 4, 1906, to dedicate what would later be called "Pennsylvania's graft-cankered Capitol." The Bull Mooser exclaimed, "It's the handsomest building I ever saw."

Word of graft was in the air as thousands jammed the City for the dedication. The public had heard talk of scandal five months before from the new state treasurer.

The president never mentioned the scandal in his speech. To him it was a wonderful building and a wonderful day. He stood on the Capitol steps with Gov. Samuel W. Pennypacker, and the Carlisle Indian Band marched by playing, "Hail, Hail, the Gang's All Here." The next day the governor received a bomb threat at the Capitol, but it was a hoax.

The graft scandal broke wide open shortly after the dedication. Big money was involved. Prominent officials were linked to fraud. Leading lawyers fought the case, and convictions were won.

The graft came from furnishing the state house, not from its construction. The building went up in four years and was finished ahead of schedule at a reasonable cost of $4 million, actually $30,000 less than anticipated. The construction was well done. The tile roof, for example, lasted 66 years without needing major repairs.

The furnishings and equipment were another story. These cost almost $9 million, or 70 cents a cubic foot, more than twice the Capitol's cost. So the final price tag on the state house was $13 million. The graft was

143

so heavy that the Commonwealth lost $4 million, even though $1.5 million was returned. Once the crime was uncovered, $6 million in equity suits were filed, and the state spent $143,000 in fees for the investigation.

Fourteen persons—including the architect, state superintendent of grounds and buildings, the principal contractor, the former state treasurer, and the former state auditor general—were indicted and ruined in the trials of 1908. Five received jail sentences, but only three were living in 1910 to go behind bars. The reputation of the governor was tainted and at least three men were reported to have committed suicide because of the disclosures.

Unbeknown to President Roosevelt, the handsome doors he walked through were part of the graft. The $850 flagpole he saw should have cost $150. The office paneling he admired cost $15,000, but should have cost $1,800. The bootblack stand in the Senate cloakroom, worth $125 in 1906, cost $1,619.30. And so it went.

The graft was so bad that Mary Cassatt, the Philadelphia heiress to the Pennsylvania Railroad fortune and an expatriate in Paris, refused to do a painting for the Capitol. Miss Cassatt was the leading woman artist of the French impressionist school. A 1902 work of hers, *Mother and Child*, was sold in 1969 for $140,000.

The story began with the burning of the old Capitol on Feb. 2, 1897. The building, 75 years old, went up in flames during the noon hour, though the fire was not extinguished until midnight. It might have started in the open fireplace in the office of Lieutenant Governor Walter Lyon, who was out of the room, perhaps at lunch. At 1 P.M. a page told Senate President Pro Tempore Samuel J. M. McCarrell of Harrisburg that there was a fire raging upstairs in the two-story building. "Get out your buckets," the chief clerk said. By the time the alarm was answered, the fire had spread to 20 rooms.

"It is preposterous and criminal that a blaze like that of yesterday should have such disastrous results in the middle of the day, at a busy hour, with hundreds of persons about the building," the *Harrisburg Patriot* editorialized.

An anonymous cynic wrote: "At last the bribers, the bribed and the unbribed, the corrupters and the corrupt, all have been smoked out."

The rain, snow, and wind, plus low water pressure, hampered the Harrisburg Fire Department. An estimated 500 tons of paper burned, though most of the important historic and legislative documents were safely stored in the two smaller, fireproof buildings beside the Capitol. The present Capitol covers the entire site of these three buildings. Some of the last business conducted included a bill in the Senate to ban standing in theater aisles and a bill in the House to prohibit liquor dealers from becoming school directors and school directors from obtaining liquor licenses. A "bushel of unanswered mail" on one senator's desk went up in flames.

No one was killed in the fire. Fourteen persons were injured, including a policeman struck by a brass chandelier. Only one of the horde of looters was arrested. Prize souvenirs were wooden legislative desks, and a few of these still exist in Harrisburg.

Eli Bowen in his 1854 *Locomotive Sketches* wrote: "The Capitol stands on a handsome sloping elevation. . . . The grounds are enclosed with an iron-rail fence, and laid out in handsome gravel walks, shaded with numerous trees, which are still young and in vigorous growth. The main building is 180 feet in length by 80 feet in width, and two stories in height. It is a plain but substantial brick building, sufficiently characteristic of our old Commonwealth. A large circular portico, faced with six heavy stone columns, constitutes the front entrance to the building. In the interior is a large rotunda, with a high dome overarching, from which is entered the Senate chamber on the left, and the Hall of the Representatives on the right." The dome had "a directory" of names scratched and scribbled on it by visitors, and the Capitol clock tolled its last at high noon.

The taxpayer loss was estimated at $1.5 million, because the state house was insured for only $200,000.

After the fire, the Legislature transferred its quarters to Grace Methodist Church. It was the first time, the *Patriot* said, that "the whole Legislature will go to church."

Within eight days, a bill was offered that the capital be taken back to Philadelphia, as of Jan. 1, 1899. "For 100 years legislators with brains have kept the Capitol out of Philadelphia and the reasons for doing so then are good now," the *Patriot* editorialized. Gov. Daniel H. Hastings, whose daughter, the late Mrs. Ross A. Hickok, was planning her coming-out party at the Governor's Mansion and would reside in Harrisburg for another 60 years, said the Capitol should remain in the City and be rebuilt immediately.

That September 30, the contract for designing the new Capitol was awarded. The cornerstone was laid on Aug. 10, 1898, and the trowel used by George Washington for the nation's Capitol in 1793 was borrowed from the Freemasons for the ceremony. Yet the fight to transfer the capital first to Philadelphia, or then to Pittsburgh, Lancaster, Allentown, Reading, Somerset, and Montoursville, continued. With Harrisburg's Cong. Marlin E. Olmsted leading the defense, the last House bill to remove the capital was defeated on May 8, 1901, by a vote of 103–75.

The Legislature in 1901 created a commission to construct the Capitol at a cost of $4 million. Legislative acts in 1901, 1903, and 1905, however, turned the power of furnishing the building over to the Board of Public Grounds and Buildings. An act read: "The State Treasurer is hereby authorized and directed to pay out of any moneys in the Treasury not otherwise appropriated . . . such sums as may be required . . . for furnishing . . . , which shall be done only on the written orders of the Board of Public Grounds and Buildings." The Building Commission, having done its job so efficiently, lost the power to direct the important spending project where graft would be an easier matter to arrange.

Governor Pennypacker to the end of his life in 1916 maintained that no matter how the Board of Public Grounds and Buildings operated, the completed Capitol was still $5 million cheaper than either the nation's Capitol or Philadelphia's City Hall and was much less costly than Pennsylvania Station in New York. Pennypacker liked to say that no special taxes were needed to pay for a 475-room building larger than St. Paul's Cathedral.

The Governor misstated the case, however. He thought it was important that the guilty architect could say it "was the cheapest building of its character in the country." The roar of outrage was not against the $13 million pricetag of the Capitol. It was against the $4 million worth of graft. Pennypacker in later years wrote a small book on the subject. He prefaced his remarks with the text from Deuteronomy 27:18, "Cursed be he that maketh the blind to wander out of the way."

In the third year of the Pennypacker Administration, 1905, one of the most remarkable upsets in Pennsylvania political history occurred. William H. Berry, 53, a Democrat and former mayor of Chester, was elected state treasurer by 88,194 votes over Republican J. Lee Plummer. The previous year Republican Teddy Roosevelt had carried Pennsylvania for the presidency by 505,519 votes. Berry was the only Democrat elected to a state office between 1897 and 1911.

The first thing Berry found on his desk was the bill for the Capitol flagpole, inflated by almost six times its proper cost. The new treasurer immediately made a study of his own office and found that the paneling, worth about $1,800, cost $15,000; that the ceiling, worth about $500, cost $5,500, and that the flooring cost $90,000, though not worth a hundredth of that price. From his south-wing office, he began to poke in the corners of the rest of the Capitol, and then he shouted graft. Newspapermen filed muckraking tales of the fraud, with Berry supplying the details.

"It cannot be successfully denied that the Commonwealth got a good job in the Capitol, but the prices were outrageous and they ought not to stand," he said. Meanwhile, with the gubernatorial elections coming that November of 1906, the Pennypacker Administration charged Berry with being a political opportunist.

To answer graft rumors, the innocent Pennypacker, prior to the October 1906 dedication, authorized a study of expenditures and said: "And now I bid farewell, I hope forever, to that malodorous scandal which followed so closely upon the completion of a marvelous and commendable achievement and whose purveyors may be likened to those vile fish that swim in the wake of a good ship, her prow buffeting the seas and her flag flying proudly in the breezes of Heaven, but seek only to feast their appetites upon the offal which is cast overboard."

After the dedication, the rumors got worse. By October 24, Pennypacker was obviously disturbed. "I know of no graft," he said. "I do not believe there has been any. I do not like the term." The *Philadelphia North American* answered the Governor: "He is probably the only one among the 7 million people in Pennsylvania so childlike and bland."

The *Patriot* on October 29 published its findings, revealing that its filing cabinets cost $278 while similar ones in the new Capitol cost $2,470. The diffierence, the *Patriot* noted, was more than a workman on the Capitol was paid in a year for his labor.

As late as January of 1907, Pennypacker's attorney general, Hampton Carson, said, "I do not hesitate to say that, in my judgment, there is no trace of crime."

In the election of November 1906 Edwin S. Stuart, a Republican from Philadelphia, won, despite the graft scandal, by 48,364 votes over Democratic reformer Lewis Emery, Jr. When bachelor Governor Stuart took office on Jan. 14, 1907, he vowed to make an honest investigation. Historians credit Stuart with doing just that. The Republican senator from Indiana County, John S. Fisher, conducted a thorough probe, gathering facts which led to court convictions. For Fisher, it led to the governorship in 1927, and Fisher Plaza is named for him.

The day after the Capitol's dedication, Treasurer Berry stopped payments to contractors. He had found, among other things, that the pavement around the Capitol cost 31.5 cents a square foot when it should have cost about 18 cents. But by that Oct. 7, 1906, much of the heavy grabbing of cash had taken place. At one time, the Commonwealth was ahead in payments to contractors by $950,913.

John H. Sanderson, a Philadelphian and the major contractor for furnishing the Capitol, perhaps was the chief culprit. For decades afterwards, items in the Capitol were jokingly named for him, such as the

"Sanderson tubs," as the umbrella stands he bought for $14 and resold for $73.60 were called. He paid $40 for an 8-by-4-foot mahogany table and resold it for $1,472. Two rostrums, which should have cost $2,060, cost $90,748.80. Mahogany clothes trees, costing between $5.65 and $12 each, went for $73.60. Rolltop desks, valued at $33, were sold for $220.80. A corner cupboard worth $50 was sold for $625.60. The $60 sofa in Treasurer Berry's office cost $552.05. The andirons in the same office were inflated too.

Sanderson did "an excellent business selling air to the State," as one newspaper put it. Yet many of the Sanderson items were solid pieces of period furniture, and endured 50 or more years of hard bureaucratic use. Today they are valuable antiques, reselling for something as much as the State originally paid for them.

The purchasing system may not have been unique for the era Matt Quay called "shaking the plum tree," but it was certainly imaginative. Desks, chairs, chandeliers, andirons, marble mantels, and countless items were bought per foot. "Per foot" meant lineal, square, or cubic measurements, often with augmented dimensions that were the result of exaggerated guesses. Sometimes the packaging dimensions were used. Poundage and tonnage were brought into play when a contractor could turn them to his favor.

Harper's Weekly covered the graft case and T. Everett Harry wrote: "It is more wonderful than any of the schemes for getting public money invented by New York's famous Boss Tweed in his most zealous days." Under this type of deal, the $4 million Capitol structure got a $2 million lighting system. "One can find no other building in the world lighted at such great expense," Harry wrote.

In court, the counsel for Sanderson claimed that he was guilty of generosity but nothing else. "Where in all the evidence of the Commonwealth," asked Harrisburg attorney Charles H. Bergner, "is there a word to show that any of these men received a penny that did not belong to them? There is not a word." Sanderson, in fact, claimed that he supplied 1,092 additional square feet of furniture for the House and Senate free of charge.

The prosecution retorted by showing how Sanderson, a chubby fellow with the look of a walrus, operated. The Senate bootblack stand, still in use, cost $50 to make and was purchased by Sanderson for $125. It is 64.5 square feet. At the inflated rate of $18.40 a square foot, the price should have been $1,186.80, but Sanderson added a $432.50 mark-up to that, though he did supply two wooden chairs and four brass footrests. "It's a shame to take the money," prosecutor James Scarlet said sarcastically in the courtroom.

Owen Wister, the Philadelphia author of the famous western novel, *The Virginian*, did his own investigating. He concluded that there were at least six ways in which the taxpayer was being cheated.

The idiotic poundage price, for example, was set at $3.85, but even this was not enough. The state ended up paying $4.85 a pound for furnishings. Weight was charged for when it did not exist. The beautiful chandelier in Room 100 was paid for at a price based on 900 pounds, when it actually weighed 755 pounds. Materials were leaded to increase their weight. As a result, the chandeliers in the House weigh more than 3.5 tons.

For all the fixtures in the Capitol that should have cost $569,000, the state paid $2,041,523.

Wister also found that the bronze was fake, the castings dishonest, and the gold-plating a sham.

Senator Fisher is quoted on page 419 of the *Legislative Record* of 1909: "The expert of the commission estimates that the value of all bronze work found on cases is less than one-fourth of the price paid." The entire furnishing job, the Senator said, has "marked evidence of duplicity and deceit."

Two marble slab benches, a marble-lined swimming pool, and a marble shower bath were to have gone into the Capitol under the original plans, but when the scandal broke these were canceled.

While the quality of workmanship on the Capitol was never questioned—much of it is excellent—investigators found numerous instances in which specifications were disregarded. Solid mahogany was to be used in the brackets and moldings in such places as the Governor's Reception Room and the Senate Caucus Room. Today the fake brackets can be seen. They are part wood and part composition. A pigeon once got into the Reception Room and chipped the mahogany veneer, revealing a plaster composition underneath.

The gallery rails in the House and Senate are not bronze, but brass.

Perhaps the worst thievery was achieved in the glass mosaic frieze bands for the main rotunda of the Capitol. The plan was for "Tiffany Faverile opalescent glass or its equivalent in every way." Today there is no Tiffany Faverile glass to be found in the Capitol. The grafters put in material from the Assembled Tile and Slab Co. of Pittsburgh and then charged $24,089 for what should have cost $9,656.

The art work, such as the Barnard statuary, and the craftsmanship, such as the tile in the Capitol, were purchased by the Commonwealth at reasonable prices, however. The artists did not share in the graft.

The Capitol Graft Case, one of the most sensational of its day, went to trial Jan. 27, 1908, at the old Dauphin County Courthouse at Market and Court Sts. It was Commonwealth Court, and sitting on the bench was President Judge George Kunkel, one of Dauphin County's greatest judges.

Some of the best lawyers in Pennsylvania were in the case, drawing fees rumored to be as high as $25,000. In fact, it was said that one lawyer came just to help pick the jury, and he left with $25,000 in his pocket. Admission to the courtroom was by ticket only.

Four men, each of whom had posted $60,000 bail, faced the court in the first of several trials. They were chief contractor John H. Sanderson, former superintendent of public grounds and buildings James H. Shumaker, former auditor general William P. Snyder, and former treasurer William L. Mathues. Snyder was a physician, a graduate of the University of Pennsylvania Medical School, former Chester County Republican chairman, a former legislator, and twice president pro tempore of the Senate. Mathues was a lawyer and a leader in the Delaware County GOP machine.

Joseph M. Huston, of Philadelphia, the brilliant young architect of the Capitol, was granted severance.

The four men on trial were charged with conspiracy with intent to defraud the state of $19,308.40. Items included in the fraud charges were 65 sofas at $2,260.40 and 145 clothes trees at $4,157.20. The maximum penalty was two years and $500 fine.

The Commonwealth threw a battery of talented lawyers against the accused. Deputy Attorney General Jesse Cunningham of Harrisburg was in charge. Cunningham later became a Superior Court judge. Others for the state were M. Hampton Todd, John Fox Weiss, Sen. John E. Fox, and the most able of all, James Scarlet of Danville, as skillful a trial lawyer as ever practiced in Pennsylvania.

"If a man throws the dice and five sixes come up, it is unusual," exclaimed Scarlet. "If he throws them a second time and five sixes are shown, it seems strange. If he throws them three times and five sixes turn out, it seems remarkable. If he throws them four times and five sixes turn out, it seems wonderful. But if he throws them five times and five sixes are up, it seems miraculous." Scarlet concluded that the accused had played with "loaded dice."

The defense admitted to bad policies, but argued that mistakes should not be confused with conspiracy. Here is an excerpt in the cross-examination of former auditor general Mathues:

Q. "But you paid them (the bills) without knowing whether they were correct or not?" A. "I did. . . ."

Q. "What did you understand was the foot measurement?" A. "I have never understood that. . . ."

Q. "Did you ever try to understand it?" A. "No, sir. . . ."

Q. "How would you understand the bills, how would you audit them, if you did not understand that?" A. "I depended entirely on the architect. . . . I may have been a little easy. . . ."

Q. "For my own satisfaction, just tell me what mental processes you underwent when you audited a bill?" A. "I . . . saw that the additions and multiplications were correct. . . ."

Architect Huston was claimed to be an agent of the purchaser, the Board of Public Grounds and Buildings. On February 18 former Governor Pennypacker, once a judge, took the stand and testified that he had no knowledge of the graft that went on during his administration. "How long did you place faith in Mr. Huston?" prosecutor Scarlet asked. "I may say down to the present time," Pennypacker replied. "I think his work was a great achievement." "It certainly was," Scarlet said.

The former governor's reputation suffered at the trial. As a youth he had been in the militia marching to the Battle of Gettysburg and had slept on the old Capitol steps wrapped in a red horse blanket. Boss Matt Quay, his distant cousin, made him governor in 1902.

"Governor Pennypacker was here as a witness," said Cunningham in court, "and what he didn't know about matters on the Hill impressed everybody. According to the testimony in this case, Governor Pennypacker was deceived." Cunningham called him an "honest old man." But for the defense's case, Cunningham said it was "false as hell."

Excitement was so high at the trial that at one point the 28 Pinkerton men on duty arrested an underwear salesman in the City for attempting to influence the jury. It was proven quickly that the charge was false.

The jury, with Joseph H. Dunkel, a pipefitter from Swatara Township, as foreman, went out on March 13 and took eight hours and 36 minutes to find the four guilty. The day the verdict was returned, Edwin Austin Abbey announced from New York that he had finished his inspirational paintings for the Capitol dome.

Other graft trials were held, including one of a congressman from Marietta who was found innocent. In all, five persons were convicted. The case eventually went to the State Supreme Court and the verdicts were upheld. By 1910, however, when the litigation ended, Sanderson and Mathues were dead. Shumaker, Snyder, and Huston did go behind penitentiary bars.

It was charged that architect Huston received 4 percent on the furnishings. He angrily complained to the press that he was an artist and that mankind has always slapped artists into jail. He said the Athenians gave the great Phidias $40,000 in gold to do a statue of Athena for the

Parthenon. When the statue was finished, the Athenians complained Phidias had kept some of the gold and put him in jail. The man who designed the Paris Opera House got the same treatment, said Huston, who had modeled the rotunda steps after those of the Opera House.

The Capitol Graft Case established precedents. In the Turnpike Cinders Case in Dauphin County Court in 1958, references were made to the 1908 trials and a brief history of them was included in the judicial record. It was never a point in the Capitol case that the trials should not be held in Dauphin County, but in the cinders case this issue was raised. Judge Homer L. Kreider pointed to the precedent set by Judge Kunkel in 1908 and said Dauphin County, serving until 1970 as Commonwealth Court, had jurisdiction.

The revelation of the Capitol scandal made little political difference to Pennsylvanians. The electorate apparently was resigned to dishonest leadership. "Pennsylvania is not rottener than she ever was," wrote Owen Wister, "but merely as rotten as ever she has been."

Matt Quay, his son, and the state treasurer had been indicted for fraud in 1898. He was barred from the U.S. Senate, but put back there by an understanding Pennsylvania Legislature. Said Quay in 1900: "Pennsylvania is honest, her people are honest, her officials are honest. And of all this union of states, Pennsylvania is the fairest and the happiest, and the most intelligent and best governed." At Quay's death in 1904, Sen. Boies Penrose took over and ran the corrupt machine even more expertly, earning for himself a statue in Capitol Park.

Treasurer William H. Berry, the hero of the case, never won public office again. He was succeeded by a Republican in 1908, and by 1910 the Democrats would not even run him for governor. He did run as an independent reformer, however, getting 252,732 votes more than the regular Democratic candidate but losing to Republican John K. Tener by 33,487 votes. In 1912, Berry sought the office of state treasurer again, but lost in the landslide. He died in 1928, and it was not until six years later that George H. Earle III put the first Democratic administration in the new Capitol.

Owen Wister angrily wrote in the muckraking magazine *Everybody's*:

"The people of Pennsylvania walked last autumn by thousands and thousands through their new Capitol, and to most of them it was superb and beautiful. Its total lack of individuality and distinction, its great aimless bulk, its bilious, overeaten decoration, its swollen bronzes, its varicose chandeliers, expressed their notion of the grand and the desirable. Now that they have learned that it was all another robbery, and that their carved mahogany is mostly putty, they are not much disturbed. Do not pity them. They deserve everything they get, for Pennsylvania is today a government by knaves at the expense of fools."

To Wister, "The people of Pennsylvania are not self-respecting. In the place of self-respect they substitute an impregnable complacency." The Pennsylvania Dutch have a "servile acquiescence" about government, he said, and "no Dutch county has ever turned its boss out." The Quakers have the same acquiescence plus timidity. The Pennsylvania Irish for their part would vote for "despotism" at the drop of a hat. "And the rest of us, Anglo-Saxons, Jews, Italians, Bulgarians, Hungarians, Polish and Germans are not such good citizens either," he wrote. "Lethargically prosperous, Pennsylvania is all belly and no members, and its ideals do not rise higher than the belly."

At the time of the graft scandal, most Pennsylvanians thought their Capital grandiose, perhaps even worth the fraudulent cost overrun. President Roosevelt, Governor Pennypacker, and Treasurer Berry regarded it as a majestic edifice. Covering two acres, the Capitol with its exterior of Vermont granite and its interior of marble, mahogany, bronze, and tile is simply the most impressive building in Central Pennsylvania. It is an anthology of architecture. The 26,000-ton dome, towering to 272 feet, is modeled after that of St. Peter's in Rome. The Italian marble staircase is a copy of the grand staircase of the Paris Opera House. The Italian Renaissance style was used for the exterior of the building, while there is Greek Doric in the Senate chamber, Corinthian in the House chamber, and Ionic in the Supreme Court. Today the Capitol is the center of a 65-acre complex of 11 major buildings, housing 15,000 employees. In 1970 it was insured for $129 million, at a premium cost of $176,730.

On the 100th anniversary of Lincoln's birth, Feb. 12, 1909, both President Roosevelt and Vice-President Charles Fairbanks were in town —the only time a president and vice-president have visited Harrisburg the same day. Fairbanks commented: "The State Capitol is a magnificent building, but it is lacking in one respect. The surrounding park is not adequate for so large and imposing a structure. As I said, the building and its decorations are works of art, but a large park to show properly the beauty and magnificence of the building is badly needed." It still lacks that setting.

The state house, really, is impressive only for its size and extravagance. "The Capitol," wrote Owen Wister, "is not a good work. Outside it looks as much like all other capitols as any banana looks like the rest of the bunch. Inside it is a monstrous botch of bad arrangement, bad lighting, bad ventilation, and the most bloated bad taste." Amy Oakley in her *Our Pennsylvania* of 1950 wrote, most accurately of all, "Distance undoubtedly lends enchantment to the Capitol."

SIMON CAMERON

Simon Cameron

. . . His Gray Eminence

Simon Cameron is the biggest name to come out of Harrisburg and the patriarch of its most famous family, the Cameron-McCormick clan.

He is a major, but defamed figure in American history. He was considered for the presidency in 1860 and mentioned for the vice-presidency in 1856, 1860, and 1864. He was President Lincoln's secretary of war for 10 months. For 20 years he was a U.S. senator, and his son, J. Donald, inherited his seat for another 20 years.

Most importantly, Cameron was the organizer of the most powerful and enduring state political machine in the nation's history. His Pennsylvania went Republican in every presidential election from 1860 through 1932, and in the same period elected 14 Republican governors and only one Democrat. Cameron's Grand Old Party controlled 34 consecutive State Senates and 32 of 34 State House majorities.

154

To Carl Sandburg, Cameron was "the most skilled political manipulator in America." To Pennsylvania's most noted economist, Henry C. Carey, writing to Abraham Lincoln in 1861, Cameron was "the very incarnation of corruption." To President James K. Polk, he was a "managing tricky man in whom no reliance can be placed."

Harrisburg's first mayor, William H. Kepner, paid tribute to Cameron's political prowess by toasting him as "a Pennsylvanian who has never forgotten his native state." Even his foes, as the *Lancaster Daily Intelligencer* editorialized at his death, regarded him as "successful but not noble."

Though he had an international reputation and a fortune of at least $2 million, Cameron was a remarkably simple man, both in his living style and in the way he played politics.

True to his Scotch-Irish and German farmer ancestors, he was systematic. He lived his retirement years from 1877 to 1889 at his Front St. Mansion or at his Donegal Springs country home. He would rise before 8 A.M., have toast, a chop, or a few soft-boiled eggs, and then receive visitors. At 11 A.M. Cameron always had champagne. He drank it at that time of day for 50 years, claiming it added 20 years to his life. For lunch he would have roast beef, vegetables, and then usually a baked apple, which he especially enjoyed. For supper he dined on grits and oatmeal. Cameron did not like pastry. He said pie-eaters die young.

Bedtime usually was 11 P.M., and he would read himself to sleep. Cameron said he never dreamed.

He napped in the afternoons and browsed in his library. He said he was a "literary fellow." He certainly was curious about books and people, though his own writing and oratorical talents were nil. He wrote no memoirs and told no tales of what had happened in his crowded political career. His taciturnity was a trait shared by his family and by virtually all his successors in the leadership of Dauphin County Republicanism.

Cameron is discredited for saying: "An honest politician is one, who when he is bought, stays bought." But his most recent and most thorough biographer, Dr. Erwin S. Bradley, a graduate of Penn State, claims this quote cannot be documented. Yet Cameron did write on an envelope after winning his Senate seat in 1857 in a contest in which bribes were offered and accepted: "How strange it is that so many men are governed by a belief that I am willing to buy them." And in 1866 he wrote to a newspaperman about his rival, Gov. Andrew G. Curtin: "He is truthless, corrupt and mercenary, without even faith to those who would buy him."

Cameron enjoyed exceptional health in his 90 years, and with Calvinistic fortitude he endured a number of misfortunes. His son Simon lived to age 64, but was mentally retarded and had to be cared for at home. His oldest son, Maj. William Brua Cameron, died at age 38 in the Civil War. A younger brother, Col. James Cameron, was killed at Bull Run, the first Pennsylvania officer to fall in the war. Four of his 10 children died in childhood and his wife, Margaretta, preceded him in death by 16 years.

The Cameron name from his lineage survived him by only 70 years. His granddaughter, Miss Mary Cameron, died in Harrisburg in October of 1959. A great-granddaughter, Mrs. Elva Cameron South, a granddaughter of Maj. William Brua Cameron, is still living in Pittsburgh. The direct Cameron-McCormick line expired in January of 1964 with the death of Miss Anne McCormick, a grandniece.

The wealth of Cameron endures yet, though the last substantial holding of land, 190 acres of the old Cameron farm at Lochiel, between Harrisburg and Steelton, was sold in October of 1968. Simon bought the farm in 1841 and turned it over to J. Donald in 1872.

"Loose gray clothes hung from his tall, slim frame," wrote Carl Sandburg. "He was smooth of face, sharp-lipped, with a delicate straight nose, a finely chiseled mask touched with fox wariness. As he pronounced dry and pretendedly forthright decisions, Cameron's face was more often mask than face. He wrought effects from behind the scenes."

There was this grayness to Cameron, in his hair, his eyes, and his style. He had the "austere look of a Covenanter," as one historian noted. He was such a devout Presbyterian that he once made it a point to get a rose from the grave of John Calvin. He always lived modestly for a man of his means; yet he could spend lavishly for political purposes or when using government money as secretary of war.

He was satisfied, as few men are, with his own material gains. Power, not greed, motivated him. It is said, with some exaggeration, that never in his 32 years of public service did he ever use his position to make a dollar for himself; but he did use his position and influence repeatedly to make dollars for others. "I don't have to be dishonest to make money," he said at a Harrisburg banquet honoring him. "I can go out in the street in the normal course of business and make more money than my detractors."

Cameron was an affable and polite man, especially in small gatherings. He was worldly but not aggressively domineering. Despite the masculinity of his eaglelike face and his dignified bearing, he had a strangely weak voice. He was reticent and always under control, except for one notable instant on the Senate floor in 1847 when he was challenged by a drunken Mississippi senator. With a lightninglike blow, Cameron knocked the man unconscious.

Cameron was shrewd in his private life, as well as in the political arena. He made it a point to marry well. His wife was the daughter of Peter Brua, a director of a Harrisburg bank. His son, J. Donald, married the daughter of the president of the Dauphin Deposit Bank. One daughter married the editor of the *Patriot*. Another married Wayne MacVeagh, an excellent lawyer who became Republican state chairman and attorney general for President Garfield. Another daughter married a Centre County judge. Family ties were important.

Only when he was 78 and retired was Cameron exposed as foolish in a private affair. Mary S. Oliver, a federal employee known as the "Widow Oliver," claimed that when Cameron was 75 he took improper advantages of her and made an offer to marry her. She sued for $50,-000. Cameron won in court, but paid legal fees. It was not the money that hurt, but such stinging home state editorial comment as, "Old Simon, you gay old dog, you!"

Cameron was born March 8, 1799, in a log house in Maytown. He was the son of a poor Scotch-Irish tailor and tavern keeper. His mother was a country girl from a Palatinate German family. There were six children. When Simon was nine, the family moved to Sunbury, where the father, Charles Cameron, soon died.

At age 11, Cameron was accepted into the home of a childless Jewish physician, Dr. Peter Grahl. The doctor and his brother-in-law, Lorenzo Da Ponte, a Jewish-Italian émigré, got Simon started on his self-education. At 17, Cameron became an apprentice with the *Northumberland Gazette*. He completed his training at the *Harrisburg Republican* and rose to be assistant editor. At 22, he was an editor in Doylestown, and then he spent some months in Washington. At 25, he borrowed $400 from an uncle and became part-owner of the *Republican*, merging it with the *Pennsylvania Reporter*. Before he was 30, he was out of active journalism, was a silent partner in Harrisburg publishing, had a rich wife, and had earned the first $20,000 of his eventual fortune.

As a newspaperman in 1824, he entered politics as a delegate from Dauphin County to the Democratic state convention. For exactly half the rest of his life, he was a Democrat. That is one reason he became a different kind of Republican from Andrew Curtin, Thaddeus Stevens, or Lincoln, all of whom came up through the Whig Party.

For 21 months, from 1828 to 1830, he was adjutant general under Gov. John Andrew Shulze, who was married to the sister of the wife of John Cameron, Simon's brother. Cameron was never in the army, but he retained the title of "General" and was addressed by this in Harrisburg, not "Senator."

Cameron laid the groundwork for his political success and his personal wealth in the 15 years between 1830 and 1845. He was an early supporter of Gen. Andrew Jackson and rose to leadership rank in the Pennsylvania Democratic Party. He was a key backer of James Buchanan until 1345, when they had a permanent falling out. Meanwhile, in 1838 Cameron rejected a sure bid for Congress. He had other interests at the time, but it was the start of his lifelong pattern of never going before the public to win elective office.

For an entrepreneur with Cameron's common sense, business was brisk. He was in canal building, railroading, iron, printing, banking, and real estate. He and his brother James had a network of railroads, including the Northern Central, which almost doubled its profits while Cameron was Secretary of War. Cameron ran the Middletown Bank, which held state funds while issuing its own notes and made unexplained profits while he was the federal agent for the Winnebago Indians in 1838.

If Simon Cameron ever acted politically against the best interests of the railroads, it is unrecorded. He played railroad politics to the hilt, and the power and money he derived from his railroad colleagues enabled him to be the master of the Pennsylvania Republicans. As Gideon Welles said, "The railroad controls Pennsylvania, and Cameron has had the adroitness to secure it."

With his inside connections to county organizations and the legislature, Cameron was an excellent lobbyist for the banks as well. In 1838 he wrote to Philadelphia Banker Simon Gratz for financial assistance: "It is but fair that the banks in the city should incur some of the expenses necessary to their safety. I should not under other circumstances accept anything from them. But you know a man cannot live at Harrisburg on the winds."

He avoided holding any local or state public office that would crimp his style. When his man, State Sen. David R. Porter of Huntingdon, was a candidate for governor, Cameron advised him to absent himself from the Senate during the campaign, because it was "a very unsafe spot for a politician." Meanwhile, Cameron secured Porter's brother James a Dauphin County judgeship.

In 1845 James Buchanan left the U.S. Senate to be secretary of state. Cameron captured his seat with a legislative vote of 67 to 55. He did it with some Whig votes, a few of which undoubtedly were purchased. The man he beat, George W. Woodward, 36, of Wilkes-Barre, then was named by President Polk to the Supreme Court, but Cameron viciously blocked the appointment.

Cameron served in the Senate until 1849, and six years later attempted to return. The 1855 unsuccessful try was as disgraceful an episode as ever occurred in Pennsylvania politics. At one caucus, 90 legislators produced 91 votes. Five joint sessions were called to get 67 votes for a candidate. Cameron got the most, a high of 59, but Andrew Curtin walked out with 29 Know-Nothing, Whig, and dissident votes and a majority never could be achieved. This was the beginning of the 30-year war between Cameron and Curtin.

No senator could be selected in 1855, but the following year, with a newly elected legislature, former Gov. William Bigler was chosen. By 1856 Cameron was a Republican. At the first GOP national convention in Philadelphia he was mentioned for vice-president, and would have done more for the defeated Frémont ticket than the New Jersey governor selected.

In 1857 Cameron returned to the U.S. Senate. This time it was unabashed bribery that did it. In fact, Cameron became the only Pennsylvanian to go to the Senate when the opposition controlled the legislature. Two Schuylkill County Democrats and one from York County were taken care of, and Cameron got exactly the required 67 votes. Cameron was never unmindful of a favor. Thirty years later he was still paying the coal bill for the widow of one of the turncoat Democrats.

Cameron was a genius at manipulation. Legislative selection of U.S. senators lasted until 1914. In Cameron's day, there were 133 Pennsylvania legislators. If a candidate controlled, or bought, just 34 votes of the majority caucus, he had the election. Cameron's expertise started with getting his men named House speaker and Senate president pro tempore.

Once again Cameron was in the Senate only four years, this time until he joined Lincoln's cabinet.

He led a divided delegation to the 1860 GOP convention. Dauphin County the previous year endorsed him for president, but he begged off. "The Presidency is so very far above my ambition or qualifications that it has not really entered my head," he said. On the first ballot he received 50½ votes, and on the second he threw his support to Lincoln and started the landslide. He might have had the vice-presidency, but he did not want to risk a nasty fight to get it.

Cameron was secretary of war for 10 months, and he turned in a disgraceful performance.

It is doubtful if anyone could have won laurels in the War Department, for it was as disorganized and unprepared as the nation was to fight a long civil war. Cameron had little administrative talent for such a task and, furthermore, he was distrusted by many, perhaps even by President Lincoln himself. Lavish expenditures and fraudulent contracts were common, but Cameron made the War Department a haven for his favorite game, patronage.

"He exhibited extraordinary pains to execute one simple favor," his biographer Bradley notes. Initially the department had five employees from Pennsylvania. Cameron hired 22 more. He made the boss of South Philadelphia the chief clerk, and his assistant secretary for transportation was the vice-president of the Pennsylvania Railroad. Soldiers were transported in PRR boxcars at twice the cost they should have been. A thousand horses were purchased at Huntingdon, a third of which were blind or diseased. The *New York Times* exaggerated, but there was a grain of truth in its statement that he "converted one-half the population of Pennsylvania into contractors."

The best story about Secretary of War Cameron is probably apocryphal. Thaddeus Stevens complained to Lincoln that Cameron was mismanaging the war effort. "You don't think Mr. Cameron would steal, do you?" Lincoln is supposed to have asked. "Well, he wouldn't steal a red-hot stove." Lincoln enjoyed that remark so well that he passed it on to Cameron, who did not see the humor. Stevens returned to Lincoln and said, "He is very mad and made me promise to retract. I will now do so. I believe I told you he would not steal a red-hot stove. I will now take that back."

Cameron said his operation was "strictly economical," but in January of 1862 Lincoln removed him and made him minister to Russia. The Senate took four days to confirm him, by a vote of 28–14. In April, the House voted 79–45 to censure Cameron. The action embittered Cameron, as it would anyone. Lincoln, keeping on Cameron's side, wisely issued a statement that the Pennsylvanian was no more to blame for the faults of the War Department than he himself. Long after the war, in 1875, the House made Cameron a happy man by unanimously rescinding its censure resolution.

Simon Cameron's lasting achievement was to build the Pennsylvania Republican Party.

During the Civil War, his major role was to keep Pennsylvania safe for the Union, and this is why Lincoln kept on friendly terms with him. Lincoln won the Commonwealth in 1860 by 89,159 votes, but his margin dropped to 20,075 in 1864. Governor Curtin's re-election in 1863 was closer. Pennsylvania, especially its business interests, never fully backed Lincoln.

Cameron constructed the Pennsylvania GOP by manipulation, fund-raising, patronage, and a variety of secretive tactics. He was not a boss and certainly lacked solid control in Philadelphia and many sections of the state, but he was first among equals in the Republican high command. He made it clear that business, the farmers, the general public, and certainly the party workers could profit by endorsing his brand of Republicanism.

Cameron played personal politics, in that he dealt with key individuals in every sector of the state. He used newspapers such as the *Harrisburg Telegraph*, the *Philadelphia Bulletin*, and the *Pittsburgh Gazette*, and cooperative editors were rewarded, often with postmasterships.

His talents were exactly what was needed to develop a political machine. He was practical, patient, persistent, and seldom stubborn. He accepted temporary setbacks, though not defeat. He had a skill for making the public believe he was more powerful than he really was. He was not doctrinaire, except on the need for a high protective tariff for his fellow Pennsylvania businessmen. On the racial issue, he was neither an abolitionist nor a bigot. Most of all, it was instinctive for him to reward friends and punish enemies.

He boasted that he never was false to his constituents. The year of his death, he wrote: "When I am gone all I ask is that people may say that I did the best I could and was never untrue to a friend."

Cameron was in Russia only a few months, resigning the post at the end of 1862. The Democrats took a combined one-vote majority in the Pennsylvania legislature that year, but Cameron thought he had a chance to return to the U.S. Senate. "The urging of Cameron's followers to have him re-enter the Senate was somewhat analogous to inciting a land animal to come out of the water," Bradley writes. "The Senate was Cameron's perfect medium—the one which he had mastered and in which he felt perfectly at home." Before the joint session to name the senator, as much as $100,000 was bid for a single vote. Cameron, however, was defeated, 67–65.

He purchased the John Harris Mansion, then 97 years old, on April 1, 1863. Cameron made a two-story addition and added the brick building in the rear. There he entertained U. S. Grant, the Carnegies, and others. The mansion today has his picture, a desk, a grand piano, two sofas, his French porcelain dishes, a chair, and his candelabra. His name is still on the brass doorbell. At his death the mansion went to his widowed daughter-in-law, Mrs. Richard J. Haldeman. The Haldeman family in 1941 turned it over to the Historical Society of Dauphin County.

In 1867 Cameron at last was renamed to the U.S. Senate, and he stayed there ten years, six of them as chairman of the Foreign Relations Committee.

The 1867 Republican legislative caucus was a critical one, for it determined that Cameron and not the more liberal, outgoing Governor Curtin would direct the Republican Party. With superb infighting, Cameron won the caucus, 46 votes to Curtin's 23. Thad Stevens got seven votes and Galusha Grow, five. At the joint session, Cameron won easily over Edgar Cowan, the Democrat, 81–47. To garner votes, J. Donald Cameron and Wayne MacVeagh worked diligently. It was Cameron's luck that MacVeagh was his daughter's fiancé in the summer of 1866 when Cameron Republicans were campaigning for the legislature.

The 1867 defeat ended Curtin's hopes of leadership, though at the end of his life he went to Congress as a Democrat. Grow was Lincoln's first speaker of the House in 1861, but the Cameron Republicans redistricted him out of his seat. He did not get back to Congress until 1894. The Cameron machine played rough with apostates.

Cameron was an undistinguished senator. He authored no major legislation and did little other than play partisan politics and protect vested interests and plutocrats. He voted for the conviction of President Andrew Johnson, and that vote was almost enough to cause national embarrassment.

In 1876 Cameron secured the post of secretary of war for his son, J. Donald, who, in turn, through his exceedingly skillful machinations, enabled Rutherford B. Hayes to win the presidency in that year's disputed election. Hayes, however, refused to reappoint Cameron's son. In a bold move, Simon Cameron resigned his Senate seat and had the Pennsylvania legislature give it to J. Donald, in what was called "The Cameron Transfer."

"Pennsylvania is Cameron's state, and there is no reason why the Camerons should not represent it in the U.S. Senate," the *New York Tribune* had said in 1874 when Simon initially thought that both he and J. Donald should be in the Senate together.

Simon Cameron's 12 retirement years were spent in leisure and travel, though he retained his interest in Republican politics. He was unhappy about criticism, but he was a much honored man nevertheless. Cameron County was named for him, as well as a coal town in West Virginia. Cameron, S.C. is named for J. Donald. Bucknell University awarded him an honorary doctorate, and he presented it with a gift of $1,000.

When J. Donald, a widower, married Miss Elizabeth Sherman, 24 years his junior, Cameron neglected to attend the wedding. She was the niece of Gen. William T. Sherman and Sen. John Sherman, and Cameron had never gotten along with Senator Sherman.

On June 19, 1889, Cameron was at his Donegal home when he was stricken with paralysis. He died on June 26 at 7:51 P.M.

"Neither fulsome eulogy nor ungenerous criticism befits the occasion of the death of one whose prominence for many years as a public character gives abundant opportunity to his friends to indulge in the one as well as to his enemies to excuse themselves for resorting to the other," the *Patriot* editorialized. He was a man, the paper said, who raised political disciples. "In the management and control of his party, General Cameron never had a rival. All opposition went down before his political skill. The Republican organization was as wax in his hands."

His body was brought by train to Harrisburg. At his mansion, he lay in an oak casket, garbed in a black suit and high collar, with a scarf of black silk tied under his chin. He had been a Harrisburger for 67 of his 90 years. Both the Harrisburg Press Club and his old Typographical Union No. 14, still in existence, sent flowers for their card-carrier.

The Rev. Dr. George S. Chambers, his long-time pastor at Pine Street Presbyterian Church, conducted the simple ceremonies on June 29. Cameron was buried in the large family plot at the Harrisburg Cemetery. He lies beneath an eight-foot granite stone whose inscription reads: "Simon Cameron, a printer-editor, Adjutant General of Pennsylvania, elected for four terms as Senator of the United States, Secretary of War, Minister to Russia."

J. D. CAMERON

J. Donald Cameron

. . . *The Forgotten Cameron*

J. Donald Cameron not only lived up to his father's expectations and served a duplicate 20 years in the U.S. Senate, but he put Rutherford B. Hayes in the White House and in his quiet way made the Camerons even more important to Harrisburg.

He was one of the six children of Simon Cameron who lived to adulthood, but he was the important Cameron after his father's retirement in 1877.

James Donald Cameron—but always known as J. Donald or Don Cameron—was born May 14, 1833, at Middletown. He went to school in Philadelphia and then on to Princeton, class of 1852. His first job was to clerk in his father's Middletown Bank, but within a few years he was president.

In 1855 he married Mary McCormick, the only daughter of James McCormick, a lawyer and president of the Dauphin Deposit and Trust Co. Don and Mary had eight children, six of whom lived to adulthood. Their lone son was James McCormick Cameron, who never had any children to carry on the direct Cameron name. Don's brother Brua had a son, so the male ancestry of Simon Cameron lasted another generation.

Don had three important brothers-in-law. Wayne MacVeagh, with whom he was close, was a liberal Republican and GOP state chairman as a young man. He eventually became President Garfield's attorney general, the third of the Cameron family to be in a president's cabinet. James Burnside was a judge in Centre County and kept the Northern Tier in the Cameron camp. He was killed in a fall from a carriage in 1859.

Richard S. Haldeman was the third brother-in-law. His father was the president of the Harrisburg National Bank and the founder of New Cumberland. Haldeman, two years older than Don, started the daily *Patriot*, served two terms in Congress and late in life was defeated for the State Senate by just two votes by John B. Rutherford. A Democrat, Haldeman was an outspoken opponent of Cameron Republicanism. He lived at Bunker Hill, north of Wormleysburg.

Don had five daughters. Mary Cameron remained unmarried. She was active in Harrisburg civic affairs until her death in October of 1959, and was the last Harrisburg Cameron to pass from the scene. Eliza married the son of U.S. Supreme Court Justice Joseph P. Bradley. It was Justice Bradley's vote and that of House Speaker Samuel J. Randall, a Philadelphia Democrat who was the son of a friend of Simon Cameron, which made Hayes the President in 1876. Eliza Bradley lived her last years with her sister Mary at 407 N. Front St.

Don in later life turned much of the business of the Cameron enterprises over to his son, James, and his grandson, Joseph Gardner Bradley. Bradley, a Harvard lawyer who died at age 89 in 1971, ran the Cameron mining interests in West Virginia, making them a three-county, 81,000-acre empire and achieving national headlines in 1952 for his bloody battle with John L. Lewis's United Mine Workers. At his death, a West Virginia editorial writer said: "He was the last of the old-time coal barons whose hideous handiwork will depress visitors to our state for the next 100 years, but whose personal integrity and sense of honor compels admiration nonetheless."

Don Cameron believed in laissez-faire economics just as much as his grandson, but he had a social consciousness. He and Wayne MacVeagh were among the founders of Harrisburg Hospital. He sought to attract industry to the city, developed experimental, low-income housing, gave the Cameron Extension to Harrisburg to start the park system, advocated the conservation of River Park, and had City Council rename 11th St. as Cameron St. in honor of his father. His Lochiel Farm is now the site of the Harrisburg disposal plant. The Harrisburg Area Community College is on other Cameron land.

While his father was preoccupied as a politician, U.S. senator, and Lincoln's secretary of war, Don Cameron ran the banking, manufacturing, and railroad interests. As president of the Northern Central Railroad, he expanded its line from Buffalo to Baltimore and south. With his brothers-in-law, Henry and young James McCormick, he developed the Pennsylvania Steel Co., later sold to Bethlehem Steel in Steelton, and the Central Iron and Steel Co. With the McCormicks as they expanded their ownerships in local bridge and traction companies, Don more than doubled the family fortune and by 1914 had established a $4 million trust fund.

In politics, Don had his father's ability, energy, and shrewdness, and was every bit as tight-lipped and secretive. He gave unstintingly of his time, his talent, and his money to the Republican organization. The Pennsylvania GOP ranks probably never had a more faithful worker. He is "as Republican as Paul was a Christian," the *Harrisburg Telegraph* said.

Don lacked his father's easy charm. Without his father's dramatic political career, J. Donald would never have earned recognition in his own right as a skillful manipulator.

Don and MacVeagh did much of the undercover work enabling Simon Cameron to win the senatorship from Gov. Andrew G. Curtin in 1867. This was the critical Cameron victory, the one which established Pennsylvania Republicanism for the rest of the century.

Don led the fight against the presidential nomination of James G. Blaine in 1876. That same year his father had President Grant make him secretary of war, a job Simon had failed in. But Don did not fail. The full story of exactly how Don manipulated southern votes against Samuel J. Tilden probably will never be known, but he was the key to the GOP triumph.

Hayes astounded everyone by not renaming Don as secretary of war. He wrote in his diary on March 14, 1877: "Cameron and Logan [John A., of Illinois], greatly urged all day. I told C [Cameron] I could not appoint him. Too many of the old Cabinet had good claims to remain, to recognize one, without appointing more would not be advisable."

Tom Scott, president of the Pennsylvania Railroad and a close friend of the Camerons, arranged a special train to carry Hayes from Ohio to Washington. The train was in Marysville, appropriately enough, on March 2 when Hayes was awakened early in the morning with the news that his presidency was assured.

Hayes probably was behind in his diary jottings. On March 10, two days after Simon Cameron's 78th birthday, the old senator announced his resignation, effective March 12. The night before, a Sunday, the Camerons entertained all the Republican legislators at the John Harris Mansion. Each legislator was confronted individually, with no opportunity to consult colleagues or constituents. The next day at 1 P.M. the Republicans caucused at the State Library, and by a vote of 131 to 1 the nomination went to Don. The joint ballot on March 20 was an easy 146 to 93 victory for Don.

"They make no fine pretenses of political morality they do not possess," the *Patriot* editorialized after the Republican caucus.

Like his father, Don spent more time in his two decades in the Senate playing politics than being a statesman. He was the Republican national chairman in 1880 and sought a third term for U. S. Grant, a family friend. True to Cameronism, Don believed a politician's first duty was to secure jobs for friends. He never neglected patronage.

Reticent, unemotional, but judicious, he worked in the anterooms, the committees, and the caucuses. Henry Adams called him "a lump of clay." After a rare speech of Don's that was interesting, Adams commented that either MacVeagh or Don's wife must have written it for him. He was a high-tariff advocate and, oddly enough, espoused the cause of free silver, the one stance of his that did not please many of his fellow Republican leaders in Pennsylvania.

Don was returned to the Senate by the Republican-controlled Pennsylvania Legislature in 1879, 1885, and 1891. In 1894 he was mentioned as a possible presidential candidate. It was not taken seriously, but rather it bothered him as "a troublesome tin-kettle tied to one's coattail," in Henry Adams's observation.

In January of 1897, though only 63, Don Cameron retired voluntarily. He was pressed to leave by an old henchman, the unscrupulous Matthew Stanley Quay, a native of Dillsburg who had a summer home near the Camerons' Donegal Springs home. Quay took Don's seat in the Senate.

Don's wife Mary died in 1874, before he became a senator. Four years later in Cleveland he married Elizabeth Bancroft Sherman, the daughter of an Ohio judge and the niece of Gen. William T. Sherman and Sen. John Sherman. Elizabeth was 21, titian-haired, vivacious, intelligent, and the Jacqueline Kennedy of her day. Don was 45, dull, and married to a woman younger than his oldest daughter. The result was very quickly an unhappy marriage.

The Camerons resided at 21 Lafayette Square in Washington, and Henry Adams, 40, a widower, lived across the park. "She is very young, pretty and, I fear, bored, and her middle-aged Senator is fighting a boss fight in Harrisburg. So she came on Friday, wailed about Harrisburg, and was quite frank in her remarks about men and things," wrote Adams early in his 40-year acquaintanceship with Elizabeth. As she lost interest in her husband, she gained interest in such friends as Edith Wharton, Henry James, and Adams.

Don and Elizabeth had a daughter, his sixth, Martha, born in Washington on June 25, 1886. There have been years of speculation, but Ernest Samuels, the Pulitzer Prize biographer of Adams, is certain that Don was the father and not Henry Adams, who was childless in his only marriage. Martha eventually married an Englishman, who became Sir Ronald Lindsay, ambassador to the United States. Ironically, she, her father, and Henry Adams all died in 1918.

Mrs. Cameron traveled much of the time and was in Paris when Don died. She stayed out of Harrisburg after that, and died in Dorset, England, in August of 1944.

Don Cameron spent his 22 years of retirement in business, experimental farming, and travel. He was among the first to introduce Jersey cattle into Southeastern Pennsylvania. Unlike his father, he dropped out of politics entirely. He died on Aug. 30, 1918, at Donegal. Services were held at his home at Front and State Sts., and burial was at the Harrisburg Cemetery near his father.

His son, James, took up the business interests, but had none of his father's or grandfather's enthusiasm for politics. He was handicapped by a hearing problem, which may have accounted for his being shy and soft-spoken. James went to the Harrisburg Academy, Phillips Exeter, and Harvard. He was rich, handsome, and an impeccable gentleman.

James did not marry until he was 62, in 1927, to a Harrisburg widow, Mrs. Anna Scott Robinson. For their honeymoon, they went to Europe. He was one Cameron not interested in travel, and it was his first trip abroad. Before his marriage, he lived with his sisters Mary and Mrs. Eliza Bradley at 407 N. Front St. After his marriage, he lived at 319 N. Front St. and at an estate he built at Kings Gap. James' wife died in 1944 and he died at 84 on Oct. 26, 1949, at Donegal, just as the other Camerons had.

VANCE McCORMICK

Vance McCormick

. . . *The All-American*

Vance Criswell McCormick, the last major figure in the Cameron-McCormick dynasty, was Harrisburg's most distinguished citizen for 45 years. He was the youngest and among the finest mayors the City ever had. He ran for governor in 1914, and was the Democratic national chairman for the re-election of President Woodrow Wilson in 1916.

He was an open, competitive, achievement-oriented "capitalist," as he bluntly described himself. In contrast to the taciturn and secretive Camerons, he was outgoing and was the rare idealist in the family, noted for its Scotch-Irish pragmatism and its German conservatism. He was patrician, but not an ostentatious man. A friendly, fashionable bachelor for years, he was a receptive man and not austere. One of his delights, for example, was to have his police friends to his Front St. mansion for a formal dinner.

Vance McCormick had a civic consciousness none of the other Camerons and McCormicks could match. He did not differ from them just by being a Democrat, but he was a Wilsonian progressive, believing in reforming the hard doctrines of property rights and government's subservience to business. His philosophy was not unlike that of Winston

169

Churchill, whom he knew in the 1920s and had as a guest to Harrisburg. He and Bernard Baruch were financial intimates of President Wilson.

Though progressive, McCormick was an old-line Democrat out of the Grover Cleveland wing of the party. He did not readjust his philosophy to the Roosevelt New Deal. As early as 1902, when he was mayor, he opposed a minimum wage law for City employees. Never in his politics did he receive much support from labor, and never did he seek it.

He was an ardent prohibitionist and refused to back Al Smith in the 1928 presidential election. The *Patriot-News* did not accept its first liquor advertisement until April of 1951, or almost five years after his death.

McCormick was born June 19, 1872, in Silver Spring Township, Cumberland County, the son of Col. Henry McCormick and Annie Criswell McCormick. His Aunt Mary was the first wife of Sen. J. Donald Cameron. His grandfather, James McCormick I, was president of the Dauphin Deposit Trust from 1840 to 1870. His father was president from 1870 to 1874 and his uncle, James McCormick II, president from 1874 to 1908. A distant relative was president then for four years, succeeded by Donald McCormick from 1912 to 1945. Donald was Vance's first cousin and his bachelor neighbor on Front St. It was Donald in 1913 who donated the 103-acre McCormick Island to the City.

Vance's father, Colonel McCormick (1831–1897), commanded a company of volunteers in the Civil War and almost lost his life in a mining exploration of the West. California Gov. John Bigler, a native of Perry County, invited the Colonel to stay, but he decided to return to Harrisburg, where he became prominent in business and public affairs.

Vance never had any children of his own. His older brother, Henry Buehler McCormick, married but never had children. The McCormick sister, Anne, remained unmarried. She died at age 85 in 1964, the last Harrisburg member of the Cameron-McCormick clan. Miss Anne was a dedicated civic worker. For 30 years she was a Girl Scout commissioner. She was active in the Community Chest, the Civic Club, and the Historical Society.

Vance had five bachelor McCormick first cousins, Donald, Henry, William, James, and Robert. Thus the Harrisburg family name of McCormick, like that of Cameron, lasted only three generations.

McCormick went to the Harrisburg Academy, and later he was a trustee for many years. He went on to Phillips Andover Academy and captained both the football and baseball teams.

He was at Yale from 1890 to 1893. He captained the freshman

football and baseball teams, and in his sophomore year was a varsity back on a team which won all its games without being scored upon. In the 19 to 0 win over Princeton, McCormick drop-kicked a field goal, which counted for five points in that era. In his senior year, McCormick was quarterback and captain. Yale won all 11 games and scored 435 points to its opponents' zero. On successive Saturdays, McCormick led his team to shutouts over Penn, Harvard, and Princeton, and Walter Camp named him to his 1892 All-American team.

The 5-foot-6, 185-pound McCormick was a teammate of some of football's immortals. End Frank A. Hinkey was All-American four times, guard Pug Heffelfinger, three times; halfback Bum McClung, twice, and McCormick, once.

McCormick was deacon of his Yale class and vice-president of the college YMCA. His classmates rated him "the most popular" and "the greatest social favorite." The yearbook commented: "The wind and the waves are always on the side of the ablest navigator."

In 1907 McCormick was awarded an honorary master of arts degree from Yale. He succeeded President Taft on the Yale Corporation in 1913 and served until 1936.

It was while he was at Yale that he registered as a Democrat and was vice-president of the Cleveland-Stevenson Club.

After Yale, McCormick returned to Harrisburg. He rejected offers from colleges and prep schools, but became the unpaid coach of the first Carlisle Indians intercollegiate team. His 1894 team won but one game out of nine, but in 1895 it won four out of eight games. McCormick helped start the famous football tradition at the Indian School which led to the exploits of Jim Thorpe in 1911 and 1912. He was succeeded as coach by his fellow Yale All-American, W. O. "Wild Bill" Hickok, who later became a noted Harrisburg manufacturer.

With the death of Colonel McCormick just before the turn of the century, Vance became a director of the Central Iron and Steel, the Dauphin Deposit, the Harrisburg Bridge Company, and other enterprises in coal, lumber, and railroading. But just being a corporate executive was not enough for Vance McCormick.

McCormick took his first step into elective politics in 1900, when he won a seat on Common Council as a Democrat from the Fourth Ward, which was always his voting district. His residence was at 301 N. Front St.

In 1902, at age 29, McCormick became a candidate for mayor, to succeed Dr. John A. Fritchey, a Democrat. Running with McCormick were John K. Royal, later mayor, for city treasurer, and William M. Gastrock for city assessor.

The Republicans also slated a young man, Dr. Samuel F. Hassler, 34, known as "Handsome Sam" and in later years distinguished for his work against contagious diseases.

The *Harrisburg Telegraph*, purchased by E. J. Stackpole in 1901, backed the Republicans, while the Orr family's *Patriot* supported the Democrats.

"Mr. McCormick is a rich man only in the sense that he has money," said the *Patriot*. "He works more hours every day than most men of less estate." Of the opponent, the *Patriot* editorialized, "Dr. Hassler is a genial gentleman, a good citizen and an excellent physician," but it intimated that he was not half the Harrisburger that McCormick was. The *Telegraph* countered for Hassler, "His opponents have tried to create the impression that he first saw the light of day at the North Pole or somewhere else far away from Harrisburg." Actually he lived only a few blocks from McCormick, at Second and State Sts.

The campaign's major question was the $1,090,000 bond issue for Harrisburg improvement, a historical effort which overshadowed the Democratic and Republican club rivalry in the City's 10 wards.

Both candidates supported the bond issue, but McCormick was the more outspoken. "Our town management may be afflicted with a malignant cancer but it needs other than a graduate and practitioner in surgery to get at its roots and draw the deadly poison," he said. Gov. William A. Stone spoke for the Republicans: "Let your bathtub run full of city water any morning without filtering it and then look at it. You might as well go down to the tannery and bathe in a vat. It might take your hair off, but you would come out clean. Debt is not a disgrace nor is it a serious impediment. It has always been and always will be the forerunner of prosperity."

To the tune of "Marching Through Georgia," the *Telegraph* printed a song: "When we stroll at the riverfront upon a summer's day, the perfume that we must inhale is not like new-mown hay."

Election day was February 18. McCormick won, 7,066 to 4,503, and the bond issue went through, 7,319 to 3,729. Royal defeated John J. Hargest. The Republicans, however, captured eight of the 10 seats on Select Council and 12 of the 20 on Common Council, while the School Board remained under Republican control.

McCormick took office on April 1, 1902, and guided the City through the most expansive era in its history until then. The filtration plant was built, limited flood control established, the park system expanded, the Camp Curtin School at Maclay St. opened, and other projects begun. The Reading Railroad Station was built. Meanwhile, the new State Capitol was under construction.

"The City was cleaned up morally and physically as fast as this active young man could bring it about," said Dr. J. Horace McFarland, one of the founders of Bellevue Park and a national figure in conservation.

In the first decade of the century, Harrisburg grew in population by 14,000, or to 64,186. It was the seventh largest city in the Commonwealth, only slightly smaller than Erie and Wilkes-Barre.

After one term as mayor, McCormick left office to devote himself to business, civic, and statewide political interests.

As mayor on Aug. 1, 1902, McCormick acquired the *Patriot*. He stated his purpose in print: "In politics it will be Democratic, representing the highest principles and best traditions of the party, but endlessly free from the control of any political faction or individual which conflicts with public good. . . . It will always unite with its newspaper contemporaries and all good citizens to increase the prosperity of our City and make secure its honor, its peace, its happiness."

The *Daily Patriot and Union* was founded in 1858 by Richard J. Haldeman, a son-in-law of Simon Cameron. Haldeman, a Yale graduate, two-term congressman, and a Democrat, was editor until 1865.

McCormick alertly founded the *Evening News* on Feb. 15, 1917, a week after the *Telegraph* absorbed the *Harrisburg Star-Independent*. It was the last of more than 40 major newspapers in Harrisburg's history. As it was McCormick's innovation, he was always especially concerned about it.

After McCormick's death, the *Patriot-News*, with a combined circulation of 84,000, was sold by his widow on Aug. 26, 1947, to Edwin F. Russell, 33, formerly with the *Newark Star-Ledger*. Russell became the Harrisburg publisher for newspaper magnate Samuel I. Newhouse of New York. On Jan. 19, 1948, the *Patriot-News* bought the *Telegraph*, and on Good Friday, March 25, the two sons of the late E. J. Stackpole announced that the next afternoon's edition would be the last. The *Telegraph* was founded in September of 1831 and went daily in 1856.

McCormick was still new in the newspaper business when he used his *Patriot* in 1906 and 1907 to help uncover the Capitol Graft Scandal. When the Democratic Party finished last in a three-way gubernatorial race in 1910, he set about recouping the fortunes of the party from their lowest ebb in history.

In 1912 McCormick was a delegate-at-large to the Democratic National Convention at Baltimore, playing a key role in the 46 ballots to get his friend Woodrow Wilson the nomination.

Two years later he courageously decided to run for governor, though only one Democrat since the Civil War had been victorious.

Teaming with President Wilson's progressives, McCormick in 1914 routed the Jim Guffey machine that controlled the hapless Pennsylvania Democrats. In the Commonwealth's first primary in history, May 19, McCormick won the gubernatorial nomination by defeating Michael J. Ryan, city solicitor of Philadelphia and a Guffey man, 47,034 to 22,-822. Cong. A. Mitchell Palmer was on the McCormick ticket and won the nomination for U.S. senator.

McCormick's platform was good roads, abolishing the county commissioner weak minority representation that often led to corruption, strong child labor legislation, civil service, woman suffrage, and more home rule. With the support of Teddy Roosevelt's Bull Moosers, McCormick attacked bossism, specifically "Penroseism." Subserviency in the Republican Party to Boies Penrose, he said, "was enough to make the judicious swear and the angels weep."

The Penrose candidate was Dr. Martin G. Brumbaugh, who was both Philadelphia school superintendent and president of Juniata College, a Pennsylvania German every bit as devout as McCormick. Brumbaugh claimed he had "no entangling alliances." He won by 135,325 votes, a margin provided by Philadelphia and Allegheny counties alone, though the Republican machine also carried McCormick's own Dauphin County. McCormick did win 46 of the state's 67 counties.

"I have made the best fight in my power for what I believe was the good of Pennsylvania," said the 42-year-old McCormick, "but the party in power (Wilson Administration) was made to bear the blame of business conditions due to the European war. This combined with the organized opposition of the liquor interests defeated me." Joe Guffey, the nephew of Jim, later claimed that the liquor interests put $600,000 behind Brumbaugh.

Forty years later in John O'Hara's novel, *Ten North Frederick*, a character said, "If Vance McCormick can stand up for the Democrats, I can stand up for our side." Joe Guffey in his memoirs commented on the McCormick era: "The Democratic Party in Pennsylvania was no place for an opportunist."

McCormick never again ran for elective office. In 1916 President Wilson named him Democratic national chairman, a post he held for four years. He rejected offers to be in the cabinet or be an ambassador, preferring to remain in Harrisburg. He served on the American War Mission to London and Paris. He was on the War Trade Board at $1 a year. He accompanied the President to Versailles as an adviser, and supported the League of Nations.

In 1920 the Wilson era was over. McCormick was a Democratic delegate to the 1920 and 1924 conventions, and then he dropped out of prominence in national politics. McCormick, however, remained a stout-hearted Democratic publisher to the end, though his community often was as much as eight to one Republican.

McCormick's first presidential endorsement, in 1904, was Judge Alton B. Parker over Theodore Roosevelt, a preference he wisely did not try to justify. William Jennings Bryan, James M. Cox, and John W. Davis were other losers he backed. Only in 1928 did he refuse to support the Democrat, and that was because of Al Smith. But McCormick refused to endorse Herbert Hoover either. In 1932 he went for Franklin D. Roosevelt, calling him "as good as Wilson." He backed FDR again in 1936, this time with the slogan "Better Off Under Roosevelt." He stated that FDR made the GOP look silly.

By 1940, however, McCormick had a change of heart. "The New Deal has not kept its word to abandon social and economic experiments which failed," he wrote in a November 4 front-page editorial. Almost to prove it himself, he listed 26 reasons why FDR should be turned out. The New Deal had not kept faith with McCormick's old-line Democratic idealism. For example, he disliked public housing. He was thinking in terms of non-profit corporation housing, a concept in which he was far ahead of his times.

For the Roosevelt-Dewey campaign of 1944, McCormick's last, the *Patriot-News* supported the Republican again. In succeeding national elections, McCormick's successors backed only one Democrat, incumbent President Lyndon B. Johnson in 1964.

Both McCormick and his first cousin, James McCormick Cameron, waited until they were 52 to marry. And they married widows. McCormick, two years older, wed Mrs. Gertrude Howard Olmsted on Jan. 5, 1925, while Cameron married Mrs. Anna Scott Robinson in 1927. The cousins otherwise were entirely different. "Vance talked all the time of being a Democrat," said a Harrisburger. "James didn't say a thing, and you knew he was a Republican."

Vance, who broke from Cameron-McCormick Republicanism, married into a family of true-blue Republicans.

Mrs. Olmsted, a native of Richmond, Va., was the widow of Marlin E. Olmsted, who represented Harrisburg in Congress from 1897 to 1912 and died in 1913. If McCormick's Democrats had not captured Congress in 1910, Olmsted and not Champ Clark probably would have succeeded the famous Joe Cannon as Speaker of the House. It was Olmsted, the first president of the Harrisburg Country Club, who broke Dauphin County's traditional two-term, rotation-of-office principle for congressmen. He was a conservative, highly successful corporation lawyer, with interests in lumbering, railroading, and real estate. McCormick had been an usher at his future wife's wedding with Olmsted.

Olmsted lived at 105 N. Front St. and would entertain President Taft and Joe Cannon, while up the street McCormick dined with Woodrow Wilson and Congressman Palmer. A common misconception is that Olmsted Airport was named for him. It was named for Lt. Robert S. Olmsted of Vermont, who was stationed at Middletown and was killed in a balloon accident in 1923.

The Olmsteds had five children. Their daughter Gertrude remained in Harrisburg and married Spencer G. Nauman, of the law firm established in 1871 by Simon Cameron's son-in-law, Wayne MacVeagh. Mrs. Nauman became a Distinguished Daughter of Pennsylvania and a founder of the Harrisburg Area Community College. A Republican, she won election to the Harrisburg Charter Commission in 1968.

Mrs. McCormick outlived Vance by almost seven years, and died at age 78 on Jan. 24, 1953. She was a national vice-president of the Girl Scouts and was on the board of the national YWCA. She was one of the organizers of the Harrisburg Symphony and the Art Association. She and Vance had their country home at Olmsted's Cedar Cliff Farms along the Yellow Breeches.

McCormick promoted all forms of municipal improvement. He encouraged professional planning, sponsored public concerts, backed such events as Kipona, helped organize what became the United Fund, and campaigned for the building of the Market Street Underpass, new high schools, paved streets, and the riverfront steps. He was on the boards of the Harrisburg Hospital, the Red Cross, the State YMCA, and Penn State, the latter from 1908 until his death. In his newspaper he fought the good, though often futile, fight against fraudulent elections, unfair property assessments, and what he, a Calvinist, saw as social immorality.

McCormick died at Cedar Cliff on June 16, 1946, at the age of 74. Services were conducted at his Pine Street Presbyterian Church, where for years he had been a lay leader. He was buried in the Harrisburg Cemetery near the other Camerons and McCormicks.

The Dauphin Deposit became the executor for the McCormick estate, and in 1964 the stepdaughters, Mrs. Nauman and Mrs. Jane Mc-Millan of Grosse Point, Mich., formed the Vance C. McCormick Fund. It and the Anne McCormick estate began making generous contributions to a variety of community enterprises, large and small. The Community College, founded in 1964, received grants to establish its campus at Wildwood Park. On April 1, 1969, the college dedicated its $1.5 million McCormick Library, in honor of the brother and sister. Mrs. Nauman said at the ceremonies that to her stepfather, Harrisburg was "always his home, always his love, always his first consideration."

ED BEIDLEMAN

Ed Beidleman

. . . Gubernatorial Hopeful

Of all of Central Pennsylvania's politicians, the most unfortunate was Edward Ensinger Beidleman. Twice Beidleman sought the governorship, and twice fate canceled him out. The third, and most assuredly successful, chance was to have come in 1930, but Beidleman died on April 9, 1929, and Gifford Pitchot went on to win.

When Beidleman's death at age 56 was announced, his old pal, M. Harvey Taylor, then chairman of the Dauphin County Commissioners, said, "God only gives you one friend like Ed Beidleman." Beidleman was Taylor's mentor, though he was only three years older than Taylor.

A different breed from the traditional Central Pennsylvania politician, Beidleman was not content to be a big fish in a small pond. He had the ambition to fight for high office and put his name before the Pennsylvania electorate. The Camerons never risked a statewide vote, and Taylor only did so once. Traditionally, Harrisburg Area politicians are too timid even to suggest they would be worthy of advancement, and they seldom espouse a cause greater than localism. It is a strange Harrisburg malaise. Beidleman was more forthright, and that might explain why the community had such affection for him.

Beidleman collapsed of a heart attack while giving a speech before the Parent-Teachers Association at Edison Junior High School. He had a second heart attack at home and died within a day at the Polyclinic Hospital. At his funeral in Pine Street Presbyterian Church, 3,000 Harrisburgers lined up to pay their respects. The Capital flag was flown at half-mast. All the streetcars stopped at 2 P.M. for a minute's silence. Virtually every fire bell in Dauphin County was tolled.

The old Courthouse, where Kresge's is today, had tolled its bell at the passing of Lincoln, Garfield, Cameron, and McKinley. Shortly before Beidleman's death, the bell had been removed from the belfry. President Judge William M. Hargest and Commissioner Taylor ordered it put back, and for the last time the Courthouse bell tolled—56 times for each year Beidleman lived.

Beidleman's death was such a surprise that a story spread that only a few weeks before he passed a medical examination to have his life insurance increased from $10,000 to $100,000.

A public campaign paid for a special headstone and underground vault for Beidleman and his wife at the Harrisburg Cemetery. An endowment was established for the maintenance of the gravesite.

Beidleman was a teetotaler and nonsmoker. He was addicted to soft drink, which he consumed by the gallons, and to hard candy, which he carried in his pocket and distributed to the street kids while he had his own mouth full.

His father was Tom Beidleman, who had a grocery store at Lochiel. Beidleman, born July 8, 1873, at Derry and 12th Sts., grew up knowing just about everybody on Allison Hill and in Shipoke. These were his constituents. In the early 1920s, when the community argued about the need for a new high school, Beidleman insisted that if Uptown Harrisburg got a school, then Allison Hill should have one too. This is why Harrisburg not only built two high schools, but both of them in the same year.

Beidleman won class honors at old Harrisburg High on Chestnut St. in 1892, and then studied law under Judge Samuel J. M. McCarrell, who introduced him to politics. In 1904, at age 31, Beidleman began two terms in the State House. He moved to the State Senate in 1912, winning election by only 462 votes. This was the year of the Bull Moosers, and former President Theodore Roosevelt was very popular in Harrisburg. Beidleman was a regular, but he had his name also listed in the columns for Roosevelt candidates and for decoy third parties cunningly established by the Pennsylvania GOP organization. The result was that Beidleman picked up a critical 934 votes from the Bull Moosers and 130 from the Progressives and won, even though on a straight-ticket basis he polled fewer votes than either the candidate of Roosevelt's Washington Party or the regular Democrat.

For one session in the State Senate, Beidleman was president pro tempore. Taylor, who was later to hold the post for a record eight sessions, got on Beidleman's staff payroll.

Every morning Beidleman held what he called his "war board" in the drugstore at the Penn-Harris Hotel. He drank his soda pop and talked politics with the boys. Then he would walk down Third St. to his law office, and every favor-seeker in town would besiege him. The stroll was Beidleman's politics at its best. He practiced law with Arthur H. Hull and Thomas D. Caldwell, and was a fine defense attorney and an excellent counsel for the streetcar and railroad companies. Juries had a habit of voting Beidleman's way, and judges never seemed to be unsympathetic to his requests.

In his public life, he belonged to virtually every club in town. He and Taylor were leaders in the campaign that raised $750,000 to build Zembo Mosque.

Beidleman was conservative, but as a legislator he authored the railroad full-crew law, the streetcar motorman-conductor law, and workmen's compensation. His private secretary was a black man, W. Justin Carter, a local lawyer. Beidleman was so popular with the blacks that he pleaded with a ward leader once that he not be given every vote, but he was. "They love you too much to listen to reason," the ward heeler explained. Beidleman, however, never agitated for black civil rights, nor did he support woman suffrage. As Dauphin County boss, he did bring an end to the local breweries' contributing free beer to the Republican picnics, but then he did not drink beer.

Beidleman was lieutenant governor from 1919 to 1922. He was Boies Penrose's choice to run for governor in 1922, but Senator Penrose died on Dec. 31, 1921, a week before he was to announce that the Harrisburger was the man. The result was that Pinchot broke the organization and became governor.

The way was clear in 1926, but the GOP had its worst fight in history. Bill Vare defeated incumbent Sen. George Wharton Pepper and Governor Pinchot in the fraudulent U.S. Senate primary. Beidleman, now on Vare's team, was cheated in the gubernatorial. The vote was John S. Fisher, 652,944, and Beidleman, 634,521, with Cong. Tom Phillips and former Gov. John K. Tener sharing 128,502 decisive votes. Beidleman had the state by 13,325 votes, until Allegheny County turned in a delayed 31,748 plurality for Fisher. Though Fisher would never discuss the matter, Beidleman probably was counted out in Pittsburgh, with his paper ballots floating down the Ohio River. That is the confession Taylor got at the 1928 GOP national convention from a drunken Allegheny County politico. Before the count-out on the night of the election, Harrisburgers paraded by Beidleman's brick house at Market and Evergreen Sts. for a victory celebration.

After the 1926 primary defeat, Beidleman was never the same man. Ironically, he never lived through the Fisher Administration.

M. HARVEY
TAYLOR

Taylor-made

. . . The Master Politician

Maris Harvey Taylor personified the modern history of Harrisburg. An unrivaled success for decades, he mirrored in personality and philosophy the majority of his constituents. With few exceptions, he knew what his people wanted and how much they would pay for it.

He ran the political family and was called, appropriately enough, "Pop-pop." He devoted 70 years to active politics, 46 of them as an elected official. He holds two Pennsylvania records, for being Republican state chairman for 16 years and for being Senate president pro tempore for 16 years also. In addition, he has the Dauphin County record for serving 24 years in the State Senate.

"I was ambitious, naturally," he said in 1970, "but I claim this—I was always honest. There isn't anybody in Pennsylvania that can say they had to put the 'fix' on Harve. I'm proud of this."

Theodore H. White, author of *The Making of the President* series, visited Harrisburg in 1964 to see Gov. William W. Scranton, a presidential possibility. White chatted with Harve Taylor and emerged flabbergasted. "Why he's straight out of *The Last Hurrah*. I didn't think people like this existed anymore," exclaimed White. "He's a piece of Americana. He should be in the zoo with the buffalo."

Beneath the cracker-barrel, aw-shucks exterior of the boy from Shipoke was a shrewdness that was both deceptive and occasionally overrated. Obviously a man of high intelligence and native wit, Taylor would joke, "I'm not a college graduate and don't know the right words." He brushed off his competitiveness with, "I like people. Never

180

go to bed hating anybody." And he explained his conservatism with, "You don't buy a piano when you can't pay your debts."

"The trouble with writing about Harve," observed veteran reporter John Scotzin in 1963, "is that you can't get him down on paper. His folksy way, the inflections in his voice when he just makes a speech—and he can make great speeches—and that wink of the eye are the improbable talents of the man that don't show up on paper."

When he first ran for the State Senate in 1940, Taylor attempted to elucidate his philosophy:

"I believe in sound, clean, honest, economical, progressive, constitutional government, the kind the Republican Party has given to Harrisburg and Dauphin County and is now giving to Pennsylvania. I was born in Harrisburg and have lived here all my life. All that I have, or hope to have, for myself or those dearest to me, is dependent upon the welfare and prosperity of this community as a whole. My personal interests are as one with those of my neighbors."

Newspaperman Hiram G. Andrews, of Johnstown, a year younger than Taylor and three times Democratic House speaker, made this assessment:

"Years ago this writer wrote an article about Taylor in which we contended that he would have to make a choice, deciding whether he wanted to be a statesman or just a politician. He decided that he wanted to be a politician. He has been in the Senate many years, but there are no legislative crusades, no important legislation, with which he has been prominently identified throughout the years.

"Many of the men who sought recognition by means of their legislative accomplishments aren't with us anymore. Taylor, however, remains [in 1963] a part of the legislative picture—not because he is an economics specialist or an expert in the realm of fiscal legislation. Taylor remains a part of the Harrisburg picture, not because he has studied legislation, but because he has been the most astute student of human nature that Dauphin County, or the State of Pennsylvania for that matter, has produced during the present century."

As much as any man, Taylor built Harrisburg from a provincial urban area into one of the nation's largest state-government complexes. A spoilsman with abilities and instincts that matched Simon Cameron's, Taylor created jobs and spread them among the faithful. He gave his electorate uncommonly low taxation for decades, in part because his city hall and county courthouse were never adventurous on public projects. At the same time, he bargained for privileges for local and statewide business interests that will endure long beyond his death, many of them still hidden from view and others now institutionalized as an accepted relationship between government and commerce.

He estimated he got at least $30 million in state money sent Dauphin County's way while he was in the Senate. The favors—or "turning stones," in his words—that he did must be infinite.

Major scandal, flagrant vulgarity, overly harsh tactics, and a "public be damned" attitude were never a part of the Taylor operation. Cunning, a rough player and yet principled, Taylor was Calvinistic enough to want nothing of the Boss Hague or Jim Curley image or methods.

For more than half the Taylor years, Dauphin County was as vice-ridden as many counties in Pennsylvania. Fraudulent voting, payoffs, and fictitious registration names were not uncommon. Yet the favoritism, the arm-twisting, and the quiet part of the Taylor machine operation were, in an important matter of degree, at a far higher standard than practiced elsewhere in communities with similar one-party domination. Even when the Dauphin County GOP's behavior was outright objectionable, there was little sustained criticism of it and virtually no serious opposition.

After Taylor left elective office, the local Pete Wambach Gridiron Show always concluded with a 12-verse song, "Oh Where, Oh Where Has Harve Taylor Gone?" The chorus expressed the sentiments of the Taylor community: "The common folk want to know, / Since Harvey's gone everything is wrong, / Oh, where, oh where did he go? / For 60 years we were in a rut, / Things weren't awfully good, /When politicians said 'Kiss my butt,' / At least you knew where you stood."

Taylor never lived in any other community, and he rarely left Harrisburg, even for vacations. Numerous times he could have had himself elected to Congress. "I'm never ashamed, like some I've heard about, but proud to say I'm from Harrisburg whenever I visit the big cities," he said when he was eighty. "I love this town where I was born. My favorite song is 'Dear Old Harrisburg, I'm Strong for You,' by Tom Francis." For New York Timesman Homer Bigart covering the Harrisburg 8 Trial, he described Harrisburg as "a pretty well-settled community," but he was anxious that orthodoxy not be misinterpreted as dullness. "Mr. Taylor noted, with a sly wink, 'You can have fun in this town,'" Bigart wrote.

He never regarded himself as a "political boss," but rather as a chairman of the board. The bosses, in his way of thinking, operated in the big cities and were always Democrats.

Two aspects of the Taylor legend that he himself especially encouraged were his winning ways and his longevity.

For 18 years Taylor went to the Kentucky Derby with his friends from the Pennsylvania Railroad. It was his trick to lay bets on all the horses in the featured race, making sure he would have a winner and his friends could say, "There's that Harve again." On the first day of the Pennsylvania lottery, Taylor came up with three tickets making him eligible for the $1 million drawing. As John Scotzin observed, it was classic Taylor strategy to have plans A, B and C, so as to "always be able to fall back and still win something he wanted."

A three-drink man and a firm believer in "you're just as old as you think, not as old as you feel," Taylor always seemed to be the senior man in any crowd. No contemporary national politician came anywhere near duplicating his geriatric feats.

In the early 1960s Al Clark, sports editor of the *Patriot-News*, pleaded with Taylor to have the state permit interscholastic basketball in the Farm Show Arena. "Over my dead body," snapped Taylor. "The terms are acceptable," Clark answered. Taylor laughed, switched his vote, and made it possible.

Taylor got a relatively late start to reach elective office, not making City Council until he was 30. He was not a state senator until he was 64, but he lasted until he was 88. He made it to his mid-90s with the zest of a man half that age.

"Always paid my church dues in advance," was his explanation— and that's true; he paid in December for tax purposes. At age 80 he took a physical examination for a $10,000 life insurance policy and passed "with flying colors." Said Taylor, "The doctor told me that I was good to 100. That's pretty encouraging when it comes from an insurance doctor."

A month after his 94th birthday, it was reported he suffered a heart attack. Newsman Duke Kaminski telephoned him.

"I don't know where they got that crap," shouted Taylor. "I wasn't in any hospital and I didn't have a heart attack. Politicians know I haven't got a heart—just a gizzard. I'm in fine shape. As usual, I was the first one into the office this morning. My heavens, that's the worst piece of misinformation."

Kaminski took the opportunity to ask the invariable question as to what he attributed his robust life:

"Women, as I told Jack Bell of the Supreme Court not too long ago," answered Taylor. "But I suppose it's moderation in all things. I still like a drink occasionally. Better make that regularly. Bourbon's my favorite. I like its after-taste. Scotch is only a perfume. I take a beer or two every now and then. I'm not going to stop drinking when I get a kick out of it. It's a stimulant and good for me. Of course, I lay off for a day or two after getting one too many to clear out my system.

"I like to eat, particularly shell fish, but here again I never have too much at one sitting. Breakfast for me is a glass of orange juice, but I eat often the rest of the day.

"I have no truck with medicine, although late at night I may pop a Tum into my mouth to settle my stomach. I have no trouble sleeping.

"Be sure to tell my friends that I'm as well and ornery as ever."

He was an iron man, 5-foot-11, 172 pounds and trim, who laughingly outlived the longevity tables.

Harve Taylor was born June 4, 1876, a month before the American centennial and the same year as Willa Cather, Jack London, and Konrad Adenauer. He was born at 115 Conoy St., a half-block from the Susquehanna, in the first ward of Shipoke, or South Harrisburg. Down the street was the Harris Park Elementary School, his only alma mater.

He was the second child of Morris C. and Catherine Rishel Taylor, natives of Lancaster County. His older brother, B. Edward, became a businessman and eventually was a city assessor. William, Charles, Mame, and Sara were the other children. Taylor's father worked at the nearby Chesapeake Nail Works, later Central Iron and Steel. He gave his son the middle name after Capt. John C. Harvey, the paymaster at the mill.

As a schoolboy, Taylor had as many as three newspaper routes at one time. "Hard work never hurt anybody," he admonished in his later years. "That's the whole secret of living."

He left grade school at age 12 to take a 66-hour-a-week job with his father at Central Iron, laboring first in No. 2 mill but eventually becoming a clerk. The elder Taylor and the father of W. Harry Baker, prominent statewide GOP leader, were puddling foremen together at the mill. Harve worked for Central Iron for 24 years.

Young Taylor was an excellent athlete. He played on Harrisburg's first YMCA basketball team and was a halfback in sandlot football. For the 1901 Harrisburg Athletic Club, he was the star southpaw pitcher, noted for fastballs rather than curves. Paid $2.50 to pitch for a Harrisburg fire company, Taylor defeated Gettysburg's southpaw Eddie Plank, a year older than himself. In one game at Island Park, Taylor three times worked a fake wild-pitch play with his catcher to pick runners off base. Once he pitched for the Harrisburg Academy, though he wasn't a student there. Vance McCormick rewarded him with a bottle of ginger ale and let him shower instead of bathe in the river.

Taylor was lefthanded in everything but penmanship. He blamed that on his grade school teachers who forced him to write righthanded.

While living on Bailey's Row, Taylor married a neighborhood Shipoke girl, Bertha May Shertzer, on Sept. 15, 1897. They had two children, Dorothy, who married Lewis G. Kraybill, later courthouse superintendent, and Stewart, who entered the insurance business with his father. Stewart has a son, M. Harvey II, and the Kraybills a daughter, Francis. There are three great-grandchildren, including M. Harvey III. All the Harveys happen to be lefthanded.

The Taylors had an exemplary marriage that lasted more than 65 years. Though never in the public eye, Mrs. Taylor remained the adoration of her husband. As Taylor chuckled to audiences, "She used to say, 'Be a good boy and don't look at the girls.' Now she says, 'Watch what you eat.' " In her final years when she was hospitalized, Taylor never missed a day visiting her.

At age twenty-two in 1898, Taylor started in politics by being elected to replace his father, a school director, at the GOP county convention. His fellow mill workers had wanted Taylor to buck the organization, but his father advised, "Don't break up the organization. Try to break into it." Said Taylor later on, "From that minute, I have been a regular Republican, sticking to the organization at all times, never leading any independent movements."

Harve Taylor announced for public office for the first time on Jan. 26, 1907. With no opposition in the First Ward Republican primary, he ran for City Common Council. On general election day, February 19, he led the ticket with 431 votes, 100 more than a fellow Republican, George G. Young, a grocer who also was elected, and 230 more than Democrats Gustave Hanson and Joseph B. Pollock.

Prior to the election, the *Harrisburg Patriot* asked the 20 Common Council candidates if they would accept free passes from the Central Pennsylvania Traction Co. Taylor was one of nine who refused to answer.

Taylor took office on April Fools Day of 1907, at the age of thirty. His first vote was against spending $65,000 for a 54-inch sanitation dam, and Taylor's vote made the difference as the dam was defeated by one vote. Actually, as an old swimmer in the Susquehanna, he personally wanted the dam, but his Shipoke constituents were convinced it would cause a flood.

He stayed in Common Council until 1912, when he was elected to the higher chamber, Select Council, to succeed his boyhood friend, Harry F. Sheesley of Shipoke, who had taken Taylor's father-in-law's seat. Sheesley went on to head the City Ash and Rubbish Bureau for 30 years.

Taylor was a Select Councilman until 1913, when the new salaried, five-man, single-council form of government for third class cities was ordered by the State Legislature. He then became a regular councilman, as well as superintendent of parks and public properties. During his two years in this post Taylor became an avowed progressive. He was so energetic that it cost him the 1915 election, teaching him a lesson about his neighbors' penchant for conservatism that he never forgot.

"The thing I still have the greatest pride in," he noted 41 years later, "was that I took over to get all those elm trees planted you've seen on Front St. That's the one thing I am proud of, that and the Hardscrabble."

Hardscrabble was a three-block area of tattered frame houses and shacks on the riverfront, from Herr to Calder St. It was the neighborhood of the "river rats," families as poor but much more slovenly than those of Taylor's Shipoke. Taylor carried his fight through the courts to get Hardscrabble razed. In October of 1914, condemnation proceedings were completed. Where once Hardscrabble stood, the Sunken Gardens and the park greenery are.

Taylor also got a bridge for the Cameron Parkway, a new entrance to Reservoir Park, the first community playgrounds, and began to modernize the fire department by getting rid of three horse-drawn apparatuses. Meanwhile, the tax millage rate dropped from 9.5 to 9.

The 1915 election was held November 2 for four seats in Council. Taylor ran sixth in a field of eight candidates, polling 4,570 votes but needing 250 more to retain office. He lost despite one-sided support from the Stackpoles' *Telegraph*. Taylor's referendum for a $60,000 fire apparatus loan passed by 4,442 votes. Curiously enough, the day before the election, half the Sylvan Heights orphanage burned down and 119 girls were led to safety. Considerable damage would have been avoided if the fire-fighting equipment Taylor wanted had been available.

Though a junior politician, he left office with an unusual tribute. Taylor Boulevard along Reservoir Park was named for him.

While a councilman, Taylor joined Zembo Temple in 1913, nine years after it was chartered. In 1929 he was building chairman for the $850,000 Zembo Mosque and three years later was potentate, a post his son Stewart later held in 1940.

After he was defeated, Taylor established his insurance and surety business, initially with his brother Ed and then with his son. He named the firm "M. Harvey Taylor and Son" before Stewart was out of Penn State. The company prospered. Taylor did both private and public business, and as late as 1968 his firm was the agent for virtually all of Dauphin County's liability, casualty, and comprehensive insurance. On Capitol Hill, he kept an eye open for the interests of his profession. After his 1964 defeat, Taylor was made the state's insurance broker of record by Governor Scranton, but he turned his commissions over to the Association for the Blind, his favorite charity, for people "who can't see sunshine."

After his Council defeat, Taylor was out of office four years. County boss Ed Beidleman, though only three years older than Taylor, was Senate pro tem and named Taylor the clerk of the Senate.

In 1919 Beidleman, then lieutenant governor, selected Taylor to run for county recorder of deeds. "That was my big political break," Taylor said later. "I walked away with it, after people told Beidleman that I couldn't win." Taylor defeated D. W. Shaffner, the Democrat, by 9,030 votes.

The county recorder in those days was paid by the fees he collected. They propelled Taylor into the middle class. He sent his son Stewart off to Penn State. After 48 years of living in Shipoke, he bought a house on Second St. Though on the way up, Taylor did not forget his old neighbors. "Mostly the poor get in trouble," he said when in his nineties. "The rich are just as bad, but too smart."

After being recorder, Taylor was named chief county clerk. Upon the death of Henry M. Stine in 1925, Taylor became a commissioner. He was re-elected for two full terms. In 1928 he attended his first GOP national convention as an aide to Beidleman, carrying the "prescriptions," or illegal liquor, for his friends. Taylor subsequently was a delegate to eight national Republican conventions. In his last election campaign, the primary of April 25, 1972, the 95-year-old Taylor sought to be the oldest delegate at the Nixon convention, but he suffered a surprising defeat. He lost Dauphin County by 202 votes, and thereby lost the congressional district by 129 votes.

As a county commissioner from 1925 to 1935, Taylor directed the building of more roads than had been constructed in any previous period. He ran a remarkably conservative county for one which was urbanizing rapidly. In 1934 he proudly proclaimed that after 149 years Dauphin County had a debt of only $1,114,500, or about $55 per capita in the midst of the Depression. Taylor also kept the county and city Republican during the New Deal.

Commissioner Taylor developed a personalized political machine, with people who knew the vote in all 153 precincts, knew how to raise funds, and were committed to Dauphin County Republicanism and Harve Taylor himself. "You can't win elections without courthouses, city halls and township offices," he said. "I'm dedicated to the proposition that all men are created equal—if they are Republicans." With good-naturedness towards friends, severity towards enemies, and gusto at all times, Taylor collected such able lieutenants as Robert E. Woodside, Thomas J. Nelley, Bill Cunningham, Carl B. Shelley, Dr. William

K. McBride, Homer Kreider, Joe Demma, Charles Barnes, Dr. James K. Lowen, and Oscar Lingle. A high percentage of the prominent bankers, lawyers, and physicians, as well as the leading families like the Baileys, Doutrichs, Wilsbachs, Halls, Stackpoles, Reilys, and Kunkels were close to him. He was the true "game politician," playing for power and affection, in a definition offered by political scientist Arnold A. Rogow, a native Harrisburger.

As Taylor broadened his statewide influence, he developed ties with politicians such as Henry Lark, Mickey Watkins, Jim Duff, Bob Fleming and George I. Bloom. He was particularly close to Bill Reiter, vice-president of the Pennsylvania Railroad and its chief lobbyist; Harry Davis, the lobbyist of the Pews' Sun Oil, and John Sollenberger, of Hershey Chocolate interests.

After Ed Beidleman's untimely death in 1929, an informal triumvirate was formed to manage the Dauphin GOP. On it with Taylor were Alex S. Cooper, the State Senate librarian, and Sheriff William W. Caldwell, the grandfather of Judge William Caldwell and former State Rep. Thomas Caldwell.

Taylor emerged the sole leader after winning a rugged primary fight on Sept. 15, 1931. Caldwell and Cooper, with the support of Governor Pinchot, formed "The New Republicans" to battle Taylor's candidate, George Hoverter, for a third term as mayor. Taylor was running again for county commissioner under the slogan "Honorable, Honest and Upright." Unquestionably, forged poll tax receipts for the privilege of voting were issued by both sides, because 36 ballot boxes were held for recount, but Taylor's team won by almost 4,000 votes.

With the backing of millionaire reactionary Joseph M. Grundy of Bristol, Taylor became state Republican chairman in 1934. He left it in 1937 after being at odds with oilman Joseph N. Pew of Delaware County, but regained it from 1942 to 1954 after managing the gubernatorial campaign of Edward Martin.

As GOP chairman in 1934, Taylor made his one bid for statewide elective office. He sought the post of secretary of internal affairs, but the Democrats behind George M. Earle swept the election. Taylor lost to Thomas A. Logue, of Main Line Philadelphia, by 86,638 votes, even though Republicans had a 1.25 million registration lead. Taylor had a 55,279 registration advantage in his home county, but carried it by only 14,764 votes. He lost Cumberland County by 1,279 votes, but the West Shore did not stay stalwart Republican during the New Deal as the East Shore did.

In 1940 the State Senate seat from Dauphin County was open and Harve Taylor took it for himself. In 1936 George Kunkel, a conservative Democrat, son of former Republican Judge George Kunkel and the second cousin of Cong. John C. Kunkel, had become the first Dauphin County Senate Democrat in 80 years. He wisely declined to risk his luck again in 1940, even though it was another Roosevelt presidential year. Kunkel settled for four terms as minority county commissioner, winning elections with Taylor's quiet support.

Taylor and George N. Wade of Camp Hill both entered the State Senate in 1940. Wade drew seat 33 and Taylor seat 34. Wade, never close to Taylor and with different political ties, outlasted Taylor into the 1970s, though he never rose to the leadership positions that Taylor did.

Taylor was re-elected senator five times. He became president pro tempore in 1947 and held the post a record 16 years. No one in Senate history, dating back to 1791, was pro tem for more than two terms. The job is one of the most powerful in Pennsylvania. Not only is its holder second in line for the governorship, but it has the privileges of selecting committee chairmen, scheduling legislation, running patronage, guarding the contingency fund, and being the focal point of the lobbyists' attention and generosity.

A power in closed-door caucuses, where the real work is done, Taylor played a major role in pushing through Governor Duff's conservation package, blocking Governor Leader's tax program, and furthering most of Governor Scranton's desires in 1963 and 1964.

"To me Harvey was simply a formidable opponent who had the capacity to veto almost any legislation that would be passed in the House and come to the Senate," recalled George M. Leader in 1972. "As a matter of fact, he had in an indirect way, a powerful influence in the House as well. We did an investigation on the distribution of insurance commissions. The amount of money distributed by Harvey to Republican candidates was considerable; so that by the time they came into Harrisburg as legislators or senators, they had someone who had already demonstrated his friendship in a rather substantial way. This doubtlessly was one of the real contributing factors to his power."

With skill, positioning, and power, Taylor got patronage jobs for Dauphin County, advanced friends to judgeships, protected favorite interests, cared for the apparent wishes of a majority of his constituents and, above all, serviced the needs of his Republican Party. As a Senate member of the General State Authority, he had an additional power of the purse. He fought for the extension of the Capitol complex and saw to it that state rentals went to the right people.

"I'd rather be a senator than president of the United States," he once said. As Senate president pro tem, he led a Republican cut of $58 million from Governor Lawrence's budget, shouting, "No more gravy for Davey." Lawrence quipped back, "Most of you will agree with me that probably the best qualified man in Pennsylvania to discuss gravy is Senator Taylor."

Taylor's finest term as Senate leader was his last one, in 1963 and 1964, under Governor Scranton, whom he called "the smartest damn governor I ever saw" and whom he vigorously backed for the Republican presidential nomination. Contrary to his reputation as a conservative, Taylor pushed Scranton's sales tax to 5 percent. Getting Republican support and noting that each of the 45 Philadelphia Democrats in the Legislature had voted against it, Taylor lashed out when he inscribed the bill, "They want millions for the city but they refuse to help raise the money to balance the governor's budget. As far as I'm concerned, they'll get scant consideration from me. In fact, we'll make it all even and give them nothing."

Scranton delighted in Taylor. "Of all the traits and characteristics of him, the greatest is loyalty," the governor said in 1963. For Taylor's birthday in 1964, Scranton threw a lavish party at Hershey.

Scranton told *Fortune* magazine in 1964:

"One must realize that politicians are persons—personalities. They're not likely to have strong ideological convictions. But I knew Taylor was absolutely loyal to Governor Duff, and yet Duff's program was as progressive as we've had in modern times. I knew it wasn't so important— his being a reactionary—if (1) you liked him, and he knew it, and (2) if the thing you were asking wasn't political suicide. Taylor is very much of an individual. The key to him is that he's 87 years old and has never been defeated. He doesn't want to go out of politics or retire in defeat; he has an unlimited pride in this. He knows I like him—I do, very much—but I never ask too much of him. If he can't do something, I don't hit him over the head."

They did part company briefly when Taylor objected to the Constitutional Convention, which was killed in 1963 before it was accepted in 1967. "It wasn't the Constitution that he was against," explained Scranton. "All he cared about was that he'd be alienated from some political leaders and his sources of power."

Taylor's vivid personality, as much as his power, brought him ample rewards.

In 1951 the Senate, with Taylor abstaining, voted to name the north bridge over the Susquehanna for him. Taylor in 1943 had first sought the Forster Street bridge project. The Taylor Bridge opened Jan. 24, 1952. Standing in the chilly winds, Taylor exclaimed at the dedication, "It's embarrassing for me to talk. I don't deserve this compliment. It's damn embarrassing." The irony is that in John O'Hara's 1948 novel about Harrisburg, *A Rage to Live*, a character wins the mayorship because he has an obsession that a bridge be named for him.

Prior to the 1968 GOP national convention, Taylor was a Nixon man, when many Pennsylvanians were for Nelson Rockefeller. Presidents Hoover and Eisenhower had had Taylor visit them in the White House, so on June 16, 1969, President Nixon had him back, along with former Gov. John S. Fine.

The old Shipoke boy considered it one of the great moments of his life.

"I said I wanted to sit in the President's chair so I can tell my great-grandchildren about it—I have three, you know. So we all went into the Cabinet room and I sat in the President's chair. Now isn't that something for a man of 93? But remember, young fellow," he said to the national reporter, "we didn't ask for anything. We just talked about old times. The President said it's a real joy to meet two wonderful friends. Now isn't that something? You know, when a President says that, it's something."

Slyly, holding back his smile, Taylor added, "There were a number of intimacies about certain events I prefer not to mention."

The 45-minute visit was at noontime. While campaigning in Pennsylvania in 1968, Nixon had said to Taylor, "When I'm President, you're going to have breakfast in the White House." Taylor replied, "I don't eat breakfast."

Harve Taylor made numerous mistakes in his 33 years as Dauphin County Republican leader, but his organization was strong enough and he was quick-witted enough not to lose the public's trust. Order, conservatism, political favors, and no nasty scandals were what the public demanded, and what the Taylor organization provided. No national or state figures came out of the Taylor machine, but none was expected.

The challenge to Taylor's leadership came not from the weak Democrats but from within the Republican Party, and inevitably—contrary to the public's assumption—it was from a more conservative faction against Taylor. Ideological conflict, however, played no role. Taylor's politics were personal; so the politics against him were personal too.

The Fighting Five offered Taylor the most trouble.

In 1948 Walter M. Mumma opposed Taylor in the Senate primary. Mumma, a native of Steelton, was a county row officer just as his father had been. He founded Pennsy Supply and became a millionaire. At age 50 he decided to take on the 72-year-old Taylor. With the aid of such businessmen as Ben Wolfe and future trucking tycoon John Hall, the likeable Mumma formed a legislative ticket. Two businessmen, O. B.

Lank and Bill Lenker, and two young lawyers, James H. King and Robert Knapp, would seek Dauphin County House seats against the Taylor men. Thus was the name "Fighting Five" born. The Taylor machine survived the assault. Taylor himself defeated Mumma by 1,150 votes.

In 1950 the Fighting Five surfaced again. This time the statewide GOP was having one of its most glorious brawls. Joe Grundy and G. Mason Owlett pitted Harrisburg's Congressman Kunkel against Governor Duff for the U.S. Senate. Duff's choice for governor, John S. Fine, was challenged by millionaire Jay Cooke. Running for lieutenant governor on the Kunkel-Cooke ticket was George N. Wade. Mumma joined forces on that ultraconservative ticket by slating himself for Congress.

The Fighting Five billed itself as "a crusade against the 'Taylor nod,' " meaning his handpicking of candidates. "May 16 will mark a new era in Dauphin County politics because it will forever end the power of this political machine and restore confidence in the complete honesty of local elections," asserted Ben Wolfe.

Duff and Fine prevailed, but this time the Dauphin insurgents elected Mumma, as well as Edward S. Swartz. Mumma defeated J. Calvin "Haps" Frank by 8,118 votes, and Swartz of Hummelstown defeated incumbent R. Dixon Herman for his legislative seat. Herman went on to a distinguished career as a county and federal judge, while Swartz had a brief state career and ended up a right-wing spokesman in the late 1960s.

The "Taylor nod" was not disturbed. Although Mumma replaced Kunkel in Washington and Kunkel lost favor, following Mumma's death in 1961, Taylor let bygones be bygones—as he seldom did—and sent the gentleman millionaire Kunkel back to Congress. Even this had a sequel. In 1968 the youthful county chairman, Robert F. Smith, was challenged for his post by Robert M. Mumma, the Congressman's son. Now Taylor was in Bob Mumma's corner to topple his successor as county chairman, but Mumma lost by a county committee vote of 196 to 104.

Nobody, even with money and connections, could either control or make a permanent enemy of Taylor.

One of Taylor's worst blunders occurred in 1961 when he forced Republicans to accept Col. John Mc.I. Smith for judge. The Young Republican organization did not want the seventy-one-year-old Smith, who a decade earlier had been with the Fighting Five and was beaten in the GOP primary for judge by the hard-campaigning Homer L. Kreider. It was an embarrassing loss for Taylor when Lee F. Swope, forty, a capable lawyer from a distinguished Harrisburg Democratic family, nudged out Smith to be the first elected Democratic judge in the county's history.

"The United Republicans" emerged the following year, organized by Jim King of the Fighting Five, attorney John J. Shumaker, and Haps Frank, once a Taylor stalwart. The aim of the "United Arabs," as they came to be called, was to capture the grass-roots strength of the Taylor organization and put the county committee in new hands. They made no headway, however. Only maverick candidates could ever defeat a Taylor selection. To challenge him for precinct control was equivalent to staging a revolution, and Taylor's machine proved too broad-based and aggressive to permit that.

The only Democrat ever to successfully buck the Taylor GOP, Lee Swope was right in his timing and correct in his analysis that the Taylor establishment could be caught off guard only when the opposition was cordial, moderate, and of impeccable credentials. The previous year, 1960, Swope had challenged Taylor for the State Senate, calling him "the local untouchable." Vice President Nixon spoke on Market Square, and at the occasion Taylor described Sen. John F. Kennedy's qualifications for president as being "white teeth, a smile and gobs of money." Swope quipped back, "This would not disqualify Senator Taylor—if you're willing to count store teeth." A year later, Swope left his humor and punches at home, and he won against Colonel Smith. "It has been demonstrated in the past that you can't successfully hold up Taylor as an evil genius in Dauphin County," he observed. "The people seem unwilling to accept that line as a basis for voting Democratic."

The end of Harve Taylor the master politician came on April 28, 1964, when he was beaten by an almost unknown amateur Republican in what used to be controlled primaries in his own Dauphin County. And it was not even close. William B. Lentz, forty-three, a real estate broker in upper Dauphin County, swept by Taylor with a 3,249-vote margin. Lentz captured 82 of the 90 suburban and rural districts.

Taylor carried Harrisburg by 3,454 votes. In one of the last great efforts of his life, Charles A. "Nibs" Franklin gave Taylor a 640-4 lead in the black Sixth Precinct of the Seventh Ward, but such lever-pulling could not overcome the anti-Taylor sentiment outside the City.

The Taylor organization suffered more than just one defeat. It was opposing Blaine C. Hocker, the colorful Oberlin legislator since 1947 and a long-time Taylor crony. Hocker had pushed an in-lieu-of-taxes state payment bill for Taylor's beloved Harrisburg, but the old senator helped kill it in the Senate out of loyalty to Governor Scranton. There certainly was more than this disagreement, but Taylor backed William Landis, a Hershey teacher. Landis finished last, and Hocker led the legislative ticket. "I have nothing personally against Blaine. He was a good member," Taylor said prematurely.

The loss was a bitter blow to Taylor, especially because he had preplanned the ending of his career. In 1959 he said he would retire from the Senate in 1968, but Lentz advanced that schedule by four years.

"I don't think I was a poor loser," Taylor later commented. "I could have won this fight. It's my own fault. I didn't even have a (campaign) card printed. I want the blame to go on me for losing it. I was so busy looking after Scranton's interests in the Legislature that I didn't pay attention to my own."

Some of the reasons for the Taylor crash were just bad luck.

The Hershey interests closed the 26-year-old Hershey Junior College, which joined the new Harrisburg Area Community College. The M. S. Hershey Medical Center was started. But feelings were strong among Derry Township citizens, angry over the loss of their free college.

Three days before the election, the Harrisburg School Board announced it would tax commuters $5. Though the tax never went through and though Taylor was not the least responsible for its suggestion, it was an issue that hurt him.

But essentially the downfall was of Taylor's own doing.

His refusal to support the popular Blaine Hocker for his tenth consecutive legislative victory backfired. Precinct workers felt alienated from the eighty-seven-year-old chief, who often seemed more of an autocrat than a public servant. The League of Women Voters had to print, "Incumbent, failed to reply," because Taylor would not answer two questions.

Bill Lentz came to Taylor to see if he could run for a legislative seat, but Taylor refused to see him even though he was the nephew of the late Jimmy Lentz, who had been a county commissioner with Taylor. A former Millersburg councilman, Lentz was more conservative then Taylor, but he had more rashness in one finger than all the better-financed but only garrulous opponents of Taylor for decades had had in their entire bodies. Lentz announced on Jan. 23, 1964, and started his handshaking campaign at the Colonial Park Plaza. In all, he spent $3,-657.17, of which $17 went for lollipops to give to kids.

The day after the election, April 29, the joke in Downtown Harrisburg was, "Quite a tie-up this morning on the William B. Lentz Bridge." Governor Scranton was asked about the Taylor defeat. "You never really know the tallness of an oak until it is chopped down," he said sadly.

GEORGE WADE

Senator George N. Wade

... *Political Broker from the* *West Shore*

The indomitable George N. Wade of Camp Hill established a Pennsylvania Senate record in 1972 when he won his tenth election at the age of 79. Hospitalized for 18 days before the balloting, Wade had to make do with the public's memory of his 50 years of politicking, the last 32 of them as a state senator. Every corn soup supper he ever attended paid off. It was easy. Wade won by a margin of 10,560, or 56 percent of the vote, even though his age and health were against him.

Long in the shadow of Harrisburg's M. Harvey Taylor, the West Shore's Wade never received the attention he should have had as a colorful personality and an astute client-serving legislator. In many ways, Wade has been the epitome of the Central Pennsylvania politician.

No one in the 180-year history of the State Senate ever served longer than George Wade. He did it by being a political broker of unusual skill. Behind him were such clients as the Pennsylvania Manufacturers Association, the truckers, the insurance industry, the bankers, the veterans organizations, and other lobbies. For years he had ties with Roger W. Rowland, Mason Owlett, James Malone, and Woody Musselman of the PMA, plus the backing of the affluent families and the business and professional leadership in Cumberland County. Winning reelection was never difficult.

A natty dresser, he was the showpiece of the Senate. In his prime, he had a keen wit, a sharp memory, and an energetic style. "He's an old smoothy," said reporter John Scotzin. "He keeps a cool head and you can't get him upset. And he is one of the Legislature's hardest workers, very conscientious." Well into his 70s, he remained in topflight condition at 175 pounds. He could touch his toes without bending his knees, and often kept a schedule of 15 speaking engagements weekly.

His politics essentially was that of client-serving. Unlike Charles B. Penrose of Carlisle, the state senator who was the grandfather of Boies Penrose, Wade never got involved in national politics. Unlike Harve Taylor, he seldom had much to do with statewide Republican policy. He saw his job, rather, as that of brokering for those who enabled him to be a senator. A businessman himself, he was a business politician.

Oddly enough, Wade never won a top leadership position in the Senate. In 1967 he came closest but lost the post of president pro tempore by one vote in the Republican Senate Caucus. Taylor had held this powerful post for 16 years, and Wade wanted it dearly. But Wade had his compensations. In the heyday of Republicanism, Wade was chairman of the Highways Committee for 12 years and presided over record-making building programs.

Though a party regular and a deep conservative in matters other than patronage, Wade was flamboyant on occasion. His stand against radar policing of traffic speeders made him famous, though he waged an equally outspoken fight for toll-free bridges—and the $18 million Route 81 interstate bridge over the Susquehanna is named for him.

Wade's duels with Governor James H. Duff, quite a battler himself, made the sparks fly. Duff was anti-PMA, so Wade attacked his 1949 housing program as an example of a "streamlined, silver-streaked spending spree," making Duff's red hair stand on end. In the bitter 1950 GOP primary, Wade was the PMA-supported candidate for lieutenant governor. He lost to Lloyd Wood, by 281,484 votes, but did better than Harrisburg's Cong. John C. Kunkel, who had challenged Duff for the U.S. Senate nomination.

In 1962 Wade, at the age of 68, was the first Pennsylvania Republican to declare himself available for the governorship, but the bid went to William W. Scranton. Later Wade called Scranton the "most effective politician" Pennsylvania has had in the governor's office.

Wade was a master at political give-and-take. In 1972, for example, he angered some when he awarded his state senatorial scholarship as a prize in the annual Cumberland Valley beauty pageant. But he recouped popularity quickly when the Pennsylvania Rifle and Pistol Association endorsed him for re-election, citing him as a supporter of "constructive gun legislation," meaning no legislation at all. On the troubled issue of no-fault insurance, Wade cunningly aided the opponents of the measure while not endangering his public image. In tactical politics, Wade was as good as they come.

Wade was a self-made man with not even a high school diploma. He later received an honorary degree in law, while his son became a veterinarian and his grandson, George N. Wade III, earned a doctorate in physiological sociology. Wade could joke that each generation had a doctorate.

He was born August 13, 1893, in Emlenton in Venango County. The third of nine children, he grew up on a farm. At age 16 he went to work in the oil fields at $1.72 for a 12-hour day. Then he moved to the bituminous mines and greased coal cars. Uncles of his operated the old Pennsylvania Business College in Lancaster. They got their nephew to help remove the steeple of St. John's Reformed Church, which they had purchased for the school. For payment, they gave Wade free tuition. After this education, Wade served in France during World War I, then worked at the Hershey Creamery in Harrisburg, and finally drifted into the insurance business, where his quick mind and easy disposition assured his success. For 20 years he ranked third or better nationally in sales for the Ohio National Life Insurance Company. He also headed the Camp Hill Bank for more than 15 years, and in the first 18 years of the consolidated Cumberland County National Bank and Trust Co. was its chairman of the board.

American Legion activity got Wade into politics. He joined C. Wright Stuart, Harry Day, and Wilbur Arbegast as young Turks to take on Cumberland County GOP leader Caleb Brinton, and eventually won control. Wade served first on the Camp Hill School Board, then on Borough Council, and in 1930 made it to the State House. His closest general election came in 1932 when he needed Prohibition votes to win by 1,062.

In 1936 Carlisle's Robert Lee Jacobs, then a 26-year-old Democrat and now Superior Court judge, was elected to the Senate from the West Shore. Jacobs did not run for reelection in 1940, and Wade, seizing the opportunity, won a tough primary fight and then defeated Hermas L. Weary by 1,924 votes. That victory put him on his way, and he became an institution in the Pennsylvania Senate.

Simon Girty

. . . *Snarling Renegade*

Simon Girty, in truth or fiction, must be the nastiest character to ever come out of Central Pennsylvania. A villain, a scoundrel, a blackguard, a butcherer, a traitor, a cad, a renegade, and a degenerate, he lived his entire life with a snarl on his face and a curse on his lips. Many a pioneer's child was put to bed with the admonition, "Now hush, or Simon Girty will get you."

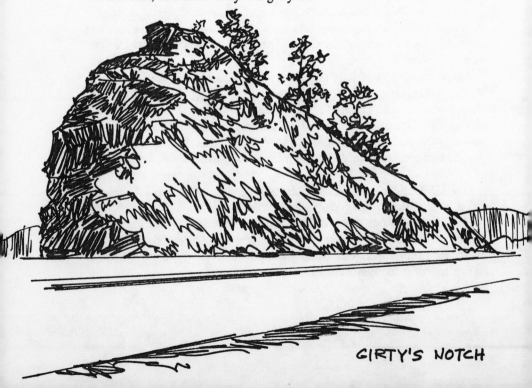

GIRTY'S NOTCH

Girty was made part of that infamous jury that Stephen Vincent Benet concocted for "The Devil and Daniel Webster." Benet, a native of Bethlehem who spent his boyhood summers in Carlisle with relatives, had Girty in the jury box as "the renegade, who saw white men burned at the stake and whooped with the Indians to see them burn. His eyes were green, like a catamount's, and the stains on his hunting shirt did not come from the blood of the deer."

Zane Grey and Thomas Boyd used Girty in their stories. In Dale Van Every's frontier novel, *Bridal Journey*, Girty blew his nose into his fingers, as the Indians did, and then advised, "When you want Indians to hanker fur war, it's allus best to let 'em work theyselves up good. And nuthin' slaps the ol' pepper to 'em like givin' 'em a captive to burn." With that said, the dark-browed, ill-natured Girty went back to chomping on his stubby clay pipe.

To Theodore Roosevelt in *The Winning of the West*, Girty was "of evil fame, whom the whole West grew to loathe, with bitter hatred, as 'the white renegade.' " He was "the most inveterate foe of whites."

Girty had the credentials to be thoroughly loathed. He was a traitor to the American cause, the friend of the savage Indians, and the employee of "Hair-Buyer" Henry Hamilton, the scalp purchaser. With better luck, Girty and his Indians would have wiped out Daniel Boone, George Rogers Clark, and even the infant Richard M. Johnson, the future vice-president under Martin Van Buren. One raiding party did murder Abraham Lincoln's grandfather and almost killed his father. And Girty's barbarity and that which he inspired in his Indian companions was not mere hearsay in the Ohio Territory and Kentucky. He himself had at least seven white scalps to his credit.

The Rev. John Heckewelder, a Moravian missionary to the Delawares in Central Ohio, saw Girty during one of his uncontrolled moods and reported: "Never before did any of us hear the like oaths, or know anybody to rave like him. He appeared like a host of evil spirits. . . . No Indian we had ever seen drunk would have been a match for him." To the parson, Girty was simply a "wild beast in human form." Oliver Spencer, a captive boy of the Shawnees, said Girty was "the very picture of a villain." His fiendish laugh, thin lips, sunken dark eyes, medium build but thick neck, the bright silk handkerchief he wore to cover a scar across his forehead, his silver-mounted pistols, Indian garb, bronzed features, and his usual hard-bitten scowl marked him as the epitome of evil.

Thus it is not surprising that Simon Girty's notoriety has endured through American fiction and nonfiction. Even the occasional revisionists have stumbled when trying to clean up Girty's dirty image. The name itself has its connotations, like Gravel Gerty, the comic strip character of the early 1950s.

His story is interwoven with legend, for the illiterate Simon Girty left no records, had no Boswell, and simply did not care about his historical standing, while at the same time his tall tale-loving frontier opponents needed a genuine villain and no mere scamp to embellish their triumphant history.

Miscreant that he was, however, Girty was not without virtues. He certainly was courageous, persistent, and loyal to the Indians with whom he cast his lot. He never cheated the red men, and that in itself is remarkable for an American of his era.

Though occasionally foolhardy, Girty always displayed the strength, cunning, and personal integrity the Indians demanded of a leader, and pale-face Girty often was given the honor of leading many Indians of various tribes into battle. Best of all, Girty was not a charlatan, or a demagogue, or a crazed revolutionist with an obsession for ideology. He simply was a scoundrel.

He was a blackguard because he switched cultures and opposed his country's willful assumption of manifest destiny. He is remembered because he had a lust and a talent for the slashing guerrilla warfare the Indians favored. And he is exceptional because over a long career of 15 years as a marked man he was too clever to be caught. Girty froze to death at 77, depriving hundreds of frontier braggarts of the revenge they vowed they would enjoy.

Simon Girty was born in 1741, the same year as Benedict Arnold, supposedly on January 16. He was born on the frontier, somewhere near Halifax. His father was a liquor-loving Irish immigrant with an Indian trader license and the reputation of a cheat. His mother was an English girl who had little luck either keeping her husband sober or providing a proper home for four boys.

When Simon was 10, his father was killed in a tavern brawl near Fort Hunter, which did not become a stockade until 1754. Conrad Richter used the locale for his frontier stories set in the era 1753 to 1764, though the present Fort Hunter dates back only to 1814 when Archibald McAllister erected the gray stone mansion with dormers. Girty's father was tomahawked by an Indian named "The Fish." A friend, John Turner, thereupon murdered "The Fish," and not long afterwards Turner married Widow Girty.

When the Indian wars came, Turner removed the Girtys and his infant son, John Turner II, to Fort Granville, now Lewistown. The Indians raided the fort, captured the family, and headed for Kittanning on the Allegheny River. There Turner was burned at the stake while

Simon and his brothers were forced to watch. The oldest son, Thomas, escaped and went to Fort Pitt. He is the only Girty to turn out right. He died at 81, a prominent Western Pennsylvania citizen. Girty's Run on the Allegheny is named for Thomas.

The Indians divided the Girty family, sending Mrs. Girty, young George, and infant John Turner to the Delawares, James to the Shawnees, and Simon to the Senecas. In later years, George and James joined older brother Simon to prey on the white man. George is said to have died drunk in the Ohio Territory during the War of 1812. James died in Canada the year before his famous brother.

Simon spent three years with the Senecas, becoming the best Indian linguist on the frontier. He not only spoke like the Indians, but he thought like them. Fine clothes, land of his own, orthodox religion, and other middle-class values—Girty disdained them all.

In 1758 Gen. John Forbes took Fort Pitt, and the following year Girty left the Senecas and headed there to be an interpreter.

Those are the facts of the youth of Simon Girty, but legend has other versions. Uriah J. Jones, a printer with the old *Patriot and Union*, in 1846 wrote a delightful but far-fetched biography, *Simon Girty, The Outlaw, An Historical Romance*. It was published by A. Monroe Aurand, Jr., of Harrisburg, and still makes great reading. Eighteen years after he wrote the book, Jones, just 46, was run over and killed by a train at the Harrisburg railroad station.

Jones sees the 5-foot-9 Girty as a cutthroat of near epic proportions, a Paul Bunyan of desperadoes. He claims Girty was born in Switzerland of a rich family, received "good moral instruction and an excellent education," and came to America when he was 21 and "for a year or thereabouts, like a gilded butterfly, he fluttered in the gay and fashionable circles in the Atlantic cities, envied by the men and admired by the women for his intelligence and great personal beauty."

When Girty tired of the city girls, in Jones's imaginative account, he supposedly moved to Girty's Notch on the Susquehanna's west bank, and there at that rock abutment organized a gang of robbers. Girty's Notch today is the only monument to Simon. Jones wrote, "Girty's Notch became the scene of many a robbery and cruel cold-blooded murder until the name of Simon Girty not only spread terror through the land, but caused the provincial government to set a price upon his head." The truth is probably that the most villainous acts ever committed at Girty's Notch are those of this era, when state troopers flag down speeding motorists on Route 11-15.

Girty's unpleasantries would have ended if he had married Edith Plunkett, says Jones. Miss Plunkett was the daughter of a regimental surgeon, Dr. William Plunkett, and the niece of the founder of Harris-burg, John Harris II. She though Girty was really "Mark Stedman." When she learned differently, she wrote a "Dear John" letter, which on Oct. 25, 1748, Girty (whom Jones has much older than other historians have) is supposed to have read. Wrote Miss Plunkett: "Thy name is infamous, and thy hands are reeking with human gore. . . . May God turn you from your erring path before it is too late, is the prayer of the heart-broken Edith." Jones says Girty reacted to the jilting by becoming even more evil. He joined with the Indians to defeat Gen. Edward Braddock, and it was here that he learned that dry wood is best for burning captives. Jones surely steps into the realm of pure fiction when he claims that Girty was on hand to crush Braddock.

At Fort Pitt, Girty was highly regarded as an interpreter, but he also was a carousing troublemaker and at least on one occasion there was a warrant issued for his arrest.

In Lord Dunmore's War against the Indians in the Ohio Territory, Girty joined forces with George Rogers Clark, Simon Kenton, William Crawford, and Col. Andrew Lewis. After the war he returned to Pitts-burgh and had difficulty earning even 50 cents a day at interpreting. At least once he was jailed.

When the Revolution came and Girty failed to be commissioned a captain, he turned renegade. On the night of March 28, 1778, he joined Alexander McKee and five others to head west for the British and their Indian allies, the Wyandots, Delawares, Shawnees, and Miamis. McKee was 6-foot-3 and the son of an Indian squaw. His father was a Pennsyl-vania Scot who had been a friend of Girty's father. An ugly, big-nosed man, McKee was totally ruthless. Teddy Roosevelt writes that actually McKee was a more able renegade than Girty, though he never achieved the fame. McKee came to a violent end. After the Revolution, he raised a stag and the animal gored him to death.

Girty, McKee, and their companions arrived at the British headquar-ters in Detroit in June of 1778. A few days later Pennsylvania officially labeled Girty a traitor and put the price of $800 upon his head. Girty is supposed to have been delighted when he learned he was worth that much.

Girty served as an informer to the British and an adviser to the Indians. The warriors trusted him implicitly, often inviting him to sit at their councils. He spoke their tongue, matched their courage, and called himself "Captain Girty." When he took part in the raids on forts and stations in the Ohio Territory, he worked as hard for scalps as any of his colleagues. Only once did he have trouble. He and a Mohawk named Captain Brant got into a drunken argument over who was the greatest warrior. Brant hit him across the forehead with his sword, and Girty was incapacitated for a few weeks.

Girty's brutality was well known; yet there was a streak of kindness in him. Henry Baker, just 18, was captured with 10 Virginians near Upper Sandusky. The others were scalped but Girty persuaded the Indians to spare young Baker. The famous frontiersman Simon Kenton was caught stealing Shawnee horses. Big, handsome Kenton, 14 years Girty's junior, had fought with Girty in Lord Dunmore's campaign. "Girty and I, two lonely men on the banks of the Ohio," said Kenton, "pledged ourselves one to the other, hand in hand, for life or death, when there was nobody in the wilderness but God and us." Chief Cornstalk had Kenton run the gauntlet eight times and three times blackened his face and tied him to the stake. But Girty did not forget an old friend and helped Kenton escape. On the way back to Kentucky, the incorrigible Kenton stole a few more horses just to make the episode profitable.

In the winter of 1781–82, American forces massacred Delawares at the Moravian shelter of Gnadenhutten, meaning Tents of Grace. Col. William Crawford followed this atrocity, for which he was not responsible, with an invasion and was captured. The colonel was tortured for three hours. He was still alive, with his flesh scorched and his ears cut off when he was tomahawked and his bloody scalp thrown in the face of captive Dr. John Knight, his regimental surgeon. Dr. Knight later escaped and reported that Girty stood by enjoying the dreadful scene. Crawford, who Uriah Jones says once refused the hand of his daughter to Girty, is supposed to have cried, "Girty, Girty, shoot me to the heart and end this torture." Girty laughed back, "How would I shoot you? Don't you see I have no gun?" It is the Crawford incident in June of 1782, more than any other, which earned Girty his lasting reputation as an archfiend.

After Crawford's 500 mounted volunteers were repulsed, Girty gathered the Indians northeast of what is now Cincinnati. As historian John Bakeless, a native Central Pennsylvanian, relates in his biography of Daniel Boone, Girty urged the Indians to invade Kentucky: "Were there a voice in the tree of the forest, or articulate sounds in the gurgling waters, every part of this country would call on you to chase away these ruthless invaders who are laying it waste. Unless you rise in the majesty of your might and exterminate their whole race, you may bid adieu to the hunting grounds of your fathers—to the delicious flesh of the animals with which they once abounded and to the skins with which you were once enabled to purchase your clothing and your rum."

Girty was in command when the Indians attacked Bryant's Station in northeastern Kentucky. Huddled in the stockade were 44 riflemen, including Boone. One of these sharpshooters aimed at James Girty, but that villain was saved by the stolen leather strap attached to his powder horn. Both the attack and siege failed. Fire arrows, including one which landed near the cradle of Richard Johnson, did not scare the frontiersmen into surrender. Simon Girty tried diplomacy, but was rebuked by young Aaron Reynolds, supposedly the foulest mouth in the fort. Reynolds shouted to the outlaw that he owned two dogs, one named Simon and the other named Girty.

Girty eventually withdrew from Bryant's Station to fight again in the Battle of Blue Licks, just north of Carlisle, Ky. It was here that Boone's son Israel was slain and Boone almost tomahawked in the bitterest fight he ever remembered having. Reynolds was captured, but before he could be tortured he overpowered an Indian guard who stooped to tie his moccasin. Reynolds knocked out the Indian and dashed away dressed only in a shirt. In later years, Reynolds joined the Baptist Church, gave up swearing, became a model citizen, and thanked Simon Girty for influencing his conversion.

The Indians took 60 scalps at Blue Licks but lost 64 of their warriors. This meant that four white prisoners must die. The five captured were told to sit on a log and stretch out their arms. Then four were stabbed and the fifth released, as Girty proclaimed that his forces had won the battle.

In one engagement, Girty had a band of Indians hide on the banks of the Ohio near Louisville while he cried "Help." When the whites came to the rescue, 24 of them were slaughtered. One pioneer, Peter Malott, escaped by swimming, but his wife and daughter Catherine were captured. Catherine was adopted by the Delawares, and four years later Girty, twice her age, married her. The Girtys had at least three children, Ann, Thomas, and Sarah.

After the Revolution, Girty tried farming near Amherstburg, across the Detroit River in Canada, but his heart was not in tilling the soil. In 1790 he joined with Little Turtle of the Miamis, Captain Pipe of the Delawares, Tarhe the Crane of the Wyandots, Blue Jacket of the Shawnees, and young Tecumseh to go on the warpath and turn back a force of 1,500 Americans. The following year there was another Indian victory. Girty ordered Gen. Richard Butler scalped, and the Indians gave him three captured cannon as a prize.

In the spring of 1793, President Washington sent three commissioners to negotiate with the Indians of the Northwest Territory. Taking Girty's advice, the Indians demanded that the Ohio River be the boundary of the United States. The president then dispatched "Big Wind" Mad Anthony Wayne with a well-trained force, including Simon Kenton as a scout, to subdue the Indians. That is what Wayne did decisively at Fallen Timbers, near Toledo, on Aug. 20, 1794. Girty was close by, but not in the battle.

The day the American forces arrived in Detroit, Girty waited until the last minute and then plunged his horse into the river and crossed into Canada. "May I breathe my last on the field of battle," he exclaimed, but he never did. He was grayed and rheumatic, no longer agile, and with dimmed eyesight when the War of 1812 came. Kenton on a government pension of $20 a month tried to visit him, but failed. And Girty got angry with his wife and for a time she left him. Always a heavy drinker, he retired to the tavern of his son-in-law.

At this point, Uriah Jones's narrative is interesting, though pure legend. Jones claims that Edith Plunkett married a man named Mayland Clayton. Girty then stole Edith away, forcing her to live with his Delaware mistress, Nuschetto. When Edith tried to escape in a canoe, Girty tomahawked her. Clayton searched for Girty for two decades, finally finding him in 1818 as an old man. Girty had turned religious, but a Jesuit, hearing only half his confession, left him in horror. Then Girty was on his knees in prayer saying, "Oh, God have mer—," when a bullet pierced his brain. Mayland Clayton stepped from a hazel bush and exclaimed, "Villain, I swore an oath to be revenged on you for blighting a flower of innocence, and my vow was registered in heaven, which has given me power for 20 years past to pursue you. Ha! Treacherous, murderous villain, my revenge is glutted and I am satisfied." At that, Indians fired a dozen bullets into Clayton. The dying Girty rolled over and said, "I forgive you, my fate is just."

The real ending was not that exciting. Girty, on a British pension, outlived almost all his old foes and comrades, a villain no more but only a shell of a man. He died during a snowstorm in mid-February of 1818. His Canadian neighbors, some of them Indians, had to hack frozen ground on the northern bank of Lake Erie to bury the greatest renegade of them all.

CUMBERLAND
COUNTY PRISON

The Legendary
Lewis the Robber

... *The Noblest Highwayman*

Though social propriety and moral rectitude are the
hallmarks of the Central Pennsylvania value system, Lewis the Robber
in the past 150 years has evolved into a genuine folk hero.

Lewis achieved much of his popularity in his own day and since because of his disdain for public officials. Even in today's enlightened era, residents of Cumberland County do not think highly of politics as a profession; so Lewis was only capitalizing on the sentiments of his community.

"If there was any class or description of people in society whom I would sooner have robbed than any other, it was those who held public office," he wrote. "Against such workers of iniquity my mind had taken a set, and I was determined never to spare them on any occasion that offered." Furthermore, Lewis was certain that Carlisle and all of Cumberland County had more "official marauders" per capita than anywhere else; so he saw it as his public duty to do much of his robbing in his native county.

Thus Lewis became a Robin Hood, stealing from the rich and giving to the poor. Dr. Mac E. Barrick has pointed out that Cumberland County in the early 1800s was at approximately the same stage of development and settlement that Missouri was in the post-Civil War era of Jesse James, another folk hero. Dr. Barrick, a native of rural Cumberland County, is the leading authority on Lewis the Robber. Formerly a professor at Dickinson College, he now teaches at Shippensburg State College and is past president of the Pennsylvania Folklore Society. He became interested in Lewis the Robber, in part, because his own family has lived in Cumberland County since 1790 and because he married into an old family whose ancestors were cronies of Lewis.

In the folklore about Lewis is the story that he went to rob an elderly lady in Perry County, getting there just before the tax collector. He heard her complaints, held back, and robbed the tax collector. Up in Mifflin County he was robbing another old lady. She owed $20 to the constable. Lewis gave her the money, had her get a receipt from the constable, and then robbed the constable of $60.

Supposedly he once caught a ride with a fellow headed for the Carlisle Fair. He was all set to rob him, but listened to his hard-luck story and just said good-bye with an "I'll keep ya in mind." In the Newville area, Lewis prepared to rob a family but heard them praying. "I couldn't rob them people after that," he said.

David Lewis was born in Carlisle on March 4, 1790. His father moved the family to Northumberland County, then died when David was 6. Lewis enlisted in the militia at age 17. He deserted and would have been executed if his good mother had not pleaded for his life. He then sawed his way out of a ball and chain to escape from the brig at the Carlisle Barracks, heading for caves along the Conodoguinet and a life of rollicking crime. He quickly became such a rogue that he won the affection of most of his Cumberland County neighbors.

He lived only 30 years, with 13 of them in the field of crime. He did some counterfeiting for a New York gang. He was imprisoned in Troy, N.Y., but with the help of the jailkeeper's daughter, Melinda, he escaped. Shortly afterward, he married Melinda. When he died, she and the family were living in Philadelphia. "I entertained for Melinda as pure a passion as ever warmed the breast of man," he wrote in his confessions. "The lovely girl had not only won my affections, but she had completely secured my gratitude and gained my confidence. Although vicious myself, I respected and admired virtue in her." He worried about them, and would not have been a folk hero if he were unmindful of the wife and kids.

Lewis made his various headquarters at the Doubling Gap Hotel near Newville, at Sterrett's Gap, in a log house on Carlisle's Hanover St., in a hut on South Mountain, and in a den near Pine Grove Furnace. Essentially he was a highwayman. He was always courteous to the ladies. He had virtue, heroism, gallantry and, of course, a sense of humor. He said that if the Legislature had given enough money to the schools, he would have gotten himself some learning and would not have had an "ill-spent life."

The dramatic end for Lewis the Robber came in 1820. He and a pal named Connelly were caught burglarizing a neighbor's house in Cumberland County. They were thrown into Carlisle Jail for the night of April 19, and the next day they were transferred to Chambersburg Jail, supposedly one of the most secure in the state. Lewis and Connelly, however, escaped from Chambersburg, just as they had done at Bedford and other prisons in Pennsylvania.

On the run, Lewis and his colleague headed up into Centre County. They robbed a wagon on Seven Mountains and were trailed by a posse up the Driftwood Branch of the Sinnamahoning Creek. There they were caught in a gun battle with the law. Connelly was slain and Lewis was shot in the right arm. Rather than have his gangrene-infected arm amputated, Lewis died in Bellefonte Jail on July 13, 1820.

The day before he died, Lewis the Robber signed a confession. It became a best-seller of sorts, and later was reprinted in such books as *Life and Adventures of David Lewis, the Robber and Counterfeiter*, published in Newville in 1890.

The Central Pennsylvania mind can be inscrutable. It can be dreadfully realistic while at the same time accepting the most farfetched rumors and inaccuracies. The legend of Lewis the Robber is mostly hokum, but it is well-aged and amusing hokum. There are far worse delusions than to believe that Lewis the Robber was a Robin Hood.

Lincoln in Central Pennsylvania

BARNARD'S LINCOLN

. . . As President-elect, at Gettysburg,

a Martyr

Abraham Lincoln gave his last major speech before becoming President in Harrisburg. He came to town on Washington's Birthday, Feb. 22, 1861, by train from Philadelphia on route to the nation's capital for his inaugural. He spoke to the Legislature and, since he was talking to an uncritical audience he did not exert himself and his speech was not notable.

"I feel, that under God, the strength of the arms and the wisdom of the heads of these masses, after all, must be my support," he said. "As I have often had reason to say, I repeat to you—I am quite sure I do not deceive myself when I tell you I bring to the work an honest heart; I dare not tell you that I bring a head sufficient for it."

It was Lincoln the total politician, and the Pennsylvania legislators cheered, as they always do, when someone downplays intellectuality.

Lincoln intended to stay that night at the Jones House, now the Dauphin Building, on Market Square. George Washington as president probably stayed there in 1794, and if so, it is one of the few sites in the United States where both men stretched out. But Lincoln never got time to sleep. After dinner, he was quietly taken in a Harrisburg transfer buggy to a darkened train in Steelton and sent on to Washington, for rumors were that he faced assassination.

Lincoln returned on Nov. 19, 1863, this time to Gettysburg. On that occasion he spoke just 267 words—the greatest speech ever made on American soil.

The night before, as he was relaxing in Gettysburg, he was asked to speak to a street crowd. His declining to say a few words were his few words. "I appear before you, fellow citizens, merely to thank you for this compliment," he said. "The inference is a very fair one that you would hear me for a little while at least, were I to commence to make a speech. I do not appear before you for the purpose of doing so, and for several substantial reasons. The most substantial of these is that I have no speech to make. In my position, it is somewhat important that I should not say any foolish things. It very often happens that the only way to help it is to say nothing at all."

As Jacques Barzun remarked, "Lincoln's purity was that of a supremely conscious genius, not of an innocent." Barzun, of the Class of 1924 at old Harrisburg Tech, made a keen analysis of that genius in an article, "Lincoln the Writer."

Lincoln's Gettysburg Address will be reinterpreted as long as the English language is spoken. As Pennsylvania's Stephen Vincent Benet said, Lincoln could give "a few speeches which make the monumental booming of Webster sound empty as the belly of a burst drum." The Gettysburg Address has what Barzun sees as the four main qualities of Lincoln's literary art—"precision, vernacular ease, rhythmical virtuosity, and elegance."

Lincoln was the most experienced courtroom lawyer ever to become president. He resolved public problems in legal concepts. As lawyers do, he sought exactness, not originality. He borrowed phrases from others—such as the famous "government of the people, by the people and for the people." He refused to use synonyms, using the word "dedicated" six times in the speech, and "lives" and "living" four times. "The great compression came after he had, lawyerlike, excluded alternatives and hit upon right order and emphasis," states Barzun.

H. L. Mencken in 1928 interpreted the Gettysburg Address as Lincoln's "Kiwanian bombast" to explain something "comprehensible to Pennsylvania Dunkards, which is to say, to persons to whom genuine ideas were not comprehensible at all." As Mencken saw it:

"One may easily imagine the reflections that the scene and the occasion must have inspired in so sagacious and unconventional a man—at all events, one may imagine the more obvious of them. They were, it is highly probable, of an extremely acrid and unpleasant nature. Before him stretched row upon row of new-made graves; around him ranged the gaunt cinders of a witless and abominable war. The thought must have occurred to him at once that—

"But before him there also stretched an acre or two of faces—the faces of dull Pennsylvania peasants from the adjacent farms, with here and there the jowls of a Philadelphia politician gleaming in the pale winter sunlight. It was too cold that day to his badly-cushioned bones for a long speech, and the audience would have been mortally offended by a good one. So old Abe put away his reflections, and launched into the tired and sure-fire stuff. Once started, the furor loquendi dragged him on. Abandoning the simple and crystal-clear English of his considered utterance, he stood a sentence on its head, and made a pretty parlor ornament of it. Proceeding, he described the causes and nature of the war in terms of the current army press bureau. Finally, he launched a sonorous, meaningless epigram, and sat down. There was immense applause. The Pennsylvania oafs were delighted. And the speech remains in all the school books to this day."

Whatever truth there is to Mencken's exaggerations, Lincoln did know his Pennsylvanians. If fate had been different, Lincoln would have been a Pennsylvania politician, not an Illinois one. His great-great-great-grandfather, his great-great-grandfather, and his great-grandfather were Pennsylvanians, living in Berks and Lycoming counties. When Lincoln was in Congress, his boardinghouse companion was Cong. James A. Pollock, of Milton, later governor of Pennsylvania. When Lincoln became president, he gave Pollock the plush job of director of the Philadelphia Mint, and "In God We Trust" was put on the coins.

Yet Lincoln was no hero to many Pennsylvanians. The old *Patriot and Union*, predecessor of the *Patriot-News*, ran the full text of Edward Everett's speech at Gettysburg and editorialized: "We pass over the silly remarks of the President. For the credit of the nation, we are willing that the veil of oblivion shall be dropped over them, and that they shall be no more repeated or thought of." The paper added: "Whatever may be Mr. Everett's feelings, he does not lack sense—whatever may be the President's virtues, he does not possess sense."

To the *Patriot*, Lincoln was "more like a well-trained monkey than a man of sense and a gentleman." And some other Central Pennsylvania newspapers agreed. The *Lancaster Intelligencer* called him "a miserable low buffoon who disgraces the Presidential chair." The *Bedford Gazette* criticized Lincoln, of all people, for a "wholesale slaughter of the King's English."

It was Franklin Weirick, editor of the *Selinsgrove Times*, however, who was the nastiest. He advised in print that young men duck the draft, that soldiers desert, and that Lincoln's sons fight in the war. In his

212   PROFILES FROM THE SUSQUEHANNA VALLEY

Christmas Day editorial of 1863, Weirick called Lincoln "a liar, a thief, a robber, a brigand, a pirate, a perjurer, a traitor, a coward, a hypocrite, a cheat, a trickster, a murderer, a tyrant, an unmitigated scoundrel, and an infernal fool." He went so far that once his townfolk got rope and were ready to lynch him if he did not shout, "Three cheers for the Union."

For the first official American Thanksgiving Day, on Nov. 26, 1863, Weirick calculated that 5,475,000 prayers had been offered for peace before the war and 16,435,000 after the war began. "What is the use of praying at all, if such an enormous quantity seems to do no good?" he asked.

Seventeen months after the Gettysburg Address, Lincoln returned to Central Pennsylvania in a coffin. He was shot fatally during the third act of the comedy, *American Cousin*, at Ford's Theatre on the night of Good Friday, April 14, 1865. The *Patriot and Union* reported the Assassination on Monday, April 17: "The National Calamity, The Assassination of President Lincoln."

Lincoln did not die until 7:22 A.M., Saturday, April 15. Two hours later, the bell at the Dauphin County Courthouse was tolled to tell the people of the tragedy. Appomattox had taken place the previous Sunday, and this was to be the first weekend of peace in exactly four years.

"The 15th of April, 1865, is a day that will be remembered by every man, woman and child in this City until the latest moments of life," the *Patriot* said on April 17. "The entire community had been looking forward to such a day of rejoicing as had never been seen within the limits of our City. Flags were flying, wreaths of evergreen, studded with beautiful flowers, were hung or prepared—the streets were already thronged with soldiers, civilians—gay and happy children were in holiday trimmings, and everything prepared for such a demonstration as would have honored our brave army for its victories and celebrated the dawn of peace. But hark! What is this whispered rumor that threads our streets and causes every face to frown with horror? 'The President, Mr. Lincoln, has been cruelly murdered.' At first it was met with an incredible look and by some was regarded as a hoax intended to affect the parade. But then there came another thrilling, stunning cry—that Mr. Seward, Secretary of State, and his son, had been simultaneously dispatched by the hand of a desperate and bloody assassin.

"No pen has graphic power to describe the scenes that presented themselves to the eye wherever it turned. Faces but moments before gleaming with prospective joy were gloomed with sadness. The emblems of rejoicing were palled in the weeds of mourning, and every heart was the sepulchre of a sorrow it could not fathom. A nation deeply mourns —nay, stands aghast at the contemplation of a deed which may prove the darkest, direst page in the history of nations."

On Friday, April 21, the remains of Lincoln arrived in Harrisburg on the funeral trip back to Springfield, Ill. The funeral train, which Gov. Andrew G. Curtin had boarded when it passed over the state line, arrived at 8:35 A.M. It was greeted by a 21-gun salute and the tolling of bells.

It rained the entire day. "The heavens all day were draped with clouds. Not a ray of sunlight appeared. It seemed as though nature, sympathizing with poor humanity, had caught the spirit of the universal gloom and had donned the garb of mourning," the *Patriot* reported.

The funeral march went from the railroad station down Market St., to Second St., up to State St. and then to the House of Representatives of the old Capitol. The hearse was drawn by four white horses, and among the pallbearers were A. Boyd Hamilton, David Fleming, Valentine Hummel, Henry Gilbert, Dr. George Bailey, and former U.S. Rep. John C. Kunkel, the grandfather of the later congressman of the same name.

"The head of the coffin was placed toward the Speaker's desk, so that as the procession filed in by twos through the main door they diverged at the foot of the coffin, passed in single file on each side, securing a close but brief glance at the face of the remains, and then receded through the temporary doorways at each side and behind the Speaker's chair into the grounds outside. The hall was beautifully and appropriately decorated and festooned with tasteful emblems of mourning," the newspaper reported.

The lines of mourners passed from 9:30 P.M. to midnight and then the next day, April 22, from 7 A.M. to 9. At 10:20 A.M. the cortege was formed to return to the railroad station.

"About 11 o'clock the whistle of the locomotive sounded departure, and the sad cortege moved slowly off. The vast concourse of people composing the procession was then formally dismissed; the military took their way to camp and barracks, and soon our streets assumed the quietness and desertion of a Sunday in midsummer," the *Patriot* said.

The funeral train went on to Philadelphia, then New York, Albany, Buffalo, Cleveland, Columbus, Indianapolis, Chicago, and finally Springfield.

Undoubtedly there were Harrisburgers who saw the live Lincoln at Gettysburg and the dead Lincoln in the House of Representatives. "It is for us the living, rather, to be dedicated here to the unfinished work which they who fought here have thus far so nobly advanced," he had told them that day at Gettysburg.

DRAWBAUGH

The Tinkerer of Eberly's Mill

. . . *Dan Drawbaugh and the Telephone*

In the 1940s, the late Roy Sheely retired to his home in Camp Hill after years of service as a telephone installer with Bell Telephone. It was only fate that Sheely worked for the telephone company. Conceivably, it could have worked for him. His grandfather, Daniel Drawbaugh of Lower Allen Township, was a claimant in the 1880s to the title of inventor of the telephone, the most valuable patent ever awarded.

Of Drawbaugh's 70 patents, 35 of them pertained to telephones. But the U.S. Supreme Court on March 19, 1888, by a vote of 4 to 3 decided that, in effect, Alexander Graham Bell and not Drawbaugh invented the telephone.

Chief Justice Morrison R. Waite, of Connecticut, wrote the majority opinion. Within four days, on March 23, at 6:30 A.M., the chief justice was dead at age 71. The court, then really 3-3 on the decision, rejected an appeal, ruling that Waite was alive when he cast his vote and wrote the opinion, and therefore the judgment stood. The minority opinion was rendered by Justice Joseph P. Bradley, of New York. Bradley's son married Simon Cameron's granddaughter, Eliza, who as a child had sat on President Lincoln's knee. Eliza Cameron Bradley for many years was a *Grande Dame* on Front St.

Daniel Drawbaugh easily qualifies as the most creative mind and strangest individual ever to come out of the West Shore. He was a mechanical and imaginative genius, but an utter fool about business, law, and publicity—three matters on which Bell was an expert.

"Originator or imitator, genius or charlatan, believe what you will, the 'wizard' still owns the distinction of almost bringing the American Bell Telephone Co. to its knees," wrote Harrisburg historian Warren J. Harder in his 1961 biography, *Daniel Drawbaugh, The Edison of the Cumberland Valley*, published by the University of Pennsylvania Press. Harder believed Drawbaugh devised the first workable telephone, as does George E. Reed, who has done considerable research on the matter. Reed, the son of the late Dauphin County state senator and the grandson of the late president of Dickinson College, is an oil lobby publicist who first became interested in Drawbaugh as a reporter for the *Harrisburg Telegraph*.

Drawbaugh was born July 14, 1827, in Bloserville, the son of a Cumberland County blacksmith and a descendant of a long line of mechanics and machinists, all poor. He did not break the string. He was in debt most of his 84 years. He had to borrow $5 to attend his father's funeral. He had 11 children, most of whom were sickly and only four of whom survived him.

Though his neighbors along the Yellow Breeches at Eberly's Mill called him a "wizard," his wife often lost patience with Drawbaugh's inability to keep up with West Shore living standards. "Dan is in that old shop, fooling his time away," she once explained to a visitor.

When Drawbaugh died at 22 S. 17th St. in Camp Hill on Nov. 3, 1911, and was buried at St. John's Church graveyard near Shiremanstown, he was able to leave his widow only $350. His three acres by the Yellow Breeches were bought by Cong. Marlin E. Olmsted.

He called himself an "inventor and designer," though he also was a gunsmith, piano tuner, and forever a tinkerer.

When he was 17, he invented a rifle. During his lifetime he invented a stave-jointing machine, a steam injector, an automatic boiler feeder, a paper bag folder, a carpet rag needle, a weather forecaster, a machine for insulating wire, an electromagnetic clock, two stamp cancellers, an automatic fire alarm, a sewing machine, equipment to make wagon wheel rims and barrels, a device to round-dress millstones, a machine to elevate grain in mills, a coin separator, and an instrument for alphabetic telegraphing.

His pneumatic stone drills were used in the construction of the Library of Congress. One of his improved water-powered motors was installed for the pipe organ at Harrisburg's St. Patrick's Cathedral. Yet at best, he earned $300 to $400 a year for his work.

Drawbaugh was exactly 20 years older than the Scotland-born Bell, and had none of the education of his rival.

In 1860 Drawbaugh began toying with using the principles of the telegraph system, then almost 20 years old, for a telephone. In 1866 he devised his teacup transmitter and mustard can receiver. This set made what is surely the world's first telephone, and it is on exhibit at the Hamilton Library in Carlisle. But legal and business advisers in Harrisburg to whom Drawbaugh turned were not so much interested in his "magnetic talking machine," as they were in his ideas for improving the use of the telegraph or for devising a self-measuring molasses faucet. It is likely that Drawbaugh was so unaware of his own shortcomings in business and promotion that he did not recognize that, above all, he needed advisers with foresight.

By 1874 Drawbaugh had his telephone in good working order, while Bell and his friend Thomas A. Watson (no relation to the IBM Tom Watson) were just getting faint echoes from their equipment in Boston. The alert Bell secured his patent on March 7, 1876, three days before the instrument really worked and the immortal command, "Mr. Watson come here, I need you," was uttered. Bell had spilt acid on his vest, and that is why he shouted. Meanwhile, it was Watson who suggested to Bell that a bell be used to summon people to the phone.

Bell made a sensational demonstration of his telephone at the 1876 Centennial Celebration in Philadelphia. Drawbaugh went down from his Eberly's Mill shop, but never considered bringing his telephone invention to the exhibition.

Drawbaugh filed for his patent on July 21, 1880. He signed his rights away to the People's Telephone Company of New York for $5,000 and a large, though never disclosed, amount of stock. Three months later the Bell Company took its bill of complaint against People's into the U.S. Circuit Court of the Southern District of New York. In a quarter-century the Bell interests fought 600 suits as party after party attempted to have the U.S. government revoke the Bell patents. People's Telephone operated in open defiance of the Bell patent, and needed Drawbaugh for its argument that it had an inventor who antedated Bell.

Bell won the Circuit Court decision, and on Jan. 24, 1887, the case reached the Supreme Court. There were 70 witnesses for Drawbaugh. Harder believed, and so does Reed, that Drawbaugh, though one of his neighbors called him "a harmless lunatic," easily predated Bell. As Reed explained, however, it was Bell who understood the merits and the scientific significance of the telephone and could interest the business community in it and promote its advancement. To Drawbaugh, it was more of a novelty or plaything. He said that if he had had $60, he would have gotten his patent in before Bell.

Drawbaugh was an inventive tinkerer. "He once spoke of conversing over a wire 'across the ocean' and he was told by the village undertaker, William Darr, to try it first across the Yellow Breeches Creek. Daniel never forgave him," writes Harder.

Myths took hold in the Harrisburg Area that Bell, unbeknown to the innocent Drawbaugh, visited him one day in a field near Eberly's Mill as he was stringing wire, and in conversation obtained the secret needed to patent his talking machine. Another version of the story is that Watson, an electrician by trade, spent several weeks visiting Drawbaugh. Still another tale is that Bell raided the Drawbaugh shop and ripped a telephone instrument from the wall to get the information he wanted. The apparent truth is that Bell was not even aware of Drawbaugh's existence until the telephone suit developed.

Drawbaugh himself never denied Bell's invention of the telephone. He maintained only that Bell did it separately and later than he.

Not discouraged, Drawbaugh spent the last years of his life working on a wireless, trying to throw vibrations across the Yellow Breeches. He never quite made it. A fellow named Guglielmo Marconi is in the history books for that one.

Silas Comfort Swallow

SILAS SWALLOW

. . . Warrior Against Sin and Drink

They do not make clergymen, politicians, and public figures anymore like the incredible Rev. Dr. Silas Comfort Swallow. Colorful and outlandish, he remains the only Harrisburger ever to run for both president and governor.

Swallow was tall and angular, and looked something like Abraham Lincoln. As he described himself: "I am a Methodist by adoption, by primogeniture, by regeneration and by flagellation." He said he followed in his mother's footsteps, and she was "an old-time shouting Methodist."

Swallow might have been the most dynamic preacher Harrisburg ever had, and the competition is keen. He had a delightful way with words, as shown in this excerpt from one of his sermons:

"One hundred thousand people in America die every year from pickling their appendices in alcohol without first having them extracted. That the little stranger may not be lonely, they also pickle at the same time the stomach, liver, kidney, heart, brain, arteries, muscles, nerves and even the bones. They soon discover that not only are these pickled, but that their owners are really in a pickle, for when they confess to have had enough of the pickling stuff, they go right on drinking it down till it is discovered that while alcohol preserves dead tissue, it rots the living and the victim of the poison must be buried in the interest of public health."

Prohibitionist "No-Swallow" ran for governor in 1898 and 1902 and for president in 1904, and did not do badly. In 1898 he polled 132,931 votes; only one other third-party candidate, William H. Berry in 1910, ever received more in a Pennsylvania gubernatorial election. In 1902

218

Swallow got only 23,327 votes for governor, but in 1904 he received 258,787 votes nationwide for president, the year Theodore Roosevelt was the overwhelming choice.

Humorist Finley Peter Dunne had his character Mr. Dooley comment on the three Prohibition presidential candidates between 1896 and 1904, Joshua Levering, John G. Woolley, and Swallow: "Cillybrated names. They were a fine lot iv ol' fellows, comin' out year afther year, to lead their little foorces to certain defeat, an' ca'mly carryin' on their campaign with ivrybody laughin' at thim. That was th' hardest thing f'r th' old heroes. . . . But they didn't mind, these inthrepid old geezers with their spectacles an' their throat whiskers. They smiled serenely, put for'ard argyments that no wan cud answer, sung 'Where Is My Wandhrin' Boy Tonight,' paid out their own money f'r hall rent, niver held a polytical job an' were niver heard about between ilictions."

But Swallow never regarded his political activity as futile. He often mentioned that he took pleasure in seeing that in his lifetime all his major goals were accomplished—the abolishing of slavery, the outlawing of lotteries, the banning of polygamy, the establishing of Prohibition, and woman suffrage.

He was an annoyance to politicians. Gov. Robert E. Pattison, a distinguished Methodist layman, had Dr. Swallow offer the prayer at his second inaugural in 1891. At the close of the ceremony on the Capitol steps, Swallow refused to ride in the inaugural parade. He said he was always ready to pray for sinners like Republicans and Democrats, but was not willing to parade with them.

Swallow accused the politicians of deliberately setting fire to the old State Capitol, but he was not taken seriously. When the Legislature was moved to Grace Methodist Church and state money was used to furnish the church for the legislative sessions, Swallow accused a member of Governor Hastings' cabinet of misappropriating public funds. He was taken to court for libel, and ultimately was convicted on two of nine charges. The one charge was dismissed, but Swallow was instructed to pay the cost. The other carried a $500 fine. Swallow appealed to the higher court and won a reversal. He then promptly challenged his prosecutors to a new trial, but they refused.

While he was involved in this public turmoil, his own Central Pennsylvania Conference of the Methodist Church suspended him from all ministerial duties from the fall of 1901 to the spring of 1902 because of "highly imprudent and unministerial conduct." On one occasion he had accused a prominent Harrisburg minister of hiring thugs to beat him up. In another incident, while he was minister of the Ridge Avenue Church on Sixth St., he saw a beer wagon stop at the home of a fellow parson.

In the true spirit of his brother's keeper, Swallow hurried over but was bluntly told by the parson that the doctor had prescribed the use of malt.

Swallow was born March 5, 1839, on a farm in Plains, just north of Wilkes-Barre. He was the first-born in a family of five children, and was named Silas Comfort after a great preacher who was a friend of his father. At the age of 14, Silas became the farmer in the family, because his father was stricken with a debilitating illness. For five years, he farmed and meanwhile at age 16 also took a job teaching in a country school during the winter months. At 19 he commuted by horseback to Wyoming Seminary in Kingston, and upon graduation began the study of law under a Wilkes-Barre attorney. His father wanted him to be a lawyer, but Silas heard "the call" and gave it up for the ministry.

In 1860, while teaching school near Hazleton, he was "prematurely licensed," in his words, as a local supply preacher. Two years later he was temporarily appointed supply pastor in the Sunbury Circuit, and eventually he received his first conference appointment to the Milton Circuit at a salary of $100 per year. He so angered the antiwar, pro-slavery members of one congregation that they padlocked the church to keep him from preaching on what he regarded as the pertinent subject of the day.

In September of 1862, he volunteered for Civil War duty, and was assigned to the 18th Regiment of the Pennsylvania Volunteers. He saw only home guard duty, but was elected a first lieutenant by his fellow soldiers.

After military service, he went back on the circuit in Berwick and Catawissa. It was in Berwick on April Fool's Day of 1864 that he had a revelation about his worst sin, that of smoking. Characteristically, he went outside and tossed his tobacco can clear over the house. He never smoked again.

Swallow married Rebecca Louise Robins, the daughter of Dr. and Mrs. Joseph Robins of Elysburg, in 1866. He took his bride to Philadelphia for their honeymoon, and there they saw the classic comedy *She Stoops to Conquer*. Before it was over, Swallow was complaining, "I'll be damned." He never went to the theater again. Similarly, he did not like dancing, did not use public conveyances on Sundays, and abhorred the "roller-skating mania."

Silas Comfort Swallow and Rebecca Robins joked throughout their 64 years of marriage about being "two birds." On at least one occasion, he was referred to in the *Harrisburg Evening News* as "Dr. Sparrow." They were great birdlovers, and when they lived in Camp Hill at Market and 17th Sts., they erected a fountain for the robins, swallows, and sparrows.

From 1868 to 1876, Swallow served congregations in Newberry, Williamsport, Milton, and Altoona. For four years he was superintendent of the Williamsport District, and for another four had a congregation in York. In 1883 Swallow took a year's leave from the ministry to be on the staff of Dickinson College, and then he returned to the pulpit in Williamsport.

While at the railroaders' Ridge Avenue Church, from 1886 to 1892, he made it one of the most exciting churches in Harrisburg. He was called "The Fighting Parson," but in addition to battling sin he also helped establish the Epworth Church at 21st and Derry Sts. and a Methodist congregation in Camp Hill. Two decades later, in 1919, when his former Ridge Avenue congregation needed $15,000 for renovations, Swallow returned to lead a house-to-house canvass, securing $12,000 of the goal from his personal and business friends.

In 1892, Swallow became superintendent of the Central Pennsylvania Conference Publishing House, with his office on Market Square. He dabbled in real estate, and was quite expert at it. He said he believed the message of Deuteronomy: "Keep the words of this covenant, and do them, that ye may prosper in all that ye do." He tithed all his life, raised orphaned children, built bird feeders, and was as generous as any man in town. Among his many contributions was $1,200 for a memorial church in Summerdale in honor of his mother-in-law.

For 10 years after he retired in 1907, he lived in Camp Hill. He intended his home to be used for retired Methodist ministers after he passed on, but he could not get agreement on that, nor on his plans for a Methodist old-age home and orphanage.

He and Mrs. Swallow moved back to Harrisburg, to 25 S. Front St., for the last 13 years of their lives. He was never fully retired, but preached and wrote constantly. The two of them attended Grace Methodist Church, where they were conspicuous for holding hands during the service. At age 70 he rented the banquet room of the old Commonwealth Hotel and invited his political enemies to dinner. He announced that, while he had nothing to apologize for, he often had been unnecessarily harsh with some who disagreed with him. He said no man should leave this world without trying to make amends and seek forgiveness. He lived almost 21 years more, the only span in his life when no one ever heard him say an unkind word about anybody.

Silas Comfort Swallow died at his home on Aug. 13, 1930, and was buried in Paxtang Cemetery; his wife died soon after. As the *Harrisburg Telegraph* said, "He was, in many ways, an outstanding man of his generation."

JOHN O'HARA

Chaucer of Carlisle
to Carbondale

. . . John O'Hara Covered the Territory

It is quite possible that in the year 2070 the most famous Central Pennsylvanian of the 1905 to 1970 era will be John Henry O'Hara. In 2070 they will look in Big Jawn's 30 books, 13 of them novels, and his 400 short stories to find out.

O'Hara was our Chaucer, covering the territory from Carlisle to Carbondale. He was preoccupied with what preoccupies us: family, status, money, sex, liquor, hypocrisy, and the waste of life. "Being a cheap, ordinary guy, I have an instinct for what an ordinary guy likes," he said candidly.

O'Hara's philosophy was that the best you can hope for is an even break. Life is a pitiless tragedy because it forces on man obligations and roles he cannot fulfill. Man's potential appears unlimited, but invariably his achievement is below his ideals and aspirations. So in his frustration, he deteriorates and disintegrates. He fights, overcompetes, and vilifies, and his dignity crumbles. Women are more nervy, selfish, animalistic, and predatory than men. They have stronger appetites for easy success and worldly conquest, so they endure a bit better.

In one of his early short stories, O'Hara has a character named Seymour M. Harrisburg. A girl down the hall is murdered. Seymour is innocent, but by the time he is done answering questions his employer does not need him anymore. He goes home to find a note in his bankbook. His wife has taken all but $10 and departed with another man. "I

222

should of done this four years ago," she scrawls. Seymour walks into the kitchen and finds she emptied the gin bottle for him.

A character named Grant violates the time-honored code of the coal regions: you do not make a pass at a girl when you are tight that you would not make when you are sober. But he does, and the treadmill of trouble starts. In the midst of havoc, he realizes he is more in love with his wife than ever. He embraces her. "Oh, I do love you, kid. You love me, don't you, really?" "Look out for my cigarette," she says.

O'Hara was a social historian, a ruthless investigator of sexual mores, and a gatherer of cultural details. What he appreciated was "class," which he defined as a patrician blend of dignity, energy, courage, imagination, humor, and intelligence—qualities which he himself had, plus a nastiness and superficiality, to make him one of the most popular writers of his day. What he said about F. Scott Fitzgerald in 1945 applies to himself: "He always knew what he was writing about, which is so, so untrue of so, so many so-so writers." Yet he was no social reformer. Actually he accepted the status quo as he chronicled its horrors.

Appointment in Samarra, his first novel, is the O'Hara masterpiece. It covers the last three days in 1930 in the life of Julian English, who at 29 was the same age as O'Hara when he wrote the novel in 1934.

Julian, the son of the leading surgeon of Gibbsville, has his marriage go sour with the former Caroline Walker, who is of upper middle-class pretensions. He is an auto dealer, mismanages his business, and must borrow $20,000 from Harry Reilly, who lacks Julian's status and is not as "socially secure." Julian drinks too much. In quick order, he quixotically throws a highball in Harry Reilly's face at the Gibbsville Country Club, tries to pick up a bootlegger's girl friend at a roadhouse, and gets into a stupid fistfight at the fashionable Gibbsville Club. Caroline moves in with her widowed mother. Finally, on December 26 at 10:41 P.M., Julian gets into his Cadillac in his closed garage and starts up the engine.

"There was nothing to do now but wait," writes O'Hara. "He smoked a little, hummed for a minute or two, and had three quick drinks and was on his fourth when he lay back and slumped down in the seat. At 10:50, by the clock in the rear seat, he tried to get up. He had not the strength to help himself, and at 10 minutes past 11 no one could have helped him, no one in the world."

When Harry Reilly hears about Julian's suicide, he expresses the common sentiment: "He was a real gentleman. I wonder what in God's name would make him do a thing like that?" Wolcott Gibbs, for whom Gibbsville was named, observed that O'Hara's characters were people with "potentially valuable lives failing, but not without some dignity, because they were not born quite strong enough for the circumstances they had to meet."

O'Hara's theme was often loneliness, and how Americans in this century try to fight it off with status, money, booze, and sex. His major weakness as a writer is that he never went far beyond describing the surface of the American scene and citizenry. But his portrayals and especially his dialogue can be brilliant. In one short story, O'Hara has a favorite character, Jim Malloy of Gibbsville, say: "On my way home, I realized that until then I had not known him at all. It was not a discovery to cause me dismay. What did he know about me? What, really, can any of us know about any of us, and why must we make such a thing of loneliness when it is the final condition of us all?"

A Rage to Live is the 590-page novel, written in 1949, about Harrisburg, "one of my favorite cities," and Dauphin County, "where my mother was born . . . the scene of some of the happiest hours of my childhood," as O'Hara says in his preface.

Grace Brock Caldwell grows up in what O'Hara calls Fort Penn, never wishes to leave, and at age 20 marries a nice New Yorker, Sidney Tate. They have a family farm near the Harrisburg Country Club. Their life is pleasant enough, with three lovely children, until at age 34 in 1917 Grace breaks loose from respectability. Her first affair is with a local housing developer, a former football star turned slob. After her husband and younger son die in the flu epidemic of 1917, she picks up with a perverted Philadelphian. Finally, she is ruining the life of an upcoming, appreciative local columnist.

Though the novel is overblown and not one of O'Hara's best, Grace Caldwell Tate is one of the great heroines of American literature. "Grace was wearing a sealskin cloak over a simple black taffeta gown, and her only jewelry was a thin diamond necklace, but she was the one," writes O'Hara. "She was what the younger women could hope to be, and what the older women, who knew her age, could take pride in." Like Tolstoy's Anna Karenina, she was socially prominent, poised, self-confident, and, not pretty, but beautiful. "Grace was the best-dressed woman in Fort Penn—but without trying. She was the handsomest—but without caring. She was the kindest—but expected nothing. She did everything the right way—but without stopping to think about it," explains O'Hara. The weakness of Grace as a heroine is that O'Hara cannot supply Anna Karenina's depth of emotional feeling and intelligence. As Orville Prescott said in his *New York Times* review, O'Hara verges dangerously close to making Grace "not a significant character but a slut."

Harrisburgers have spent more than two decades attempting to link the fictional characters of *A Rage to Live* with real Harrisburgers. It is a futile exercise. It is enough to have an O'Hara world with people, like Grace's brother, Brock, who "seemed to have determined to lead his own useless life in the way he chose, and in Fort Penn that took a perverse courage." Or Mayor George W. Walthour, who wants a bridge at Washington St. named for him. Or one of the social elite: "In her middle years Betty had become a moderately discontented woman, but that was an improvement over the whining girl she had been in her teens."

O'Hara's cultural insights, as usual, are right on the mark: "They had nothing to say against Fort Penn, but they most certainly had nothing to say in favor of it." Or, "The best blood in Fort Penn, families who by custom got things without even asking for them, because the people of Fort Penn acknowledged some kind of superiority." Or Sidney Tate's mediocre ambition for his older son, "Not a prodigy, not a shark at anything much, very likely, but a clean, decent gentleman."

Not unexpectedly, Harrisburgers accepted O'Hara's judgments with equanimity. The library added the novel to its circulation and there were no complaints.

John O'Hara was born on Jan. 31, 1905, in Pottsville, and he died at Princeton, N.J. on April 11, 1970. He never won the Nobel Prize or even a Pulitzer Prize. The Governor's Committee of 100,000 Pennsylvanians honored him posthumously. Not in the Hemingway-Fitzgerald big league, O'Hara made it to the second level with John P. Marquand and John Steinbeck.

Yet to Central Pennsylvanians, he was Chaucer. He was more right about our grossness, our grubbing for success, our romanticism, and our motivations than we may care to concede.

He told us that tenor saxophones sound flat outdoors, that men in plastic hat covers usually have cheap hats underneath, that our women do not say "half-a-dollar." He immortalized our speech: " 'Nat?' 'What?' 'I don't have to say it, do I? You know, don't you? You do know?' She nodded. 'Give me your arm.' "

Pal Joey, another of the great O'Hara characters, in his last letter "reminisses" about Berwick, Reading, Allentown, Harrisburg, Shenandoah, Scranton, and Tamaqua. "Boy I could go on with them and so could you," writes Joey. "I wish we had a chance to reminiss some nite."

As I wrote the day before his funeral: "So long, Mr. John O'Hara. You made it interesting."

J.F.K.

The Trip John F. Kennedy
Should Have Made

... Choose Dallas Instead of
Gettysburg

President John F. Kennedy was fascinated by Gettysburg, but he rejected an invitation to be there on Nov. 19, 1963, for the 100th anniversary of Lincoln's Gettysburg Address. Had that date been on his schedule, it is likely he would not have made arrangements for the weekend to go to Fort Worth, Dallas, and Austin and to stay overnight Friday, November 22, at Vice-President Johnson's Texas ranch.

226

He had been invited to Gettysburg twice in 1963. The Centennial Committee wanted him for July 4 and the 100th anniversary of the end of the battle. President Woodrow Wilson had been there for the 50th anniversary in 1913 and President Franklin D. Roosevelt in 1938 for the 75th anniversary. Two great Democrats went to Gettysburg, but Kennedy broke the tradition and made other plans.

The 10 days previous to July 4, Kennedy was in Europe. He visited Dunganstown, the Kennedy ancestral home in Ireland. He took Jacqueline to Paris and told the Frenchmen he was just Mrs. Kennedy's escort. At the Berlin Wall he said, "Ich bin ein Berliner." In Rome he met the new pope, Paul VI. Meanwhile, at Gettysburg the celebration was handled by former President Dwight D. Eisenhower and Gov. William W. Scranton.

The program in November for the 100th anniversary of the Gettysburg Address went on despite the absence of President Kennedy. Justice Michael A. Musmanno, who had once met Robert Lincoln, recited the immortal message. Marian Anderson sang. Ike, in an excellent speech, said Lincoln "knew that to live for country is a duty as demanding as is the readiness to die for it." Kennedy, preparing his trip to Texas, sent a message which was read by Lt. Gen. Milton G. Baker, chairman of the Gettysburg Centennial Commission. "Let us remember those thousands of American patriots whose graves at home, beneath the sea and in distant lands are silent sentries of our heritage," the president wrote. But a more pressing matter to him was not the heritage, but the Democratic squabble in Texas between Gov. John B. Connally and Sen. Ralph Yarborough, which he intended to resolve.

Kennedy had seen Gettysburg earlier in the year. He was at Camp David, Md., on March 30 and had his Secret Service book reservations with the Gettysburg National Park for the next day, a Sunday. It was a sneak trip. The Kennedys and their children, plus Mr. and Mrs. Paul Fay and their daughter, arrived. JFK was in sports clothes and Jackie was sharply dressed and wearing sun glasses.

The president had a new Oldsmobile convertible. The battlefield's top guide, Jacob M. Sheads, was assigned to sit beside Kennedy. Sheads, a former Army Reserve colonel, was a full-time American history teacher at Gettysburg and a part-time employee at the park. Before the president arrived, he and the Secret Service made a dry run of the tour.

The procession took off, with the Secret Service following the president. When the children got restless, JFK exercised his presidential prerogative and had them removed to the Secret Service car.

Kennedy had never visited Gettysburg before. When he saw the monument to the 28th Massachusetts unit, he went up to it. There is a

Gallic inscription, and Sheads, who had worked at Gettysburg since 1935, had written to the Irish Embassy years before for the translation. He thought he would throw Kennedy a fast one. "Do you know what that phrase means, Mr. President?" he asked. "Sure," said Kennedy. "It reads, 'Clear the way.' " And he was right. Later Sheads acknowledged that Kennedy was "an ordinary tourist, but a little more knowledgeable than most."

For Memorial Day of 1963, Kennedy sent Lyndon Johnson to Gettysburg. Johnson and his daughter Lynda Bird, both ill with intestinal infections, flew up in an outdated helicopter—travel facilities which angered Johnson so much that he later told JFK he wanted a new helicopter for any more errands he might be assigned.

LBJ at that time was a half-forgotten man. He drew little press coverage, though he was the first southerner to come to Gettysburg and talk about civil rights. "Our nation found its soul in honor on these fields of Gettysburg 100 years ago," he said. "We must not lose that soul in dishonor now on the fields of hate." Six months later Johnson was president. Pundits, remembering he had said something at Gettysburg, went back and retrieved the speech. It is now mentioned in the biographies of LBJ.

John Kennedy—like Abraham Lincoln—visited Harrisburg twice. On Sept. 15, 1960, he drew 7,000 to Market Square. The stands were opposite what was then M. Harvey Taylor's insurance office. Presidential candidate Kennedy said, "Glad to be here," and gave a mere four-minute speech. "More, more, more," the crowd shouted. But Kennedy restrained himself. He knew he would lose Dauphin County, as well as the West Shore, and he lost them big. That night 9,000 Democrats attended a $100-a-plate dinner at the Zembo Mosque. JFK stayed overnight at the Presidential Suite in the Penn-Harris Hotel, and the next day campaigned in Lancaster and York counties. He upset the odds in November by carrying the crucial state of Pennsylvania.

As president he returned here on Sept. 20, 1962, for just 4½ hours for a $100 dinner at the Farm Show Arena. The motorcade passed Seventh and Maclay Sts., where a little girl held a cocker spaniel above her head for it to see the president. Edward Kennedy had just won the nomination for U.S. senator in Massachusetts. To open his 20-minute address, JFK said, "I will introduce myself. I am Teddy Kennedy's brother."

John F. Kennedy's fourth visit to Central Pennsylvania should have been Nov. 19, 1963, but it never was and history was shockingly changed.